D0290524

CRISIS

ON THE KOREAN
PENINSULA

Also by Christoph Bluth

Korea (2008)
The Two Germanies and Military Security in Europe (2003)
The Nuclear Challenge (2000)
Germany and the Future of European Security (2000)

Related Titles from Potomac Books

Defiant Failed State:
The North Korean Threat to International Security
—Bruce E. Bechtol Jr.

Korean Unification: Inevitable Challenges
—Jacques L. Fuqua Jr.

Red Rogue: The Persistent Challenge of North Korea
—Bruce E. Bechtol Jr.

CRISIS
ON THE KOREAN
PENINSULA

CHRISTOPH BLUTH

Potomac Books
Washington, D.C.

Published in the United States by Potomac Books, Inc. All rights reserved. No part of this book may be reproduced in any manner whatsoever without written permission from the publisher, except in the case of brief quotations embodied in critical articles and reviews.

Library of Congress Cataloging-in-Publication Data
Bluth, Christoph.
  Crisis on the Korean peninsula / Christoph Bluth.—1st ed.
    p. cm.
  Includes bibliographical references and index.
  ISBN 978-1-57488-887-4 (hardcover; alk. paper)
  1. Security, International—Korea. 2. Nuclear crisis control—Korea (North) 3. Korea (North)—Foreign relations—Korea (South) 4. Korea (South)—Foreign relations—Korea (North) 5. Korean reunification question (1945–) 6. United States—Foreign relations—Korea. 7. Korea—Foreign relations—United States. 8. China—Foreign relations—Korea. 9. Korea—Foreign relations—China. I. Title.
  JZ6009.K6B58 2011
  355'.0330519—dc22

                                                             2011013856

Printed in the United States of America on acid-free paper that meets the American National Standards Institute Z39-48 Standard.

Potomac Books
22841 Quicksilver Drive
Dulles, Virginia 20166

First Edition

Contents

Acknowledgments

My thanks go first of all to Chunyao Yi, who collaborated on this project, cowrote chapter 7, and provided vital empirical research on China's policy toward the Korean Peninsula.

I benefited from the help, support, and advice from many institutions and people during the writing of this book. In particular I am grateful to Kim Chang-su and Hwang Jae-ho from the Korea Institute for Defense Analyses (KIDA) and Hankuk University of Foreign Studies, respectively; Lee Chung-min, Kim Woo-sang, and Moon Chung-in from Yonsei University; Andrei Lankov from Kookmin University; Ambassador Cho Yoon-je from Sogang University; and Park Jin, previously chairman of the Foreign Affairs, Trade, and Unification Committee at the National Assembly, for their friendship, encouragement, and advice while I was undertaking the research for this book.

Others who shared their expertise with me include Kim Tae-woo (KIDA), former unification minister Lee Jong-seok, Lim Eul-chul, Nam Man-kwon, Daniel Pinkston (International Crisis Group), Pak Haik-soon (Sejong Institute), Park Chanbong (Unification Ministry), Ted Galen Carpenter (Cato Institute), Gary Samore (then at the International Institute for Strategic Studies in the Obama administration), Scott Snyder (Asia Foundation), James Strohmaier (Pusan National University), Hyun In-taek (Korea University, unification minister at the time of writing), Stephen Flanagan (Center for Strategic and International Studies), Hazel Smith (Cranfield University), Adam Ward (International Institute for Strategic Studies), Su Jeo-seok, Yoon Young-kwan (foreign minister, now at Seoul National University), Yu Yong-weon (*Chosun Ilbo*). The opportunity for exchanges with North Korean diplomats, including Ambassador Ri Yong-ho, Thae Yong-ho, Hwang Ik-hwan, and Kim Chun-guk (director of the European Department at the Ministry of Foreign

Affairs in Pyongyang), enabled me to get a firsthand view of the North Korean perspective. My students Park Min-hyoung and Ryu Sun-hye provided invaluable assistance with fieldwork and other aspects of the research. I am also grateful for the support of the Korea Foundation, which provided two separate grants to fund the research. Some of the work was also supported by the Academy of Korean Studies. All errors and omissions in the book are of course my responsibility alone.

1

Conceptualizing the Security Crisis on the Korean Peninsula

For more than a century, Korea has been the focus of the geopolitical struggle among the Asia Pacific major powers: Russia, China, Japan, and the United States. As an old Korean saying goes, a shrimp gets crushed to death in the fight between the whales. A small peninsula on the geopolitical fault lines of Northeast Asia, Korea has suffered occupation, devastating wars, and partition. Today, it is the one place in Northeast Asia where there continues to exist a serious threat of large-scale military conflict.

THE EVOLVING SECURITY DILEMMA ON THE KOREAN PENINSULA

The division of Korea goes back to World War II, when the Soviet troops invaded the northern part of the Korean Peninsula and the southern part was occupied by the United States. Efforts through the United Nations (UN) to end the occupation and create a unified Korea were rejected by the Soviet Union, and consequently two countries were formed in 1948: the Democratic People's Republic of Korea (DPRK) in the North and Republic of Korea (ROK) in the South.

In 1950 North Korean armed forces, with support of the Soviet Union, invaded the South. The Truman administration perceived this conflict as an act of communist aggression and quickly committed forces under the aegis of the UN, which restored the status quo ante by 1953. The current division of Korea is a legacy of these events. The dividing line across the Korean Peninsula, known as the Demilitarized Zone (DMZ), was for many decades also the dividing line between the two blocs in the Cold War. Although the Soviet Union originally conceived of North Korea as a socialist client state along the lines of countries in Central Europe, Kim Il-sung was not inclined to take orders from Moscow for any period of time. As the Sino-Soviet split unfolded in the 1950s, Kim played off USSR and China against each other and sought to preserve the maximum degree of independence and freedom of action.[1]

The Korean War was a devastating setback for the ambitions of North Korean leader Kim Il-sung for the reunification of Korea as a socialist state. In the aftermath of the war the United States established a permanent military presence in South Korea, which made this objective unachievable in the short term, so North Korea focused on the reconstruction and development of their economy, though without abandoning the goal of unification. Between 1953 and 1962 the North Korean economy experienced a rapid growth in output. The emphasis was on heavy industry to fulfill the requirements of a military-industrial base, rather than consumer goods. North Korean GDP per capita exceeded that of South Korea until the mid-1970s. North Korea nevertheless received grants and loans from the Soviet Union, China, and various European socialist countries. The presence of Chinese forces in North Korea until the late 1950s relieved pressure on military expenditures.

The North Korean economy was a centrally planned economy similar to that of other socialist countries. It was organized on the principle of *juche*, national self-reliance.[2] Even though North Korea did rely to some extent on foreign economic assistance and trade, it developed the world's most autarkic economy and did not even join the Council for Mutual Economic Assistance. North Korea sought to reduce reliance on even its close ally, the Soviet Union, and create a balance between relations with China and the USSR.[3]

In the 1960s North Korea embarked on a sustained military build-up in support of a more aggressive pursuit of reunification. The size of the armed forces grew from 300,000 to about a million by the end of the 1970s, and military preparedness was absorbing an increasing share of national output. As support from its traditional allies was weakening, the correlation of forces on the Korean Peninsula was slowly changing. Relations between the two Koreas were increasingly a battle for legitimacy, defined by the contest for the "Korean nation."

As far as the development of South Korea is concerned, it went through a difficult period for the first two decades. The country suffered from political factionalism and uneven economic growth, misallocation of resources and rent-seeking behavior. Politically, militarily, and to an extent economically it was dependent on the United States.

The government of President Park Chung-hee (1961–1979) maintained societal stability and presided over a period of economic development and industrialization, but there was considerable discontent with the authoritarian nature of the regime. Relations with the United States deteriorated as human rights violations raised concerns; President Carter decided to withdraw U.S. forces from Korea in 1977 (a decision that was reversed in 1979 after 3,500 troops had been withdrawn).

In 1979, President Park was assassinated by the director of the Korean Central Intelligence Agency. After a period of government domination by the military under Chun Doo-hwan, pressure for South Korea to move toward democracy increased. Major civil society democratic movements in early 1987 and the "Declaration of Democratization and Reforms" (June 29, 1987) culminated in a new constitutional arrangement, with the presidential elections in 1987 and the election of the National Assembly in 1998.[4]

The end of the Cold War heralded a reversal of the security dilemma on the Korean Peninsula, which was the result of long-term political and economic trends. South Korea had become a prosperous country, with increasingly stable democratic political institutions.[5] The economy of North Korea, on the other hand, was in serious decline. The large-scale changes in the international system that culminated in the end of the Cold War also involved a transformation of the regional system of states in Northeast Asia. This had profound consequences for North Korea as both the structure of alliances and confrontations in which North Korea had been loosely embedded completely dissolved. The confrontational stance between Russia and China transformed into a strategic partnership of sorts, and both countries developed relations with South Korea, relations that soon became more significant in many respects than those with North Korea. Already, during the Gorbachev period in the 1980s, Soviet interest began shifting toward closer relations with South Korea. Since the end of the Cold War Russia has lost both the incentive and the capacity to provide assistance to North Korea. By 1992 both China and Russia had officially recognized South Korea.

The North Korean economy virtually collapsed with the loss of cheap energy imports, manufactured goods from Russia, and other forms of aid. In the years 1990 to 1997, the North Korean economy decreased by 42.2 percent. Agriculture, already inherently inefficient, was hit by natural disasters, resulting in serious food shortages and mass migration of starving people from North Korea to China. Material conditions of life for ordinary people have become almost unbearable.

The economic predicament is at the root of the problems of the North Korean regime.[6] The options for halting, never mind reversing, the economic decline are extremely limited. Effectively, North Korea has to obtain external support through trade and aid or credits. This is difficult because North Korea continues to represent a very unfavorable investment climate. In response to this situation, North Korea adopted what came to be called "the triple survival strategy" of improving relations with the United States, Japan, and other major capitalist countries, strengthening North Korea's "own way of socialism" in domestic policy, and gradually opening up to the outside world. From the North Korean perspective, relations with the United States were seen to be of particular importance and key to the achievement of the DPRK's security and economic objectives.[7]

The beginnings of contacts with the United States, however, precipitated a major crisis over North Korea's nuclear program. The United States suspected that North Korea was producing plutonium using a research reactor and concealing some of the nuclear material from international inspectors. In other words, North Korea was pursuing nuclear weapons. As the result of negotiations with the United States, North Korea agreed to give up its plutonium program in return for a range of political and economic concessions, including the provision of two light-water reactors for electricity production.[8] However, after George W. Bush assumed the presidency, the so-called Agreed Framework collapsed over allegations that North Korea was pursuing a second nuclear program based on uranium enrichment technology. Since then North Korea is believed to have accumulated enough plutonium for about eight nuclear warheads, and conducted a nuclear test in October 2006 and again in May 2009.

The perception of the North Korean threat is heightened by its ballistic missile industry based on Soviet-designed missiles, especially the so-called Rodong and Taepodong. North Korea has exported missiles to countries like Pakistan, Iran, Iraq, Egypt, and Libya and thereby has become one of the major proliferators of missile technology. This fact alone is a major issue of contention between North Korea and the United States. Worse, North Korea could use its missile capability to target all of South Korea as well as U.S. forces based in Japan. It has demonstrated the capability of building three-stage missiles that may in future provide the basis for an intercontinental missile capability.[9]

NORTH KOREA'S THREAT TO THE WORLD

While the threat from North Korea has become a standard part of political discourse, the articulation of the nature of this threat is surprisingly vague. A realistic threat assessment needs to be based on an analysis of the basic security dilemma on the Korean Peninsula and what we can discern about the intentions of the North Korean leadership. These issues are contested and subject to some degree of uncertainty. The total concentration of economic resources on the military and the enormous build-up of forces at the DMZ by North Korea went clearly beyond the needs for defense from a possible attack by U.S. and South Korean forces; it was designed to support a strategy of unification on Pyongyang's terms if the situation was right. Although in the first two decades after the Korean War the conventional forces of the North posed a serious threat by sheer weight of numbers and were superior to the forces of South Korea, the alliance with the United States, which was supported by the presence of U.S. forces with nuclear weapons, deterred a full-scale attack.

As South Korea fast developed its economy and the economy of North Korea stagnated and then went into precipitous decline, the military balance changed. North Korea now had to make do with old and obsolescent military equipment based on Soviet technology, whereas the South acquired more and more state-of-the-art U.S. military equipment. Nowadays South Korea would most likely win a (non-nuclear) war with the North, even without direct U.S. involvement, although U.S. forces are still in Korea and committed to be engaged if South Korea comes under attack. While North Korea could not win a war with the South, and its regime would not survive such a war, it could nevertheless inflict unacceptable damage on the South due to the large number of artillery pieces that can target the South Korean capital, Seoul, and its longer-range missiles that can target any point on the peninsula. Some missiles can even target U.S. forces in Japan.[10] There is therefore no doubt that North Korea has a robust deterrent capability, which means that the United States has no plausible military option, nor would the South Korean government want to risk any war on the peninsula.

As far as North Korea's nonconventional arsenal is concerned, it is militarily less significant than is sometimes supposed. The chemical weapons significantly enhance North Korea's capacity to cause civilian casualties in the South, but do not necessarily redress the military balance as South Korean and American forces are equipped and trained to operate in a contaminated environment. The analysis of the military balance shows that the strategic situation on the Korean Peninsula can best be characterized as a stable deterrence relationship. Nevertheless, there are significant dangers.[11] North Korea's threat to international security is two-part.

The first is the threat of proliferation. As a major source of ballistic missile technology for Iran and Pakistan, North Korea has provided potential nuclear delivery vehicles to states in crisis regions, a development that significantly affects the interests of the United States. From the American perspective, the acquisition of long-range ballistic missiles by anti-Western states such as Iran and Syria is one of the major emerging threats to international security. Moreover, Pyongyang has hinted that it might engage in the proliferation of nuclear weapons materials and technology. This threat of proliferation will persist as long as North Korea has non-conventional weapons programs.[12]

The second is the longer-term threat of North Korea's emerging capabilities. Although at present no operational missiles of intercontinental range have been deployed, that could change over the next decade or two. North Korea has not yet demonstrated that it can mount nuclear warheads on long-range missiles. However, in the medium term such a strategic threat to the continental United States could emerge. This would transform the strategic situation.[13]

At the core, the reason why North Korea represents a threat to international security is that its military capabilities constitute the main leverage it perceives it has with regard to the international community and the United States in particular. The dynamics of the confrontation and hence the sources of insecurity have changed over the decades. In the period following the Korean War, North Korea enjoyed security guarantees from the Soviet Union and China; its economy was stronger than that of the South and its military capabilities superior. The greatest source of insecurity was North Korean power, the totalitarian nature of the regime, and the ambitions of Kim Il-sung to reunite the two Koreas by force.

The end of the superpower conflict and the dramatic shift in the correlation of forces between the two Koreas altered threat perceptions. Northern leaders have articulated the threat as emanating from the "hostile attitude" of the United States. This threat has a political and a military component. The political component consists in the rejection of the legitimacy of North Korea, the unwillingness of the United States to open diplomatic relations, and the various indications that Washington would like to see a regime change there.[14] Some of the language used by the

Bush administration, such as including North Korea in the "axis of evil" and Bush's personal dislike of Kim Jong-il, the attacks on North Korea's human rights records and its missile exports, as well as the maintenance of sanctions, created an image of an implacably hostile United States that might seek any opportunity to attack. The Bush national security doctrine, with its emphasis on pre-emptive attack, added to this perception. The military component consists of the presence of U.S. forces in South Korea and Japan as well as the global military power projection capabilities, which include tactical and strategic nuclear weapons.

But how do North Korean leaders assess the threat they are facing and what are their wider strategic objectives? The opaque nature of the North Korean regime means that information about its political intentions is scarce and often unreliable. Likewise, the assessment of North Korean military programs is fraught with difficulties and has resulted in wildly different projections. In the American political discourse we can discern two different approaches to the question of the North Korean threat. Conservative commentators such as Charles Krauthammer have focused on the totalitarian nature of the regime and see the unremitting hostility to the outside world as a projection of its essential character.[15] The perpetual state of hostility at the outside world is essential to the regime's survival. The North Korean regime is illegitimate, it commits human rights violations against its own population on a large scale, and it is involved in nefarious criminal activities such as currency and drug counterfeiting. The only response to this regime is to contain it with the expectation of eventual regime change (assuming that there is no viable military option). This viewpoint became the central organizing principle of the Bush administration's first-term policy toward North Korea. Liberals, on the other hand, such as Selig Harrison[16] (echoed in the work by British academic Hazel Smith[17]) have explained North Korean behavior on the basis of the perceived threat from the United States and the serious economic problems the country was facing, and have recommended engagement and arms control. Yet another narrative, developed by the Left in South Korea and in China, blames the security crisis on the United States.

UNDERSTANDING NORTH KOREAN FOREIGN POLICY BEHAVIOR: ANALYTICAL APPROACHES

There are two different classes of theoretical approaches that scholars use to understand or explain foreign policy behavior. The first of these involves system-level theories that emphasize the structural constraints of the international system as opposed to the strategies and motivations of agents. From this perspective the relative power position is the critical factor that determines the behavior of states, whereas internal factors such as the type of political system or the actions of individuals are not significant. The second approach emphasizes domestic and social factors that account for the action of states.

STRUCTURAL REALISM

Neorealism, or structural realism, was given its classic systematic exposition by Kenneth Waltz in *Theory of International Politics*[18] and has been developed further by various scholars, including John Mearsheimer in his study *The Tragedy of Great Power Politics*.[19] Although in Waltz's conception it is not a theory of foreign policy as such, it has been widely used as a conceptual basis for interpreting foreign policy behavior. Structural realism is based on the assumption that the international system consists of states that can be described as rational actors. States are the primary actors in international politics, which is a sphere of competition.[20] This system is anarchic, i.e. it has no central authority, and its units are independent and sovereign. It is therefore also a self-help system in which states must provide for their own security and ensure their own survival. The assumption that domestic politics or the political structure of individual states is not an important factor with regard to international behavior can be expressed by asserting that states are functionally similar. Their institutional features resemble each other and through a combination of competition and imitation they are socialized into the international system.[21] In order to ensure their survival states acquire offensive military capabilities, but by increasing their relative power in the international system they also provoke mistrust and the strengthening of the military capabilities of other states. This problem is described as the security dilemma.[22]

The desire of states to maximize their power results in arms races and alliances. International relations are shaped by the balance of power. States differ primarily by their capabilities. Their balancing behavior is a function of the structure of the system (the distribution of power). Cooperation between states is limited and only in accordance with the perceived national interest. Smaller states may be satisfied with absolute gains derived from cooperation with other states; major powers will generally seek to benefit more than others through cooperation (relative gains).[23] According to Waltz, states will be satisfied with absolute gains when the international milieu is relatively benign, i.e. the level of interstate competition is not high and there is no perceived immediate threat of interstate conflict. Neorealists are skeptical with regard to the effectiveness of international institutions or regimes to promote inter-state cooperation and argue that the national interest will ultimately be the main factor that determines state behavior.[24] In Waltz's approach, neorealist theory is not determinist. The structural distribution of power in the system provides constraints on the actions state can take and rewards or punishes various forms of behavior, but different states may react to external pressures and incentives differently. Sometimes different options exist that will be more or less equivalent in terms of a state's interest. Foreign policy analysis can bridge the gap to explain the behavior of particular states.

The principal strategic options for larger powers in an anarchical self-help sys-tem are balancing, buck-passing, and bandwagoning. "Balancing" means seeking alliances with other states to balance against a major power. For example, closer strategic relations between Russia and China and calls for a multipolar system rather than one dominated by a single power could be considered an attempt at balancing against the United States. "Buck-passing" refers to leaving a larger power to deal with security threats. Much of European behavior (leaving the United States to ad-dress security in various crisis regions) is perceived in Washington as buck-passing.[25] "Bandwagoning" means that states align themselves with the strongest power.

Two assumptions of structural realism are open to question: one is that the units have similar characteristics (i.e. liberal democracies behave in the same way as to-talitarian dictatorships) and the other is that they behave as rational actors. The rea-sons to question the first assumption become apparent when we consider the example of the conflict between the Soviet Union and the United States in the Cold War. Structural realism interprets it merely as a competition between two major powers. In this account the conflict resulted in a bipolar international structure (more on that later). The two superpowers acted like the sociopolitical equivalent of magnetic poles, with other states aligning their foreign policy behavior in accordance with one pole or the other.

While this description of the Cold War system is useful in some respects, it leaves out various other factors, such as Marxist-Leninist ideology, authoritarian or totalitarian governments, and the shared Western values such as personal freedom, human rights, and democracy. It can be argued that a theory which ignores the major salient factors that determine how the agents think about the power relationships they are involved with and how they define their interests and goals is not complete. In other words, structural realism simply ignores what must be a major part of the story. The fact that structural realism does not allow for the possibility that international regimes or changing norms and identities could affect the structure of the international system may account for its failure to account for the timing and the manner in which the Cold War ended. Indeed, the fairly rapid collapse of the bipolar structure of the international system was a surprise to scholars and policymakers alike. From a different analytical perspective that takes into account the nature of the regime and the domestic structure of power, the East-West conflict cannot be understood simply as the natural rivalry between two great power systems. It was a more fundamental antagonism involving the legitimacy of different types of socioeconomic organization and the legitimacy of certain political elites for which the pursuit of Great Power interests was an essential instrument to perpetuate their own existence and ambitions.

The notion that different regime types lead to different behavior regarding international cooperation and the use of force has received greater attention due to the democratic peace theory, which states that liberal democracies do not go to war with each other. This is based on the observation that not only have there been no wars between liberal democracies, but neither are they perceived to threaten one another, and the balance of power between liberal democracies has been relevant only in the context of responses to other external threats. Some IR scholars have expressed the view that "the absence of war between democratic states has come as close as anything we have to an empirical law in international relations."[26] The extent to which the empirical evidence supports the democratic peace theory depends on how one defines the term "liberal democracy." Among the conditions for the theory to be applicable there must be a shared value system, the acceptance of international norms, and the existence of institutional mechanisms for the resolution of conflicts. There are other factors which may explain the democratic peace theory, such as the more diffuse nature of political power in liberal democracies that makes it difficult to sustain military conflicts, unless they are relatively limited in time and their objectives are widely accepted by the population. This generally rules out the acquisition of territory by force, owing to the difficulties of absorbing hostile populations in the political system and the violation of political norms involved. It also means that domestic consent to a war depends highly on the nature of the regime against which war is to be conducted—i.e. it has to be credibly described as an aggressive and authoritarian (nondemocratic) regime.

THE ROLE OF IDEAS

Neorealism sees international relations to be primarily determined by material factors, whereas other approaches emphasize the importance of ideas and values, such as the constructivist approach, which is based on the notion that power in international politics is socially constructed. In other words, international relations are not given in nature or determined by material factors alone and consequently can be altered by human practice. In the constructivist approach, elements of social reality such as perceptions of identity, norms and values, interests, fears, and culture have a significant impact on the interactions of units (i.e. states) in the international system. In the words of the constructivist scholar Alexander Wendt: "The effects of anarchy are contingent on the desires and beliefs states have and the policies they pursue."[27] We can go further than that and state that the effects of anarchy are constrained by shared norms. Although the international system is anarchic in the sense that there is no world government and each state is considered to be sovereign, in reality many aspects of the interactions between states, in particular the use of force and international trade, are highly regulated by treaties as well as international regimes and institutions.

For most of the period between World War II and 1990, the structure of the international system was determined by the rivalry between two Great Powers. This kind of system has been referred to as bipolar. The bipolarity of the Cold War was unique insofar as the two poles, or superpowers, had acquired a large stockpile of nuclear weapons that could be delivered to any point on the globe within a short period of time. Consequently they had unprecedented global reach and in extremis virtually infinite military power.

The advent of nuclear weapons modified the security dilemma and the classical approach to the balance of power. At one level, mutual assured destruction prevented direct war between the superpowers, which enjoyed an unprecedented level of national security. This resulted in a significant degree of bandwagoning. It also prevented the outbreak of war in Europe. But the intense rivalry between the superpowers still generated a great sense of insecurity and promoted conflict in other parts of the world.

The end of the Cold War and the collapse of one of the superpowers, namely the Soviet Union, resulted in a world in which the United States, with its unprecedented economic and military preponderance, assumed a uniquely powerful position. The United States became a superpower not only by virtue of its large strategic nuclear arsenal but also its conventional capabilities, which provided it with a global reach that no other power could match. This situation is frequently referred to as unipolarity, and the post–Cold War situation is described by the phrase "the unipolar moment," as coined by the commentator Charles Krauthammer.[28] The concept of unipolarity rests on the assumption that the United States has unrivalled military power and favors internationalism rather than isolationism, and that the threat of war has diminished. This analysis has given rise to an academic discourse on the nature of U.S. hegemony in the post–Cold War world, exemplified by the enlargement of NATO to extend membership to Central and East European states, including some former Soviet republics, and U.S. intervention in regional conflicts in Europe, Central Asia, and the Middle East (such as the war in Afghanistan and the invasion of Iraq).[29]

But Krauthammer's statement reveals a fundamental contradiction in this conception of unipolarity. If there is a significantly diminished threat of war, the preponderance of military power becomes less relevant. Indeed, one of the major changes in the international system—the culmination of a long-term trend—is the decline in interstate conflict. The potential for interstate conflict predicted by John Mearsheimer was nowhere apparent in Europe except on the territory of states which have now fallen apart, such as certain parts of the former Soviet Union and the former Republic of Yugoslavia. These conflicts can be interpreted either as civil or postcolonial conflicts. Instability and conflict we are witnessing in Europe are the consequences of the collapse of the Soviet Union and the Yugoslav state, which created stability on their territories by the constant threat of force. More importantly, the post–Cold War conflicts that involved significant outbreaks of violence were not interstate conflicts (such as predicted by Mearsheimer), but rather intrastate conflicts. Generally speaking, post–Cold War European states do not seem to be naturally prone to military conflict. Quite the opposite appears to be the case: the principal objective of virtually all Central and Eastern European states was/is to join various Western multilateral organizations such as NATO and the European Union and thereby accept international norms with regard to the use, and the threat of the use, of force and other consequent constraints on their foreign and domestic policies.

The international environment that emerged after the Cold War was therefore different than that predicted by some leading prominent neorealist scholars.

Other perspectives provide a sense of a deeper change. These range from *The Clash of Civilization*'s author Samuel Huntington, who sees the bipolar global power struggle replaced by new patterns of conflict and cooperation emerging along cultural lines,[30] to Francis Fukuyama, who believes in the final triumph of Western liberalism and what he calls the end of history.[31] It is not necessary to accept the whole of Fukuyama's framework or the triumphalism of some of his adherents to conclude that a major paradigm shift has occurred with regard to the role of military force in the international system and that we are indeed in a new era in which war between the major powers has become unlikely or, as some would say, obsolete.

Confirmation of the paradigm shift is evident in the increased importance of soft power for U.S. foreign policy in the post–Cold War world, as emphasized by Harvard University's Joseph Nye, who is famous for developing this concept. The paradox of American power in a world characterized by economic interdependence was that although militarily, economically, and politically the United States had a preponderance of power, it nevertheless needed to rely on international institutions and relations with friendly nations to ensure international security and stability.[32] In the course of the 1990s a new pattern of international security began to emerge. The main threat to international security no longer emanated from great power conflict. Instead, the majority of interstate conflict was confined to certain regions, like South Asia (Pakistan and India) and the Far East (the Korean Peninsula). Substate and ethnic conflicts occurred in regions with weak or failed states, such as the former Soviet south and Africa. So-called rogue states, governed by authoritarian regimes with clandestine programs to develop weapons of mass destruction (WMD), acted as state sponsors of terrorism. Rogue states are not constrained by international norms—they behave as if the international system were anarchic.

EXPLAINING NORTH KOREAN FOREIGN POLICY BEHAVIOR

At first glance, North Korean foreign policy behavior seems to fit rather neatly into the pattern of explanation offered by structural realism. At a meeting of the American Political Science Association in 2000, Kenneth Waltz cited North Korea as a prime example of how the security dilemma causes states to acquire nuclear weapons. Both North Korea's diplomacy and public statements suggest that the North

Korean leadership sees relations between states as being governed by power, and that they face a serious and persistent security threat from the United States, which is using sanctions and military threats in order to achieve regime change in North Korea. If the United States were to abandon its "hostile policy" against North Korea, lift sanctions, normalize relations, and end the military threat through a peace treaty or at least a nonaggression pact, then North Korea would not need nuclear weapons or ballistic missiles.

The structural realist explanation for North Korea's foreign policy behavior is commonly advanced in South Korea and has its adherents in the academic community. Its most prominent proponent is Bruce Cumings, who has written widely about "the U.S. role in creating Korean insecurity."[33] The most extreme version of this viewpoint, which commands significant support among younger South Koreans, has been articulated by Tim Beal, who identifies the United States as the main source of the conflict on the Korean peninsula and defends North Korea's actions as part of a "struggle against American power."[34] Selig Harrison has argued that U.S. actions create a sense of insecurity in North Korea and that its policies can be explained on this basis. This liberal view is also the basis of Leon Sigal's work; Sigal argues that North Korea was misunderstood by U.S. politicians and that while coercive diplomacy failed and brought the United States to the brink of war with North Korea, a strategy based on cooperative security would bring diplomatic success. Similarly, Ken Booth and Nicholas J. Wheeler have argued that "one important step to reassure Pyongyang that any cooperative move on its part would be reciprocated by South Korea and the United States would be for the latter, along with Russia and China, to provide the DPRK with the security guarantees it desperately seeks. Such a development . . . requires that Washington be open to the possibility that North Korea's military behavior stems from fear rather than malign intent."[35]

It is true that the North Korean regime feels under threat, but it is important to understand the source of the threat. The history of the Korean Peninsula since 1945 is not easily reconcilable with this analysis of the security dilemma. For most of that time, North Korea was undoubtedly the source of the threat, with its ambition to reunite the peninsula on its terms and under the leadership of Kim Il-sung. It engaged in various attacks on South Korean soil and abroad to kill South Korean leaders, committed acts of terrorism, and dug tunnels underneath the DMZ in order to be able to smuggle soldiers into the South.

An alternative analysis of North Korea's behavior, which has been espoused by many conservative critics of negotiating with the North Korean regimes, including prominent members of the Bush administration such as John Bolton, Robert Joseph, and Dick Cheney, as well as by George W. Bush himself, is that North Korea itself is the source of insecurity. In this view, as the Cold War ended the United States was prepared for a diplomatic opening and found itself in conflict with North Korea only when it became apparent that DPRK was diverting nuclear materials, possibly for weapons production, in violation of its obligations under the Nuclear Nonproliferation Treaty (NPT). The actions of North Korea were not a rational response to any external threat, but rather stem from the "evil" nature of the regime, a totalitarian dictatorship that brutally oppresses its own people, proliferates WMD, and still harbors ambitions for unification on its own terms. Some have concluded that negotiations with such a regime are ill-advised because they simply result in North Korea extracting benefits from the international community without dampening its aggressive ambitions.

Neither the conservative nor the liberal approach is based on an analytical framework that enables us to understand the crisis on the Korean Peninsula. The distribution of power in the international system and the general concept of anarchy are not sufficient to explain how North Korea's threat perceptions are generated.

For example, the strategic situation on the Korean Peninsula means that deterrence is both mutual and stable. North Korea has concentrated its forces close to the DMZ to such an extent that it can instantly respond to any attack. It has deployed such a large number of artillery pieces within range of Seoul that it could without doubt inflict unacceptable damage on the South. Although there are clearly weaknesses in the North Korean force posture, arising primarily from the fact that most of its military technology is now obsolete, it does constitute a credible deterrent and North Koreans are generally convinced of the superiority of their fighting morale and ability.[36]

How the North Korean leaders assess the military threat from the United States, which is central to its public discourse, is not clear. Officials in the foreign ministry who have interacted with Americans seem to think that the risk of such an attack is low, whereas the military leaders see an attack, such as a surgical strike on nuclear or missile facilities, as a more realistic prospect.[37]

Since 1994 U.S. presidents have consistently ruled out the use of military force against North Korea, due to the effectiveness of North Korea's conventional deterrent. The threat to North Korea resides primarily in the unwillingness of the United States and much of the international community to accept the legitimacy of the North Korean regime. This is why much of North Korean diplomacy is aimed at persuading or even compelling the United States to give up its "hostile policy" toward the regime, which is an intangible but nevertheless real and serious political threat.

It is unclear how North Koreans conceive of their nuclear devices as playing a military role. The source of the military threat is primarily located in South Korea, but the idea that Koreans should use nuclear weapons against other Koreans has always been considered taboo, despite the adversarial relations between North and South. A small number of devices can at best provide some kind of "existential deterrent." But if nuclear weapons were considered essential to North Korea's security, then how can we explain that until 2008 North Korea has seemingly been willing to trade away its nuclear weapons capability in return for various economic and political benefits? It seems hard to believe that the United States could offer North Korea any kind of security guarantee that would be credible to the extent that North Korea could afford such a powerful means to deter an attack.

The seeming contradictions in North Korea's behavior are explained by the fact that the most serious threat to the North Korean regime is not external. The liberal view ignores the effect of the nature and the internal dynamics of the regime on the security dilemma. The conservative view explains the behavior of the regime on the basis of its nature, but fails to analyze its nature and the sources of North Korea foreign policy behavior.

The fundamental threat that the North Korean regime faces is that the DPRK is not a viable state. Its economy is broken, its industry cannot supply the basic needs of the population, its external trade is minimal, and its agriculture cannot feed its people adequately. Significant parts of the population are destitute and malnourished; North Korean citizens are cut off from virtually all sources of information about the modern world and do not receive education appropriate to the twenty-first century. The leadership is trapped in the paradox that the country cannot sustain itself in the long term without fundamental reform, which, however, would destroy the regime.

There is no solution to this problem that would leave the existing power structure in North Korea intact. Consequently the regime is using its one asset, namely its military capabilities, to extract as much support from the outside world as is needed to muddle through and stave off collapse, while using all of the resources of the state at its disposal to control the citizenry and prevent any disloyalty to the regime or any opposition from forming.

In the subsequent chapters, you will see that the various crises in North Korea's relations with the outside world, especially the United States, are a manifestation of this internal dilemma. Although support from the outside world can mitigate the effects of the disastrous economic and social reality in the DPRK, it cannot resolve it. Every time an international crisis is resolved, another one rears its head. This explains why North Korea has defected from every agreement it has ever made. For as long as this regime persists, the United States and North Korea will experience a never-ending cycle of conflict and cooperation.

Another way of looking at this dilemma is that North Korea needs better relations with the United States in order to alleviate its security concerns and gain external economic and financial support. On the other end, the hostility of the United States is the central legitimizing principle that is used to explain all the failings of the North Korean state to its population. Thus, the regime can neither afford permanent conflict nor permanent lack of tension with the United States.

ORGANIZATIONAL BEHAVIOR AND DECISION-MAKING THEORIES

The fact that despite fifteen years of negotiations neither North Korea nor the United States have reached their objectives (if we assume that North Korea has other objectives besides acquiring nuclear devices), even though there was agreement on the basic elements of any deal, may simply reflect the irresolvable dilemma that the North Korean regime faces. At the same time, the negotiating history shows quite clearly that both the United States and North Korea missed some vital opportunities. To the outside world, North Korea's foreign policy behavior often seemed strange, to the point that it has been widely considered to be irrational. Considering organizational behavior and models of decision-making may provide some insights into North Korean foreign policy behavior.

In foreign policy analysis, models of decision-making have been developed that question the rational expectations that are at the root of system-level theories of international relations. A pioneering study by Graham Allison on the 1962 Cuban Missile Crisis, published in his book *Essence of Decision*, proposed three alternative models for the study of decision-making: the rational actor model, the organizational behavior model, and the governmental politics model.[38] The rational actor model is based on the assumption that states are unitary actors in foreign policy, and that they act in relation to threats and opportunities so as to maximize the benefits of the outcome for themselves. The organizational behavior model is based on the observation that the bureaucratic organization of governments places limits on and influences the implementation of policy to the extent of sometimes determining the final outcome. Organizational processes based on set procedures and previous experience are used to implement policy. In a crisis, due to limitations of time and resources governments do not necessarily examine all possible courses of actions, but often settle on the first proposal that seems likely to resolve the issue. Often instead of a holistic approach to a problem, it is broken up and assigned to the different parts of the bureaucracy that deal with it in accordance to established processes rather than in terms of the overall desired outcome. The governmental politics model acknowledges that the government is not necessarily a unitary actor, but that differences of interests and points of view exist within a government. Policy is the outcome of the interaction of a game between various players within the bureaucracy, and outcome may not necessarily serve the best interests of the state. In fact, it may be incompatible with any rationally conceived policy objective. Instead, it serves the political, financial, or other interests of sections in the bureaucracy or society.

Is North Korea a rational actor? This question, in terms of decision-making theory, is not about the state of mind of Kim Jong-il. Instead, it has a very precise meaning about how decisions are made and policy is formed and implemented. Possible influences on North Korean policy arising from divisions within the elite (e.g. reformers versus hard-liners, military versus civilians) will be explored further in this volume. Even if North Korea is a rational actor, there are possible limitations that explain the failure of the DPRK to achieve its policy objectives. Rationality can be bounded by limits to knowledge, an incorrect analysis of the available policy alternatives, or the employment of incorrect means to achieve the state's objectives.

In the case of North Korea, there is ample evidence that North Koreans often do not perceive the outside world and the intentions of their adversaries correctly, and that likewise the outside world and especially U.S. policymakers have an incorrect perception or are uncertain about the motivations and objectives that drive North Korea's action. Misperception of a strategic situation may be due to cultural differences or secrecy surrounding a state's capabilities and intentions.

Another source of misperception is strategic cognitive dissonance. Strategic cognitive dissonance occurs when the reality of a strategic situation conflicts with deeply held beliefs by decision-makers.[39] Cognitive dissonance is a psychological phenomenon that arises when two mutually contradictory beliefs are held at the same time. If one of these beliefs is so strong that a person is unable to question or discard it, the second belief has to be questioned in order to reduce the dissonance. Cognitive dissonance as a source of misperception and its effect on decision-making has been analyzed by Robert Jervis.[40] There are many examples of strategic cognitive dissonance. For instance, the deeply held belief in the conservative elite in the United States that the Soviet Union was seeking to change the strategic nuclear balance in such a way that it would be capable to inflict a first strike on the U.S. Intercontinental Ballistic Missile (ICBM) force led to the debate about the basing of the MX missile and the so-called window of vulnerability. The strategic analysis underlying the idea that the Soviet Union was looking to achieve victory in a nuclear war was faulty in that it incorrectly assessed the strategic balance between the two sides, both of whom were constrained by strategic arms control, and completely ignored the enormous invulnerable second strike capability based at sea.[41] The source of the cognitive dissonance in this case is the fundamental belief that the Soviet Union is aggressive and relentlessly seeks to defeat the West. The notion that the Soviet Union might be deterred by U.S. strategic forces, and therefore has accepted the need for peaceful coexistence, is incompatible with this core belief and hence had to be rejected in order to reduce the dissonance.[42]

Jervis, in his study on perceptions and misperceptions, laid the foundation of the analysis of how the psychology of leaders affects decision-making under conditions of incomplete information, stress, and cognitive bias.[43] According to Jervis, misperception can result in overestimating one's influence or capabilities. If strategic analysis does not yield a useful construct, an alternative approach to explain the failure of nuclear weapons to deter conflict is based on strategic cognitive dissonance. Deterrence fails because one side does not correctly perceive the strategic situation and is consequently willing to assume excessive risks. Any military action as a result of this level of strategic dissonance involves risks that could have catastrophic consequences.[44] How this applies to North Korea's relations with the outside world will be explored further in this volume.

The first part of this book is focused on the political and military aspects of the crisis on the Korean Peninsula. It looks at the military confrontation and North

Korea's nuclear and missile programs, and then examines the evolution of the security crisis in Korea since the partition in 1945.

The second part considers the geopolitical context. It provides an empirical account of the Agreed Framework that for some time froze the plutonium program and the subsequent multilateral efforts to deal with the nuclear program through the Six-Party Talks. Given that the various regional actors have different perceptions and strategic objectives with regard to North Korea, the book also considers the international responses to the North Korean issue from the perspectives of various stakeholders in some depth.

The problem of North Korea and its nuclear program is of crucial significance for the security and geopolitics of Northeast Asia. Apart from the fact that this situation is the most likely source of serious military conflict in the region, it is also an important factor in determining the presence and role of the United States and relations between China, Japan, South Korea, and Russia. The manner in which this crisis is ultimately resolved and the future of North Korea will determine whether the Republic of Korea remains allied with the United States and the relative positions of influence of China and the United States in the region.

2

Preparing for Confrontation

North Korea's Armed Forces and Military Strategy

The most obvious manifestation of the crisis on the Korean Peninsula is the military confrontation at the Demilitarized Zone, where two large armies are facing each other, ready to go to war at short notice. The risk of war seems ever present; soldiers are watching each other warily and occasionally exchange fire. In fact, the Korean Peninsula is the only place in Northeast Asia where the imminent outbreak of large-scale warfare is a real possibility. This threat is exacerbated by the possibility of the use of WMD. But what is the nature of the North Korean threat, and what are the risks posed by this military confrontation? This chapter will examine the military balance on the Korean Peninsula, assess the risks, and evaluate the political implications.

THE KOREAN PEOPLE'S ARMY

The current military confrontation across the DMZ in Korea developed as a consequence of the Korean War (1950–1953), in which the North's Korean People's Army (KPA) was thoroughly defeated. The conflict ended in a stalemate due to China's intervention and a decision by President Truman to end the war with a division of the peninsula at the 38th parallel. Despite a narrow escape thanks to China's support, Kim Il-sung never relinquished his ambition to reunify Korea under his leadership, and North Korea has built up substantial forces near the DMZ. In the South and in Washington, the intentions of the North were considered to be aggressive, as North Korea also engaged in terrorist attacks, made attempts to assassinate the South Korean leadership, and prepared numerous tunnels underneath the DMZ, seemingly in preparation for an eventual invasion of the South. The scale of the forces fielded by the DPRK exceeded that of the South in all categories, be it number of troops and reservists, artillery pieces, armored vehicles, or combat aircraft. But the presence of the U.S. forces, which until the late 1980s deployed nuclear weapons in South Korea, robbed any invasion from the North of any chance of success.

Today the armed forces of the DPRK include 1,106,000 active personnel. More than 90 percent (950,000) are in the army, 110,000 are in the air force, and the navy has a personnel of 46,000. There are also 189,000 paramilitary troops. The armed forces consist primarily of conscripts who have to serve for five years (minimum). North Korea also maintains a reserve force of 4,700,000.[1] About 70 percent of the active force and 80 percent of the aggregate firepower of the DPRK is positioned within 100 kilometers of the DMZ, including 700,000 troops, 12,000 artillery pieces, and 2,000 main battle tanks.

The North Korean army, which defeated the South Korean army during the Korean War and then was routed by the allied forces, has been built up steadily over the decades. In 1960 the number of troops was below 400,000 and it remained around this level until 1972. In other words, there was an increasing militarization of the DPRK over two decades to provide the military resources for reunification by force, if circumstances permitted (i.e. the U.S.-ROK alliance ended), or to defend against any aggression from the South. This militarization affected the entire structure of the society as political power rested predominantly in the military, especially after Kim Jong-il proclaimed the "military first" policy. Under this policy the military is given absolute priority with respect to material resources.

As official statistics from the DPRK are unreliable, it is difficult to estimate the true level of defense expenditures. The International Institute for Strategic Studies (IISS) Military Balance of 2009 refuses to even estimate any financial data with respect to North Korea, but experts believe defense expenditures are approximately $5–7 billion (about a quarter of GDP).[2] It is hard to overstate the degree to which the military consumes virtually all resources, as from the mid-1990s it became apparent that the only factories operating at full capacity were those producing military goods.[3]

North Korea's military strategy is offensive, designed to penetrate rapidly into enemy territory with overwhelming firepower and speed. Its operational concepts have been adapted from Soviet and Chinese military doctrine. The frontline forces are deployed in three echelons—a forward echelon comprised of four infantry corps;

a second echelon consisting of the armor corps, two mechanized corps, and artillery corps; and a third echelon with another artillery corps and two mechanized corps. The forces are protected by an extensive network of hardened shelters. Additionally, defensive forces are deployed throughout the territory of the DPRK—including a corps to defend Pyongyang and extensive coastal and air defenses—but the concentration of forces at the front line means that the Korean armed forces lack the strategic depth that is provided in South Korea by three defensive belts. About 88,000 special forces are trained to penetrate into the South with light weapons and conduct reconnaissance and special operations, possibly in advance of any major assault. In order to facilitate the infiltration of troops into South Korea in the event of conflict, North Korea has dug various tunnels under the DMZ (two of which were discovered).

The KPA is equipped with more than 3,500 main battle tanks, 560 light tanks, and 2,500 armored personnel carriers. It fields in excess of 17,900 artillery pieces, and various self-propelled guns, 7,500 mortars, 11,000 pieces of anti-aircraft artillery, 10,000 surface-to-air missiles, and various kinds of anti-tank munitions. North Korea's naval forces are mostly coastal defense vessels without the capability to foil U.S. naval operations or move large numbers of forces to the South. They consist of 158 patrol craft, 100 torpedo craft, 43 missile craft, some 26 Soviet-designed diesel submarines, some 65 miniature submarines for sending special forces into enemy territory, 10 amphibious ships, and 23 anti-mine ships. Coastal defense has been enhanced with the deployment of anti-ship cruise missiles.

The strength of the North Korean military lies in the sheer number of troops and tanks, and the training of the armed forces. However, most of North Korea's main equipment dates from the 1960s or even earlier. Thus 1,600 of the main battle tanks are Soviet-made T54 from the 1960s, and 800 are T62. The most modern tanks are North Korean adaptations of Soviet tanks, namely the Chonmaho, which was adapted from the T62, and the Pokpoongho, which incorporates various Soviet technologies, including reverse-engineered parts of the T72, which had been scrapped by the Soviet Union, and technology from the T80 and T90 models. North Korea may have up to 1,000 Chonmaho and perhaps 100 Pokpoongho. Nevertheless, the fact remains that North Korea has over the decades failed to adequately modernize its mechanized forces. It is unclear whether this is the result of strategic choices or simply the failure of the Soviet Union and China to provide the DPRK with the equipment it needed and the inability of the North Korean weapons industry to keep up with developments in other countries. This weakness also extends to the air force. North Korea has a substantial air force with some 605 combat aircraft. These are mostly older MiGs, although there are some more modern MiG-23, MiG-29, and Su-25. A significant proportion of the air force is based close to the DMZ. This means the KPA cannot achieve one of the key requirements in Soviet concepts of deep operations, namely to obtain air superiority and deploy air-deliverable ground forces.

WEAPONS OF MASS DESTRUCTION: NUCLEAR WEAPONS

At the core of the crisis on the Korean Peninsula since the early 1990s is North Korea's nuclear program. It is not known exactly when North Korea first constructed a working nuclear device: it was not until the underground nuclear test that North Korea conducted on October 9, 2006, that its capability to explode a nuclear fission device was confirmed. Although there is consensus that a fission device was detonated, it seems that the test did not go according to plan. Shortly before the test Pyongyang informed the Chinese government of the impending nuclear detonation and that it was supposed to have a target yield of 4 kT (that is, the kind of explosion that would be produced by 4,000 tons of conventional explosive). The precise yield is not known, but nevertheless there is consensus among expert observers that it was much lower (estimates vary between 0.2 and 1 kT).[4] There are many possible reasons for the lower yield, from impurities in the plutonium or improper machining of the plutonium to problems with the conventional explosives that create the critical mass or the neutron initiator.[5] However, when Siegfried Hecker of Stanford University visited the Yongbyon facility toward the end of 2006, his North Korean hosts dismissed all suggestions that their test did not achieve its technical objectives and expressed great pride in their achievement.[6]

A second nuclear test took place on May 25, 2009. On the basis of seismic data, the yield of the explosion was estimated to be in the range of 2–8 kT, with the most likely value around 4 kT. It took some time to detect the presence of nuclear particles that confirmed it was an atomic explosion.[7]

Thus it has now been generally accepted that North Korea has built nuclear explosive devices, but the question remains whether it can manufacture warheads that can fit on ballistic missiles. According to an interview conducted with officials from South Korea's Ministry of National Defense by the International Crisis Group

(ICG), North Korean engineers made significant progress in warhead miniaturization between 1999 and 2001, and are now capable of mounting warheads on ballistic missiles.[8] But so far there is no publicly available evidence that confirms these views. North Korea would need to create a device that weighs less than a ton in order to be able to use missiles to deliver it (the Nagasaki weapon weighed 4 tons and could not have been delivered by North Korea's missiles or aircraft).[9] In 2005 *Weolgan Chosun* (Monthly Chosun) journal in Seoul reported that a North Korean who defected earlier that year claimed to have worked for the Second Economic Committee of the Supreme People's Assembly that oversees munitions production. The defector stated that North Korean scientists produced at least one nuclear device with 4 kg of plutonium that weighed a ton, and were working to reduce the weight of the weapon to 500 kg.[10]

The number of nuclear devices North Korea may have is limited by the extent of its plutonium production. The reactor that produces the plutonium is a 5 MWe reactor at Yongbyon whose capacity is reasonably well known; based on the history of the reactor, independent analysts have calculated that it could have produced up to about 60 kg plutonium. (This contrasts with the official U.S. government estimate of 50 kg and the DPRK's declared amount of separated plutonium of 37 kg.) In 2009 work was resumed at two other reactors at Yongbyon, which North Korea had begun to construct but never completed, namely the 50 MWe reactor at Yongbyon, and the 200 MWe Taechon reactor. Completion of these reactors is years away, but Siegfried Hecker has estimated that the 50 MWe reactor, when completed, could generate about 275 kg plutonium per year. At present the nuclear materials available to the North Koreans is still quite limited, enough for up to 8–12 warheads, but if there is no deal to end the nuclear program this could change in the future.[11]

The statement from North Korea's foreign ministry that accompanied the 2006 test referred to the DPRK's "nuclear deterrent," and this phrase has been repeated in similar statements that have been issued since.[12] In 2008 the willingness of Pyongyang to dismantle its plutonium production facilities seemed to indicate that the DPRK would be content with a small-scale so-called existential deterrent that would enhance North Korea's already considerable ability to cause unacceptable levels of casualties in South Korea. The North Koreans understand fully that any use of nuclear weapons risks swift and devastating retaliation, but seem to believe that the existence of the capability will deter the United States from attacking North Korea or intervening effectively in the event of military hostilities. Given that the DPRK cannot compete with the United States in nuclear arms, the KPA must rely on a strategy of asymmetric deterrence.[13]

CHEMICAL WEAPONS

Given the political attention aimed at the nuclear program, it is often ignored that North Korea has a substantial stockpile of chemical weapons. They are significant, given that these weapons may be used at the outset of any conflict on the Korean Peninsula. Their impact in any military conflict would be limited, given that U.S. and South Korean forces are well equipped and trained for combat in an environment involving the use of chemical agents, but they have the capacity of causing widespread panic and massive civilian casualties. The details of the chemical weapons program and capabilities are even more obscure than those of the nuclear program, partly because production facilities are harder to identify and these capabilities have not aroused the same kind of international controversy. North Korea is one of only seven countries that have neither signed nor acceded to the Chemical Weapons Convention (CWC). However, the DPRK is a party to the Geneva Protocol of 1925, which prohibits the use—but not the possession—of chemical or biological agents in warfare. North Korea is also part of the Biological and Toxin Weapons Convention (BTWC), which prohibits the production and stockpiling of biological agents for weapons (but not for defense research), but there is no verification regime in place.[14] By contrast, the Republic of Korea signed the CWC in 1993 and completed the destruction of its chemical stockpiles by 2008.[15]

The DPRK is believed to have one of the largest stockpiles of chemical weapons in the world, with estimates ranging from 2,500 to 5,000 tons of chemical agents. These reportedly include all the major classes of chemicals, such as choking (phosgene), blister (mustard gas), blood (hydrogen cyanide), and nerve agents (sarin). According to a report by the U.S. Department of Defense, North Korea began to develop and stockpile chemical weapons after the Korean War. In 1954 the Korean People's Army established nuclear, biological, and chemical defense units on the same pattern as the Soviet armed forces. It is believed that North Korea's offensive chemical weapons program received some assistance from China. During this period North Korea developed a substantial chemical industry, as called for in the first five-year plan (1957–1961). In 1961 Kim Il-sung issued a Declaration of Chemicalization, calling for the construction of a dual-use chemical industry for civilian and military purposes. A chemical bureau was established out of the chemical department in the general staff of the defense ministry (since 1981 known as the Nuclear and Chemical Defense Bureau). In 1964 North Korea started to import agricultural chemicals from Japan, which enabled Pyongyang to obtain chemical precursors for the synthesis of mustard gas and the nerve agent tabun, and at a later date organic compounds containing phosphorus and chlorine. When the Soviet Union resumed technical assistance to North Korea, the latter received nuclear, chemical, and biological training materials. The DPRK also received small amounts of mustard and nerve agents from the Soviets. Production of chemical weapons most likely began in the 1970s. In the later part of that decade, it was reported that North Korea was producing significant amounts of chemical agents, including cyanogen chloride as well as some mustard gas and tabun. This report seemed credible as the U.S. Defense Intelligence Agency reported in 1979 that North Korea had developed protective measures against chemical weapons and that it was likely it would proceed toward the production of offensive agents. In the following years there was continued speculation about North Korea's chemical weapons program. The next official statement came from the South Korean defense minister Lee Ki-baek, who stated on the basis of a defense ministry report that the DPRK had a stockpile of between 180 and 250 metric tons of chemical weapons, including mustard gas and nerve gas.

In January 1989 the foreign minister of the DPRK, Kim Young-nam, made a statement to the effect that North Korea did not produce or store nuclear or chemical weapons and did not seek to import such weapons. Around the same time it was reported that the North Korean inventory included mustard agents, hydrogen cyanide, adamsite, phosgene, tabun, and sarin. In 1991 a military manual, *Konggyok-chon* (Offensive Warfare), published by Kim Il-sung Military University, codified the conduct of nuclear and chemical defense units. In February 1992 Kim Il-sung issued a directive to the effect that the entire population should be provided with protective masks and training in nuclear, biological, and chemical (NBC) defense. This was the first of many clear indications that Pyongyang expects a future war to be fought in a contaminated environment. In October 1992 South Korean Intelligence (then called the Agency for National Security Planning) claimed that North Korea had six centers for chemical weapons storage, each with a stockpile of 1,000 tons of agents, and that some chemical agents were kept by military units in artillery shells.

In November Pyongyang angrily denied that it had any chemical weapons, while at the same time accusing the United States of having a large stockpile in South Korea. North Korea repeated that it had no chemical weapons and declared that it adhered to international law in good faith, but declined to join the CWC despite being urged to do so by the Russian government.

In the mid-1990s there were a number of defectors that confirmed the existence of an offensive chemical weapons program and provided some details. On March 18, 1994, Yi Chung-kuk, a sergeant in the KPA Nuclear Chemical Defense Bureau, defected to the Republic of Korea. He said he defected in order to warn the world about North Korea's chemical weapons program. Although he himself was involved in work on defense against chemical attacks, he claimed considerable second-hand knowledge about the DPRK's offensive chemical weapons program and stated that the North had enough chemical weapons to destroy the South without the use of nuclear weapons. Moreover, he also claimed that North Korea could use Scud missiles to deliver chemical warheads.[16] Yi provided detailed information about the 18th Nuclear and Chemical Defense Battalion and on Factory No. 279 and the No. 398 Research Institute in Sokam-ri. According to him these facilities are responsible for the development and production of equipment for defense against chemical attacks. Yi also claimed that the February 8th Vinalon Complex is involved in the chemical weapons program. Vinalon is a textile fiber, and according to Yi the inventor of vinalon contributed to the research and development of chemical weapons. Choi Ju-hwal, a colonel in the KPA, served in the Ministry of Defense in Pyongyang from 1968 to 1995, when he defected. Choi only had second-hand information on North Korea's chemical weapons that he said he obtained from other officials. In 1997 he claimed that North Korea had a stock of more than 5,000 tons of chemical agents, including hydrogen cyanide, cyanogen chloride, lewisite, mustard gas, and various nerve gases such as sarin, tabun, soman, and V-agents.[17] Some evidence comes from the high-level defector Hwang Jang-yop. Hwang was not in charge or directly involved with programs relating to WMD, but he was one of the highest-level insiders of the regime and therefore is probably the most reliable source. On the basis of debriefing sessions with Hwang the then Foreign Minister of the Republic of Korea, Yu Chong-ha, told the National Assembly Unification and Foreign Affairs Committee on May 6, 1997, that North Korea had about 5,000 tons of chemical weapons agents and operated eight plants capable of producing 5,000 tons of agent every year.

Chemical munitions can be placed on missiles or in artillery tubes, and there is little doubt that North Korea possesses the capacity to use chemical weapons in devastating attacks against South Korea's civilian population, but North Korea's leaders are aware that this could invite unrestrained nuclear attacks by the United States. Nevertheless, this means the North Korean military has the capacity to cause large civilian casualties in the South, which is clearly instrumentalized to deter limited strikes by the United States on North Korean territory.

BIOLOGICAL WEAPONS

As far as biological agents are concerned, even less is known about any stockpiles or weaponization. In 1992 South Korea's Agency for National Security Planning reported to the National Assembly that Kim Il-sung ordered the then so-called Academy of Defense Sciences (now the Second Natural Science Academy) to develop biological weapons. A testing center was established that managed to procure samples of anthrax, plague, and cholera from Japan in 1968.[18] In 1980 the Central Biology Research Institute was established, alongside the No. 25 Factory in Cheongju (North Pyeongan Province), which is believed to have produced various biological agents and a military biodefense unit. There are various other production facilities and research centers that may be involved in research and development of biological weapons agents. Intelligence estimates of North Korea's biological weapons capabilities have become more tentative over time. In August 2005 the then commander of the U.S. forces in Korea, General Leon LaPorte, said he did not believe North Korea had weaponized biological agents, and a similar judgment has been made by the South Korean government.[19] According to South Korean government sources, North Korea may have obtained a small sample of the smallpox virus, but this remains unconfirmed and there is no evidence that there has been mass vaccination of the North Korean armed forces, which would be necessary if smallpox were to be used as a biological weapon.[20]

MISSILE TECHNOLOGY

For more than thirty years North Korea has been involved in the production of ballistic missiles, developing a large infrastructure for design, testing, and manufacture. North Korea's ballistic missile industry is based primarily on Soviet technology and was developed with the help of the Soviet Union and China. Although there are significant uncertainties about the extent of North Korea's missile capabilities, it is estimated that the DPRK has about 700 ballistic missiles.

Ballistic missiles are clearly the delivery system of choice for nuclear weapons, given the vulnerability of aircraft to air defense and the difficulties in executing a coordinated attack with strategic bombers. For this reason there seems to be an inextricable link between North Korea's nuclear ambitions and its ballistic missile program. North Korean efforts to develop ballistic missiles go back to the mid-1960s. In 1965 the Hamhung Military Academy was opened, and several departments began studying and teaching the design of missile engines.[21] The Soviet Union had rejected Kim Il-sung's requests for ballistic missiles, but in 1968 provided the DPRK with FROG-5 short-range missile systems, surface-to-air missiles, and anti-ship missiles for coastal defense. The FROGs, with a range of up to 60 km, and a payload of 400 kg, were capable of delivering conventional or chemical munitions into the Seoul metropolitan area from positions just behind the DMZ and therefore added to the capabilities provided by North Korean artillery.[22] Moscow balked at providing North Korea with more advanced missiles as relations between the DPRK and the Soviet Union deteriorated in the context of a sharpening conflict between China and the USSR. Consequently Pyongyang turned to Beijing to obtain access to more advanced missile technology. In 1971 China and North Korea signed a military cooperation treaty that included missile technology transfer and the sale of missiles. China provided North Korea with surface-to-air and surface-to-ship missiles.[23] In April 1975, when Kim Il-sung visited Beijing, a deal was concluded for North Korea's participation in a Chinese missile development project. The Dongfeng 61 was conceived as a single-stage tactical missile, based on Soviet Scud technology, with a range of 600 km and a payload of 1,000 kg. The project did not come to fruition, because when its main supporter General Chen Xilian was removed from the PRC government in 1978 it was cancelled.[24] However, North Korean missile experts may have acquired a great deal of technical knowledge as a result of their participation, which most likely assisted them when North Korea built its own version of the Scud.

Hwasong Missiles

After the end of the joint project with China, North Korea forged links with Middle Eastern countries, and Egypt and the DPRK began to collaborate on missile production. Egypt needed assistance because their relationship with the Soviet Union had collapsed in the wake of the 1978 Camp David accords. Cairo supplied Pyongyang with a few Scud-B (R-17) with its mobile launcher for the purpose of reverse engineering. By 1984 North Korea had successfully produced a number of Scud-B-like prototypes, designated the Hwasong-5. This engineering effort involved the construction of a number of new facilities, including (according to defector reports) the Sanum dong R&D facilities (also called the No. 7 Factory), the Sungni Automobile Factory where mobile launchers are produced, the No. 125 factory for missile assembly (located near Pyongyang), and the Musudan-ri missile testing facility (Hamgyong Province).

The Hwasong-5 (Hwasong means "Mars") has a range of about 320–40 km (about 15 percent greater than that of the original Scud-B) and carries a payload of 1,000 kg. It is reported serial production began in 1986 and continued until about 1991. The Hwasong-5 was supplied to Iran during the Iran-Iraq war, where it experienced combat use that allowed DPRK engineers to gain valuable technical data. In the meantime North Korea developed another version of the Scud with a lower payload and a lighter airframe, extending the range to 500 km. This missile, called the Hwasong-6, started to be deployed in 1991.

The extent of indigenous technology in these missiles remains subject to doubt. There have been various unconfirmed reports that North Korea did receive a number of Scud missiles from the Soviet Union (either officially or unofficially). The Stockholm International Peace Research Institute (SIPRI) reported that the Soviet Union provided North Korea with approximately 240 Scud-B missiles between 1985 and 1988.[25] The North Korean missiles are remarkably similar to the Soviet originals, suggesting that the modifications were minor and that the original Scud rocket motors were used.

Rodong Missiles

By 1991 the entire Korean Peninsula was within the range of North Korean missiles, but the efforts to extend the range of the Scud had reached their limits. According to the conventional account, in the late 1980s North Korea had begun the development of a medium-range missile that would have the capability to target Japan, with a range of 1,000–1,300 km and a payload of 700–1,000 kg. This missile, called the Rodong, was based on a design that required new engines and guidance systems to achieve the required performance characteristics. The concept design for it was developed by the USSR's Makeyev Design Bureau (or Makeyev OKB, a design bureau that specialized in submarine-launched missiles), and consequently this missile bears some resemblance to the early designs of the SS-N-4 (R-13) and SS-N-5 (R-21). It seems that North Korea managed to overcome the challenges of developing new engines that required four times the thrust of a Scud engine, probably with the assistance of Soviet missile engineers. Indeed, the Rodong engine seems to be of similar design as the Isayev S-2.713M engine incorporated in the SS-N-4, and the missile itself is an intermediate design between the SS-N-4 and SS-N-5. There is good reason to believe that this engine was designed by the Isayev design bureau (the former OKB-2 NII-88) that designed a number of missile engines for the Makeyev OKB. It is known that sixty engineers from the Makeyev OKB were prevented from flying to North Korea in October 1992, although a number of them subsequently made their way to North Korea by alternate routes and others collaborated with North Korean engineers by e-mail.[26]

The scale of the North Korean missile program, which developed different missile types within a comparatively short time frame, makes it appear implausible that North Korea could have achieved such a feat without a substantial transfer of technology. Working alone would have strained the capacity of countries with a far more highly developed industrial base. A North Korean defector claimed that 90 percent of the components of a factory producing missile guidance and control systems were imported from Japan.[27] While the DPRK may now have become self-sufficient in the capacity to produce airframes, tanks, and other important missile components, it may still be reliant on imports for advanced electronic components. Some analysts have become convinced that North Korea's missile program is not really indigenous or self-sufficient in any sense, but is more accurately described as procurement. Thus Daniel Pinkston from the ICG and Robert Schmucker, a former UNSCOM (United Nations Special Commission) inspector in Iraq, have pointed out that the DPRK missile program is characterized by short development timelines, few flight tests, and early production schedules.[28]

Details on the development and deployment of the Rodong are sketchy. In May 1990 a new missile that resembled what later became known as the Rodong was observed by U.S. satellites at the Musudan-ri test launch facility. In May 1993 there was a successful launch from Musudan-ri into the Sea of Japan. The missile traveled a distance of about 500 km on a high-altitude trajectory designed to demonstrate warhead separation. This was the only test of the missile by North Korea ever reported, although Pakistan and Iran tested a number of Rodong-type missiles since 1998 and it may be assumed that North Korea obtained data from these tests. The IISS North Korea dossier estimates the CEP (a measure of accuracy) of the Rodong at 3–5 km, and a report cited at GlobalSecurity.org claims a CEP of 2–4 km, but the data for such an assessment is very limited.[29]

The timeline for production and deployment as well as the size of the Rodong force remain uncertain, and the program has suffered from various technical and financial problems. Nevertheless, the rapid development of this missile on the basis of a minimal number of test flights indicates that North Korea received substantial technical assistance from abroad. Daniel Pinkston from the ICG and Charles Vick from GlobalSecurity.org have built a very substantial case that Russian engineers from the Makeyev Design Bureau actively participated in the production of the Rodong.[30] Indeed, some analysts go as far as to claim that the Rodong was designed by Russians, who played a key role in its development, or that the Rodong itself is an old missile from the Makeyev Design Bureau that never achieved operational status in the Soviet Union.[31]

The construction of missile storage sites began in July 1995, and by October of that year four launch sites had been built. Operational training of missile crews is believed to have started in 1995 as well. The Ministry of National Defense of the Republic of Korea declared the missile to be operational in 1997, and South Korean sources claimed that by 1999 nine Rodong missiles had been deployed. The deployment rates and numbers remain guesses, but most observers believe that by 2002 the DPRK had between 100 and 200 operational Rodong. North Korea also exported the missile. The Pakistani Ghauri is practically identical to Rodong, and the Iranian Shahab-3 was developed on the basis of the Rodong design with the assistance of North Korean engineers. It is believed that Iran purchased at least 10 complete Rodong missiles. Some Rodong were exported to Libya. North Korea also exported about 500 Hwasong-5 and -6 to Iran, Syria, Egypt, and Libya.

Clearly the strategic purpose of the Rodong is to hold Japanese cities, military installations, and U.S. forces in Japan at risk. The IISS dossier on North Korean military capabilities published in 2004 argues that because of its poor accuracy and low numbers, the Rodong is not effective against hardened military targets and is therefore more likely a political rather than a military weapon, unless it is fitted with nuclear warheads. Of course the use of nuclear weapons would be suicidal for the Pyongyang regime. While it may be true that the effectiveness of the Rodong remains limited, it is clear that North Korea considers the capability to attack Japan and U.S. forces in Okinawa a critical element of its defense posture. An active test program to validate the performance of the Rodong was undertaken by Iran. Iranian engineers made substantial changes to the missile, replacing the heavy steel airframe with one made from aluminum, and reducing the weight of the re-entry vehicle to 750 kg. They also lengthened the fuel tanks, achieving an extension of the range to 1,600 km. The accuracy of the missile was somewhat improved by changing the shape of the nose cone and (it appears) replacing the guidance system. This new version of the missile was called the Ghadr-1. The Rodong-2, which made its appearance in 2006, seems to be very similar to the Ghadr-1, so much so that specialists from the IISS believe that North Korea adopted Iranian technology (possibly by importing complete missiles), which now seems to be well ahead that of the DPRK.[32]

Taepodong Missiles

This became evident when on August 31, 1998, North Korea launched a new kind of missile in an attempt to place a small satellite into orbit. This missile was called Taepodong-1 by U.S. analysts (after the area from where it was launched), although the North Korean name is Paektusan-1. The Taepodong-1 missile (distinct from the space launch vehicle) is a two-stage missile. The first stage is based on a modified Rodong; the second stage is a Scud-B and -C. This combination is estimated to have a range of 2,000–2,200 km and a payload of 700–1,000 kg. The space launch vehicle is the third stage, consisting of a small ellipsoid-shaped solid motor designed to lift the satellite into orbit.

The Korean Central News Agency reported the launch of a satellite into orbit, even though in reality the launch failed.[33] The first stage of the rocket fell into to the Sea of Japan and the second stage into the water near the Sanriku coast. The third stage fired, but an unknown malfunction resulted in the failure of the satellite to achieve orbit. Although the satellite launch failed, the attempt alarmed analysts because it demonstrated the capability to manage the technical problems of building a missile with three stages. The Taepodong thus demonstrated the potential for developing missiles of intercontinental range (ICBMs).

Although it is now generally accepted that North Korea attempted to launch a satellite, the action provoked considerable outcry due to its trajectory, which was perceived as demonstrating a threat against Japan. The Japanese government denounced the event as a missile launch and stated it would reconsider its contribution to the light water reactors under the Agreed Framework, although in the end Japan resumed its support. The event also gave Japan further impetus to collaboration with the United States on theater missile defense, and on September 20 the two countries reaffirmed their commitment to conduct joint research on ballistic missile defense.

In the face of international criticism and political pressure, North Korea negotiated an agreement with Washington in September 1999, whereby in return for the lifting of a range of sanctions North Korea imposed a moratorium on long-range missile tests. This moratorium was extended more than once and remained in force until 2006, even though after the collapse of the Agreed Framework Pyongyang threatened to resume space launches and in early 2005 threatened the resumption of missile tests if no progress was made in nuclear talks. On July 5, 2006, North Korea made good on this threat, conducting a series of missile launches that resulted in the imposition of sanctions by the United Nations.[34]

The key strategic question is if and when North Korea will be able to acquire an intercontinental missile capability that can strike at targets on the continental United States. According to the IISS analysts, the three-stage version of the Paektusan-1 could deliver a small payload (100–200 kg) to targets on the U.S. mainland, not enough for a crude nuclear device and probably not enough for a chemical warhead that could cause a significant number of casualties. North Korea's plans for an ICBM capability therefore rest on the development of a larger missile, designated Taepodong-2 (Paektusan-2). According to a North Korean defector, development of the Taepodong-2 began in 1987 on direct orders of Kim Jong-il. The missile is believed to exist in a two- or three-stage variant (the latter being a space launch vehicle). The second stage is believed to have the engine from the Rodong, with a substantially larger first stage that can deliver a great deal more thrust. An alternative hypothesis is that the second stage has the rocket engine from the soviet R-27 (a sea-based missiles deployed in North Korea as the land-based Musudan).[35] Various analyses, including U.S. intelligence reports, have described the first stage as similar to the first stage of the Chinese Dongfeng-3 (CSS-2/DF-3). The IISS dossier describes the first stage as a cluster of four Rodong engines. Estimates of the range for the missile vary, with 3,500–6,000 km representing a reasonable guess based on the design characteristics, given a payload of about 1,000 kg.[36] There are reports that China provided some assistance and that North Korean military personnel paid visits to Yinchuan and a Chinese naval base in Dalian to get information about various types of ballistic missiles.[37] The 1995 U.S. National Intelligence Estimate (NIE) gave a range estimate of 4,000–6,000 km, and concluded that no country other than the declared nuclear powers would be able to attack the continental United States for at least another fifteen years. The Taepodong-2 would be able to reach Alaska or Hawaii at best.

The missile tests in July 2006 were primarily a political demonstration. In the case of the Rodong, Pyongyang essentially outsourced its testing to its customers in Pakistan and Iran, although those tests were few in number and therefore confidence in the reliability of Rodong must remain limited (especially as about 50 percent of the tests appear to have been failures). A test of the Taepodong-2 engine is believed to have taken place in 2001. The test in 2006 resulted in the early explosion of the missile, so the data this test provided must have been very limited. It was reported that North Korea initiated talks with Iran on exporting components of the Taepodong-2 to Iran, where they would be assembled by North Korean engineers. In 2004 it was again reported that Iran was considering purchasing the Taepodong-2 as the basis for an intercontinental ballistic missile and also that Russian missile engineers were assisting a solid-fuel design team at the Shahid Bagheri Industrial Group in Iran to develop two long-range missiles with a range of 5,000 km and 10,000 km, respectively. These missiles could be the Shahab-5 and Shahab-6, although Teheran has indicated that its missile developments would end with the Shahab-4. The Shahab-4 is a satellite launch vehicle that has so far not been revealed.[38] By the time Taepodong-1 program was terminated, its capabilities remained very much unproven, and it was unclear how much progress North Korea was making toward the development of an ICBM.

In September 2008 there were reports that the DPRK was constructing a new long-range missile test site at Dongchan-ri, in North Pyongan Province on the west coast.[39] On February 24, 2009, North Korea announced the intention to launch a satellite from the older Musudan-ri lauch site on the east coast using the Unha-2 space launch vehicle (essentially a Taepodong-2). South Korean and U.S. officials were quick to point out that such a launch would contravene UN Security Council Resolutions 1695 and 1718.[40] The launch with the alleged purpose of putting a satellite (called Gwangmyeongseong-2) into orbit was reported on April 5, 2009. By openly defying the UN and asserting its right to launch satellites, North Korea put the international community on notice that it was not willing to accept restrictions on what it considered to be its sovereign right to exploration of space technology. The North Korean government issued dire warnings about the consequences of an attempt to shoot down the rocket or take North Korea to the Security Council. The wider ramification of this action was the potential change in the strategic equation between United States and North Korea, because of the perception that the launch was to demonstrate North Korea's capability to fire long-range missiles that would eventually be able to target the continental United States. These developments have the potential of completely changing the strategic equation in relation to North Korea. However, the payload of the Taepodong-2 is 750 kg. More than a decade of development will most likely be needed for North Korea to be able to manufacture nuclear warheads that can be incorporated into a re-entry vehicle for either the Taepodong-2, Rodong-2, or any other missile in the DPRK inventory.

What did this launch demonstrate? Indeed the Taepodong-2 lifted off correctly and the first two stages of the missiles were operational, but the satellite did not reach orbit and the debris came down into the Pacific. It is fair to conclude that North Korea's missiles, while able to target South Korea, Japan, and perhaps even Guam, do not yet have full intercontinental capability.

There was considerable public discussion about the wise decision of the United States and Japan not to test their missile defense systems against the North Korean rocket. One reason was that this would obviously have been a serious escalation of the crisis, with unpredictable results. Moreover, the likelihood of a successful interception was probably low and a failed attempt to shoot down the rocket would have embarrassed the United States and emboldened the North Koreans. On June 12, 2009, the UN Security Council passed resolution 1874, reprimanding North Korea for the nuclear and missile tests.[41] It imposed new sanctions, expanded arms embargos, and authorized ship searches on the high seas, thus breathing new life into the Proliferation Security Initiative as South Korea finally decided to join.[42] The resolution also imposed measures to deprive the DPRK of means of financing its nuclear and missile programs and banned the exports of heavy arms in general and ballistic missiles in particular. The latter, if it could be enforced, would be a blow to Iranian and Pakistani missile programs as well as seriously restricting North Korea's hard currency earnings as the arms trade between Iran and North Korea alone is estimated to be worth $2 billion.[43] The resolution was tested soon thereafter as a North Korean ship, the *Kang Nam*, sailed toward Myanmar and was shadowed by U.S. battle ships, only to return without having docked and discharged its cargo.[44]

Musudan Missile

There are two other North Korean missile programs that need to be mentioned. In September 2003 there were reports of sightings by U.S. intelligence satellites of a new type of missile that seemed to be similar to the Soviet SS-N-6 (originally a submarine-launched missile) at Mirim airbase. On September 9, 2003, just prior to the celebrations of the fifty-fifth anniversary of the founding of the DPRK, about ten missiles and five launchers were sighted at the base (the preparation site for parades). Subsequently some analysts have expressed the view that these were merely mock-ups and that this unknown missile, which has never been flight tested and about whose development there had been no prior information, does not exist. However, information that construction on two underground missile sites in Yangdok County (South Pyongan Province) and Sangam-ri, Hochon County (Hamgyong Province) was underway seemed to substantiate the view that there might be more to this new missile program than met the eye. On July 7, 2004, in testimony to the National Defense Committee of the ROK National Assembly, then Defense Minister Cho Young-kil confirmed that North Korea had deployed this new missile.

This missile, called the Musudan, has a range of 2,750–4,000 km, and it is suggested that it is based on the engine of an SS-N-6 (R-27) with a Rodong re-entry vehicle and interstage element, thus resulting in a missile body with a diameter of 1.5 m (equal to that of the SS-N-6) but somewhat greater length than the original Soviet missile (12 m as opposed to 9.65 m).[45] It is believed to have an accuracy based on a CEP of 1.9 km. The missile has not yet been flight tested and so there is no information on its performance characteristics other than extrapolations from what is known of the SS-N-6. If the estimates for the range of the missile are correct (up to 2,400 km with a 650 kg warhead), then it could target American bases in Okinawa and Guam. Unlike others, this new system is deployed on mobile launchers. The original SS-N-6 was tested for deployment on surface ships as well as submarines, and there are fears that North Korea might seek to deploy the missiles in this mode, thereby potentially increasing the target range, although surface ships would be very vulnerable to interception. However, based on its demonstration at a military parade, it is believed that it will be deployed in a road-mobile mode. The development of the

Musudan began in 1992, when the general designer of the Makeyev Design Bureau, Igor Velichko, signed a $3 million contract with the Korea Yeongwang Trading Company. The contract was for Russian professors to teach in North Korea, but in fact involved the development of a space vehicle designated Zyb (a reference to the R-27/SS-N-6).[46] As was discussed earlier, the missile has a slightly longer airframe than the original R-27 and presumably the airframe has been reinforced to permit launch from land. It is estimated that North Korea may have a few dozen of these missiles shipped from Russia.

KN-02 Missile

The other missile of note is the KN-02, which is based on the SS-21 (Tochka) and which was first publicly displayed on April 25, 2007. It is believed that the SS-21 was procured from Syria together with solid propellant. The missiles that Syria originally acquired from the Soviet Union were shipped from Syria to North Korea in August 1996.[47] The missile has a range of 120 km and a CEP of 160 m. It is more accurate than other missiles in Pyongyang's arsenal and puts Seoul and U.S. bases in Pyeongtaek at risk. It is the only known North Korean missile using solid fuel technology.

ASSESSING THE SIGNIFICANCE OF THE NORTH KOREAN MISSILE PROGRAM

In assessing the significance of the North Korean missile program, there are several fundamental questions that have very far-reaching consequences. The first is the extent of North Korean capabilities in the field of missile technology and the potential future trajectory of the North Korean ballistic missile program. Given that the North Korean program is one of the major foundations for the Iranian and the Pakistani ballistic missile programs, this question is of significance beyond the Korean Peninsula. The evidence suggests that North Korea has made considerable investments in developing an infrastructure for designing, manufacturing, and testing advanced ballistic missiles. What remains obscure is the extent to which North Korea has mastered these technologies. It has become increasingly clear that North Korea relies on very extensive foreign assistance to develop its missiles. It is highly unlikely that North Korea has the capacity to reverse engineer Soviet missiles to the extent of mastering all the technologies involved in designing its own missiles. In the absence of access to the machines used to build and test the components of the sample, it is extremely difficult to understand the function of each of the components and to develop the processes and equipment necessary to manufacture them. The Soviet missiles North Korea seeks to reverse engineer were designed and built in the 1950s and 1960s, and the original equipment may no longer exist as the production lines have been closed for decades; whatever equipment does exist would be subject to export controls and not available on the open market.

The work of Michael Ellemann at the IISS has shown the extraordinary difficulties encountered by Iraq and Iran as they sought to reverse engineer Scuds and other Soviet-made missiles during the Gulf War. For example, Iraq spent a decade in efforts to reverse engineer the Volga engine of the Soviet SA-2, scavenging a larger number of these engines in the process, without success.[48] In a recent report published by the IISS on the Iranian missile program, the authors state:

> As Soviet and Chinese successes, and Iraqi failures, make clear, a successful reverse-engineering effort cannot rely solely on information extracted from sample components. Instead, it requires deep fundamental knowledge of the item to be replicated, or access to the original design documentation and production engineers. Iraq lacked both.[49]

Another peculiar feature of the North Korean program is that the supposedly reverse-engineered missiles bear such close resemblance to the original. Typically, the appearance and the performance characteristics of reverse-engineered systems differ significantly from the original, as demonstrated by the Soviet efforts to reverse engineer German ballistic missiles, or the Chinese version of the Soviet R-2. While the North Koreans may have varied the range and payload of the Soviet missiles slightly, these are in conformity with the performance profile of the original missile. Moreover, to develop ballistic missiles that perform with any degree of reliability and in order to determine their performance characteristics requires an intensive and disciplined testing program that is entirely absent from the North Korean missile complex.[50] As we have already pointed out, North Korea has introduced a range of missiles with almost no testing, and even the tests that were conducted involved no telemetry and therefore no data were collected; the tests were political demonstrations rather than an element of the missile design process. The Musudan resembles the Soviet sea-based R-27 so closely that it may well been shipped to the DPRK rather than developed in situ. The Rodong-2 likewise resembles the Iranian Ghadr-1 to such an extent that North Korea may have been the recipient of Iranian missile technology. It is clear North Korea does not possess an active development program for these missiles. The launchers are imported either from Belarus or China; there is no evidence of domestic launcher development. This raises the question of the extent of a truly indigenous missile technology base in North Korea and whether North Korea is more of a trader rather than a producer of missiles. This in turn affects the question of the future trajectory of the DPRK's missile program and whether North Korea will be able to achieve significant improvements in range and accuracy, so as to develop a militarily significant missile capability and extend the range to be able to strike the continental United States. If it is indeed the case the North Korean medium- and long-range ballistic missile program was virtually wholly reliant on foreign assistance, there is a question mark about the DPRK's capacity to develop an accurate, reliable, long-range missile. This is because the technology North Korea has obtained belongs to the second generation of Soviet missile technology and it is unclear whether Russia or China are prepared to make more advanced technology available, even through unofficial channels.

The close analysis of the Iranian ballistic missile program carried out by the IISS, which includes data about the support they received from North Korea, paints a very clear picture. The North Koreans and Iranians have had some success in modifying the performance characteristics of the missiles by altering the payloads, rebuilding the airframes, and modifying the fuel tanks. There is evidence that North Korea has tried to obtain components for inertial guidance systems to improve the accuracy of their missiles. The North Koreans have also produced longer-range missiles by strapping together multiple engines of the Rodong and have produced multistage rockets. However, neither the North Koreans nor the Iranians have been able to improve the performance of the engine, and there is no evidence that they are capable of manufacturing the engine itself. The engine of the Rodong, which was observed to have Cyrillic markings, looks from the outside exactly like an up-scale version of the engine of the Scud-C.[51] The Rodong most likely is a missile in the Scud design heritage produced by the Makeyev Design Bureau that was never introduced into the Soviet Rocket Forces. This missile was deemed too large for a mobile launcher and therefore not deployed; instead the Scud-B and Scud-C were developed and deployed. The Rodong produces twice the thrust of the Scud-B, and the dimensions of the Scud-B in comparison to the Rodong suggest a normalized reduction in size. The Isayev Design Bureau experienced problems with the Scud engine due to vibrations, and placed baffles inside the engine to deal with combustion instabilities, which are absent from the Rodong, where these problems do not seem to have occurred, again suggesting that the Scud-B was derived from the original Soviet version of what is now known as the Rodong.[52] The Makeyev Design Bureau faced very serious financial problems in the 1990s as the production of submarine-launch ballistic missiles (SLBM) was halted and the Russian government failed to pay its substantial debts to the enterprise. In addition to sending Russian engineers to North Korea to assist in the development of their ballistic missile program, they off-loaded their substantial inventory of missiles and components for systems that had long been decommissioned to the North Koreans, who in turn sold much of their imports to the Iranians and Pakistanis. The long-range missile development program of the DPRK relies on two rocket motors, the engine of the Rodong and that of the Musudan (R-27). Both of these are supplied by the Makeyev Design Bureau, and neither the North Koreans nor the Iranians are capable of manufacturing these engines themselves or developing new, more powerful rocket motors.[53]

This imposes serious constraints on North Korean prospects for developing missiles of intercontinental range. The development path chosen by the North Koreans for the development of longer-range missiles using several engines and a solid-fuel motor for a third stage so far has failed to produce the desired results. According to the IISS, an ICBM using the technology available to the North Koreans would weigh in the order of 120 tons with a diameter of 2.5 m to deliver a 1 ton warhead.[54] It remains to be seen whether North Korea has the capacity to build the required airframes. Such missiles, if they are ever built, will require substantial testing to establish their reliability and will be difficult to deploy in secure silos, given their size. Essentially, North Korea remains stuck in the missile technology of the 1950s and 1960s.

The unknown factor is the extent to which the Makeyev Bureau will continue to provide expertise, equipment, components, and missiles. In particular, the number of rocket engines available is likely to be limited. Moreover, the situation has changed since the 1990s. The Makeyev Bureau has benefited from Russia's SLBM modernization program and has also been tasked with the development of modern space launch vehicles, thereby eliminating the incentive for illicit sales of highly restricted technology.[55] Moreover, the Russian government has stepped up efforts to ensure compliance with the Missile Technology Control Regime (MTCR). For this reason it is likely that the supply of hardware from Russia has dried up and North Korea will have to make do with what it has acquired in the past. This means that the large-scale deployment of long-range missiles, and ICBMs in particular, may not be an option for Pyongyang.

There are consequences for those countries whose ballistic missile programs have relied on North Korean technology. Pakistan's long-range missile capability is predicated on the Ghauri, which is based on the Rodong. Pakistan has already declared that it will no longer procure missiles or components from North Korea, but this means that Islamabad will be unable to deploy missiles that can target the whole of India's territory. As far as Iran is concerned, its efforts to develop long-range missiles are subject to similar constraints. Iran has absorbed what technology it could from North Korea, and is adopting a more disciplined and sophisticated approach to missile development, which means that as the supply of Soviet components and engines runs out, the flow of ballistic missile proliferation may reverse and North Korea will become a recipient of Iranian technology, unless something is done to disrupt this collaboration. Of course, the severe constraints on North Korea's access to hard currency may limit such cooperation as Pyongyang runs out of items to barter. Overall, provided Russia and China abide by the restrictions of the MTCR (even though China is not yet a member), the prospects for ballistic missile proliferation are much more restricted than thought hitherto.

The second question regards the military purpose of North Korean long-range ballistic missiles and the impact of the program on the strategic situation in Northeast Asia. Ballistic missiles form one of the key elements of North Korea's asymmetric capabilities. The precise strategy underlying the procurement and deployment of ballistic missiles and the nature of the threat posed by North Korea's ballistic missiles remains unclear.

The threat posed by North Korean missiles at this time remains limited. North Korea has several hundred Hwasong-5 and -6 at its disposal, but these missiles with a range of 500 km are so inaccurate that they cannot be reliably used against military targets. Indeed, during the Iran-Iraq war, hundreds of these missiles were fired by both sides, without having a significant effect on the conduct of the war. The First Gulf War in 1990–1991 also demonstrated that Scud-based missiles are not very effective against military targets. The Rodong could hold targets in Japan at risk, but its reliability remains unproven. The Rodong-2 and Musudan have a greater range, but will require a substantial flight test program to achieve an operational status. Missiles could be effective antipopulation weapons if they carry chemical warheads. It is still not very likely that North Korea has been able to develop nuclear warheads that can be delivered by ballistic missiles. The payload that can be carried by the Rodong-2 and the Musudan is less than 800 kg, and based on the dimensions of the re-entry vehicle a nuclear device would have to have a diameter of 60 cm or less. Similar restrictions apply to the Taepodong-2. More than a decade of development will most likely be needed for North Korea to be able to manufacture nuclear warheads that fit these requirements.

ASSESSING THE NORTH KOREAN THREAT

Threat perception is based on an analysis of intentions and the military capabilities built to support them. For decades the North Korean threat was defined by the declared intention of the commitment of the Korean Workers' Party to "achieving a complete socialist victory in the northern half of the republic and to completing a people's revolution to liberate all Korean people throughout the nation."[56] Most analysts agree that the extreme weakness of the state since the early nineties means that while nominally the goal of unification is still maintained, the Kim regime is now exclusively focused on survival, which demands a strategy of deterrence.

Some analysts have argued that the military doctrine of the Korean People's Army and the pattern and manner of deployment of its forces suggest an aggressive intent.[57] Although there is some truth to this, the statement needs qualification. The North Korean capital Pyongyang is located just 120 km north of the DMZ, so a defensive force posture would require similar patterns of deployment, to impede an advance toward the capital along the Gaesong-Munsan and the Chorwon Valley approaches. Moreover, Soviet military thought, which to some extent informs North Korean thinking, has always emphasized the counteroffensive as a central part of defense strategy.

The fact that the bulk of North Korean forces are deployed within reach of the DMZ must not be overinterpreted, given that from the KPA's perspective this is the direction from which any threat is to be expected. Heavy fortifications throughout the country are designed to provide a deep defense to prevent the country from being overrun.

An assessment of the military balance is therefore not very straightforward, because most of North Korea's military equipment dates from the 1950s and 1960s and is not comparable to the advanced military equipment the ROK has been able to develop and purchase. Analysis of the comparative capability of weapons technology based on observations from the 1991 Gulf War indicates that modern Western weapons systems are two to four times better than older Soviet-designed systems. In particular, North Korea lacks the target acquisition and precision-guidance and space-reconnaissance capabilities of its opponents.

In the early decades after the Korean War, it was generally believed that North Korea had a military advantage over South Korea and that the security of the Republic of Korea depended critically on the support of the United States. The United States deployed around 50,000 troops (the numbers varied over the years), which were considered to be a tripwire for massive reinforcements from Japan and farther afield. Until the end of the 1980s, U.S. forces in Korea were also equipped with nuclear weapons stationed on the peninsula. However, as South Korea developed into a modern industrialized state, it modernized its armed forces to the point that most analysts would agree that the North Korean armed forces (leaving aside nuclear weapons) are no match for those of the ROK.

It is true that there is a significant numerical imbalance. South Korea's active military personnel stands at 687,000, compared with 1,106,000 for North Korea. South Korea has 2,360 main battle tanks, compared to more than 3,500 fielded by the KPA. But South Korea's battle tanks embody modern technology and are both faster and have superior firepower to the bulk of North Korea's, which are mostly equipped with technology dating to the 1970s or earlier. Particularly impressive is the Type 88 K1 battle tank, based on a design provided by General Dynamic Land Systems (then Chrysler), which designed the U.S. M1 Abrams battle tank. It incorporates state-of-the art firepower and armor, and is highly maneuverable. The ROK army has 1,000 K1, and its other main battle tanks are also far superior to most North Korean equivalents. For example, South Korea, rather than North Korea, was able to purchase the advanced Russian main battle tank, the T80. In addition to main battle tanks, the ROK army fields 2,480 armored personnel carriers and light tanks, 115 attack helicopters (including 60 Cobra), more than 100 unmanned aerial vehicles (UAV), 10,774 artillery pieces, some 6,000 mortars, 1,130 air defense missiles, and a dozen Hyunmu surface-to-surface missiles based on U.S. technology (range 180 km, payload 500 kg). When it comes to the air force, the story is similar: numerical imbalance is more than compensated for by superior capability. The ROK air force has 468 advanced fighters, which include 39 F-15 Eagle and a 165 F-16. The ROK navy, too, is far superior to its North Korean counterpart. Including marines, the total South Korean navy personnel is 68,000 strong and consists of three fleets: Donghae (East Sea), Pyeongtaek (Yellow Sea), and Busan (South Sea). There are 47 principal surface combatants, including 10 destroyers, 9 frigates, and 28 corvettes. The navy also has 12 tactical submarines and ships and aircraft for amphibious, special warfare, anti-submarine, and other types of operation.[58] The official assessment of the U.S. Department of Defense is that as far as the overall military balance is concerned, South Korea enjoys a significant advantage over the North.[59] This judgment has been confirmed by various independent analyses.[60]

The security guarantee from the United States and the U.S. forces stationed in the Republic of Korea remove any doubt about who would prevail in a war. At the beginning of 2009 the United States had 25,241 personnel stationed on the Korean Peninsula. They were comprised of the 8th Army under Pacific Command (17,130), 254 U.S. navy personnel from Pacific Command, and 7,857 from the 7th Air Force. There were about 300 fixed-wing aircraft in the vicinity of Korea deployable in any crisis (including aircraft based in Japan and on nearby aircraft carriers).

Currently the headquarters of USFK (U.S. Forces Korea) is based at Yongsan in Seoul under the command of Gen. Walter L. Sharp. However, it has been agreed that U.S. forces will redeploy to the Osan-Pyeongtaek area 75 km south from the Han River, which runs through Seoul. This means that only South Korean forces will be forward deployed at the DMZ. Another important change in relations between the armed forces of the ROK and the United States is the agreement to transfer wartime command of ROK forces to Korea (in place of the Korean-U.S. combined forces command, led by the U.S. commander in wartime).

The redeployment puts American forces beyond the reach of North Korea's artillery, thereby enhancing their capacity to respond to an attack. If major hostilities were to break out, existing operational plans call for very substantial reinforcements of up to 500,000 American troops. The second issue is the timeliness of reinforcements, given that a surprise attack could very quickly create realities on the ground. Independent experts believe that U.S. troop levels could be tripled within three days, but transport for a heavy army division would take twenty to thirty days and the entire reinforcement operation would take longer (two to three months). By this time the decisive phase of combat operations is likely to be already completed.

The United States and the Republic of Korea have conducted large joint exercises, called Team Spirit, involving about 200,000 troops, and a smaller annual Ulchi Focus Lens exercise involving 75,000 troops. These exercises have always drawn sharp criticism from North Korea; for example, in 2008 the exercise Key Resolve (which involved only 6,000 additional U.S. troops) was denounced as a "war game aimed at a northward invasion."[61] Every time such exercises are held, North Korea puts its forces on a war footing, which consumes scarce resources such as fuel. From the point of view of the United States and the Republic of Korea, the exercises demonstrate an excellent level of combat readiness and coordination.

Whether the operational plans can be implemented will also depend on U.S. commitments elsewhere. The substantial American troop commitments in Iraq and Afghanistan raise serious doubts in this regard. Privately South Korean specialists have expressed deep skepticism that reinforcements in the event of war would be on the scale envisaged in the operational plans.[62] Indeed, Michael O'Hanlon from the Brookings Institution estimates that "we could cobble together a couple or three divisions I think, using equipment not in depot, from the six to eight divisions here now (not in Iraq or Afghanistan). But it would be only about half of what the war plans call for."[63]

Assuming the war plans can be implemented, the United States would deploy the modern equivalent of five heavy divisions and more than fifteen fighter wings, exceeding North Korea's capabilities even without counting the formidable forces of the Republic of Korea. This assumes that the allies would not use nuclear weapons, which remains an option in extreme circumstances.

O'Hanlon and Mike Mochizuki have published a detailed analysis of a scenario in which North Korea attacks in order to occupy the South.[64] In the 1990s it was assumed in the United States that a surprise attack by North Korea might be successful in capturing Seoul in the early phase of the conflict. Such a conflict would involve heavy artillery bombardment, the use of surface-to-surface missiles, and the rapid movement of armored forces across the DMZ. However, O'Hanlon and Mochizuki's analysis shows that given the failure of North Korea to adequately modernize its mechanized and armored forces, and the technological gap between the armed forces of the two sides, it is doubtful that North Korea will be able to achieve this objective. Military readiness has declined as the levels of training, equipment maintenance, provision of fuel, et cetera, have plummeted. North Korean forces would face the bulk of the South Korean army across a 250 km front without any hope of either gaining air superiority or suppressing the artillery or air defenses in the South. Quite to the contrary, U.S. and ROK air forces would establish air superiority for themselves very quickly. Thus the advancing forces would be extremely vulnerable, and during the advance their supply lines would be subject to interdiction. With about 500 aircraft, allied forces have the capacity to destroy several hundred enemy armored vehicles every day. Moreover, much of the terrain is unsuitable for armored vehicles, channeling the attacking forces into narrow corridors. In tank engagements with ROK armored divisions, the more advanced forces of the South would prevail. Meanwhile, massive air attacks on targets throughout North Korea would begin with sea-based Tomahawk cruise missiles and heavy bombers based in Guam and Okinawa. Another decisive advantage for the allies is that they boast all-weather day-and-night capabilities. Indeed, North Korea has nothing that matches allied reconnaissance capabilities, which include joint surveillance target attack radar system (JSTARS) aircraft, RC-7B reconnaissance aircraft, and of course U.S. space-based assets.[65]

Given this situation, it is clear that North Korea's asymmetric deterrence strategy is focused on countervalue targets. This strategy has both military and psychological aspects. The deployment of such a large number of artillery tubes within range of Seoul means that the North Korean military could inflict large casualties and severely damage the South Korean economy. Although the South Korean army has the capability to track and locate artillery positions by radar and swiftly destroy them, it is not possible to prevent each artillery tube from firing at least five and possibly more shells before it is pulled back or destroyed. This means thousands of artillery shells could be fired at Seoul before all the artillery tubes are destroyed. North Korea has hundreds of ballistic missiles that can reach any target on the Korean Peninsula and can be launched against targets in Japan and as far afield as Guam. The missile warheads may be conventional, chemical, biological, or nuclear, although (as discussed earlier in this chapter) there is no conclusive evidence yet that North Korea has mastered the technical requirements to place nuclear devices on missiles. Although these weapons are not very accurate, and therefore are not very suitable for destroying important military targets, they can cause significant damage and inflict massive casualties, especially if they are armed with chemical munitions (let alone the use of nuclear warheads). The key strategic issue is whether North Korea will be able to target the continental United States. If its nuclear and missile programs continue without restraint, the DPRK might eventually acquire such a capability.

The psychological component of asymmetric deterrence is to convey the willingness to assume much greater risk than the opponent. This is based on the presumption that both South Korea and the United States are averse to civilian casualties. North Korea is projecting a kind of nihilistic attitude to military conflict on the peninsula—that it is willing to risk a major catastrophe and engage in brinkmanship backed up by the threat of military action. This obviously involves a large element of bluff. The Kim regime is clearly preoccupied with its survival, it is neither suicidal nor irrational, but it seeks to extract maximum leverage from its military capabilities, and their cultural mindset is that such that military capabilities are perceived as the true and only currency of political power. Finally, North Korea also seeks to leverage its weakness in its relations with the outside world. A collapse of the North Korean state could create a situation that might become extremely difficult to manage for its neighbors, in particular South Korea and China. Indeed the countries in the region have a great stake in preventing an uncontrolled dissolution of the regime, which would create chaos and a massive refugee crisis with possibly highly armed people streaming into China and across the DMZ, resulting in a humanitarian catastrophe.

To some extent, the North Korean strategy is effective. South Korea indeed has much to lose in the outbreak of military hostilities on the Korean Peninsula. The United States has considered military options for a pre-emptive attack and rejected them because of the likely economic and human costs. Although President Lee Myung-bak was under severe pressure to respond forcefully to the sinking of the *Cheonan*, a South Korean naval ship, in 2010, he refrained from military action (except for joint exercises with the U.S. navy to demonstrate resolve) and confined the response to economic and political sanctions.

In the public discourse, the nuclear program pursued by a rogue state is identified as a serious threat, but the nature of this threat is rarely clearly articulated. Since the early 1990s the nuclear program seems to have served two distinct purposes. One is to provide a deterrent against the threat from the United States; the other is to serve as a bargaining tool to deal with the economic and political threats to the regime. These two functions are ultimately incompatible for as long as the international community insists that the nuclear program is traded in return for underwriting the Kim regime. The problem for North Korea has always been that it has only one card to trade. This means anything it will get in return will have to be enough to mitigate all conceivable future threats to its existence, but it has been difficult to conceive of a package that can achieve all that. Consequently North Korea has been trying to trade its card bit by bit, postponing the day when it will finally have to give it up.

Now we have reached a stage when North Korea will insist on keeping at least some nuclear devices and will dismantle the plutonium program in return for economic support and political and security guarantees. The Obama administration has made it clear it is not prepared to recognize North Korea as a nuclear power and is not interested in any negotiations that will not lead to complete nuclear disarmament. So far it remains unclear what policy the U.S. administration plan to pursue in order to constrain North Korea's nuclear program from expanding once and for all.

Clearly any use of nuclear weapons either on the Korean Peninsula or farther afield would invite a devastating response that would destroy the regime completely. The problem is that North Korea's strategic capabilities will encourage greater risk-taking at a lower level, in accordance with the stability/instability paradox identified by the international relations scholar Glenn Snyder.[66] Given the propensity of the Pyongyang regime to use military threats as tools of diplomacy, the United States will at some point find itself in a situation of greater risk and may consider its options to become more restricted. A secular increase in the quantity and quality of North Korea's arsenal is also undesirable, as it will induce a much greater sense of insecurity in the region and may provoke countermeasures, such as the deployment of missile defenses or even the acquisition of nuclear weapons by Japan and/or the Republic of Korea. Although this latter possibility still remains distant, it is clear that all the powers in the region have an interest in finding an effective way to constrain North Korea's nuclear ambitions. Another threat that has been identified is the prospect that North Korea might proliferate its nuclear capabilities to other regimes with unpalatable ambitions. North Korea has been a major supplier of ballistic missiles to Pakistan and Iran. Worse, there is evidence of North Korea's nuclear collaboration with others, such as Syria. In the Syrian case, on September 6, 2007, Israeli jets attacked and destroyed a suspected nuclear facility where North Korean specialists had been assisting the Syrians.[67]

Neither side on the Korean Peninsula has any real interest in initiating armed conflict. In this sense, it can be said that there is a stable system of deterrence. At the same time, the use of military threats for political purposes, the level of North Korea's brinkmanship, and the fundamental instability of the regime which could collapse or degenerate into fights between internal factions means that there remains a significant risk of inadvertent escalation of conflict to the level of full-scale military hostilities. This is why the situation on the Korean Peninsula continues to represent a major risk to international security in Northeast Asia.

3

North Korea and the World

From Soviet Colony to Failed State

The North Korean state came into being as a result of the division of the Korean Peninsula at the end of World War II, when Japanese occupation of Korea ended with the arrival of the United States and the Soviet Union. This chapter will chart the development of the DPRK from a Stalinist people's republic in the sphere of influence of the Soviet Union to a failed and isolated state and explain the emergence of the totalitarian system of government in the hands of the Kim family, which continues to exercise a stranglehold over the country to this day.

THE ORIGINS OF THE DPRK

The Japanese had arrived in Korea in 1905, and Imperial Japan formally annexed the territory of Korea five years later.[1] At that time Korea had a largely underdeveloped agricultural economy.

In addition to exerting total political control, by the ruthless use of violence if deemed necessary, the Japanese government sought to increase agricultural production in order to meet Japanese demand for rice and attempted to integrate the Korean economy with that of Japan. It built up industrial capacity, especially in the North, and invested in infrastructure, including transport, utilities, and education. However, most of the large-scale enterprises in Korea were owned by Japanese companies. The Japanese authorities seized arable land and sold it to Japanese willing to settle in Korea, resulting in an increasing Japanese ownership of land, reaching 52.7 percent in 1932. Japan sought to dominate Korea socially, and to effectively destroy Korean culture, in what has been described as cultural genocide. Koreans were required to learn Japanese, which became the official language of government, commerce, and education, and had to adopt Japanese-style names. During World War II many Korean women were abducted from the countryside and served as so-called comfort women in military brothels, a form of sexual slavery. Even though the Japanese modernized Korea's industry and education, improving Korea's human capital, their thirty-five-year rule of Korea left a legacy of hatred of the oppressors and a strong feeling of nationalism that to some extent persists to the present day and is especially evident in North Korea.

The occupation provoked the formation of a Korean independence movement, which engaged in various forms of action against Japanese rule. On March 1, 1919, a group of nationalist leaders read out a declaration of independence, but demonstrations against Japanese rule throughout Korea were brutally put down by the authorities, resulting in more than 7,000 deaths. Some of the principal leaders of what came to be known as the Samil Movement (also known as the March First Movement) formed the provisional government of Korea in Shanghai on April 13, 1919 (it later relocated to Chongqing). Among them were Rhee Syngman, a conservative nationalist who until 1925 served as president and later became the first president of the Republic of Korea; Kim Gu (born Kim Chang-am), who served as president from 1940 to 1948; and Yi Dong-hwi, a prominent socialist who established the first communist group in Korea in 1918, known as the Korean People's Socialist Party (*Hanin Sahoe-dang*), in Khabarovsk, Siberia. The provisional government did not achieve any international recognition, except from the Nationalist Chinese government. Although Yi Dong-hwi was the first premier of the provisional government, he resigned as the Korean communist movement was developing closer links with the Soviet government in Moscow, which supported it financially. Yi returned to Manchuria in 1921 to organize a guerrilla campaign in northern Korea. He eventually died in Siberia in 1928.

Kim Il-sung (1912–1994), a nom de guerre adopted by Kim Seong-ju in the 1930s, would later portray himself as the father of the communist resistance against Japanese rule. According to official North Korean history, he single-handedly led the anti-Japanese liberation movement and a revolution for Korean independence that culminated in victory in 1945. This narrative constitutes the central myth that legitimates a regime whose leadership, army, and ideology were forged in the resistance against the Japanese. Of course, this account is grossly exaggerated. Kim did not play a prominent role in either the independence movement or the Communist Party until 1934, although he later became one of the leading figures. In 1929 he was arrested by the Japanese just after joining the underground communist youth group. The official history promulgated by the Korean People's Army states that Kim Il-sung formed the army on April 25, 1932, but like much of the official version of his role in the communist movement and the anti-Japanese resistance, this bears little relation to reality. The Korean People's Army originated with the Korean Volunteer Army (KVA) formed in Yan'an (China) in 1939 by Kim Tu-bong and Mu Chong. The KVA fought against the Japanese alongside Chinese communist forces who supplied weapons and ammunition. Toward the end of the war, when Japanese forces had been defeated, the KVA entered Manchuria where more ethnic Koreans joined it, before crossing into Korean territory. By September 1945 the KVA consisted of 2,500 fighters. By October of that year, the Soviets started to organize security in North Korea using Korean fighters and the KPA was formally established on February 8, 1948.

In 1931, the Japanese occupied Manchuria (technically known as Inner Manchuria, consisting of three provinces in Northeast China bordering Russia) in order to create a buffer zone between Korea and Russia and exploit Manchuria's natural resources. The leading role in fighting the Japanese in southern Manchuria was played by Chinese fighters trained and supplied by Communists. Kim Il-sung acquired some fame as a guerilla fighter when he led an attack across the Manchurian-Korean border on the town of Pochonbo in June 1937, as during those years it was rare for guerillas to be able to penetrate this border. In 1939–1940 the Japanese had become more successful at suppressing the resistance, killing all the top leaders of 1st Army in which Kim was a commander. With the Japanese on his trail, Kim Il-sung decided to flee to the safety of Soviet territory in late 1940. For the next few years he was based in the village of Viatsk near Khabarovsk in Siberia. In February 1942 his wife Kim Jeong-sook gave birth to a son named Yura (diminutive form of the Russian name Yuri), later to be known as Kim Jong-il. Kim Il-sung became a captain in the Soviet army's 88th Brigade, which did not take part in the campaign against Japan, and Kim stayed in the Soviet Union for the duration of the war. [2] After Japan surrendered, Soviet forces occupied the Korean Peninsula north of the 38th parallel under an agreement with the United States, whereas American forces occupied the more populous South, including the capital, Seoul, as well as the Japanese mainland. After the end of the war the 88th Brigade was disbanded. Kim Il-sung was sent to Korea to become an aide of the Soviet *kommendant*, who was tasked with keeping the city of Pyongyang under control. After failing to reach Korea by land due to a damaged railway bridge, on September 19, 1945, Kim Il-sung arrived at the northern port of Wongsan on a ship called the *Pugachev*.

The Soviet forces that entered and occupied Korea were mostly units from the 25th Army; once the remaining Japanese forces surrendered, the Soviets had the task of ruling this territory. The Soviet military was effectively in charge in dealing with Korea until early 1947, albeit answerable to the authorities in Moscow. The commander was Colonel General I. M. Chistiakov (succeeded in April 1947 by G. P. Korotkov), but the person who played the key role in supervising both the Soviet military and the local authorities in North Korea was a political commissar by the name of T. F. Shtykov. In the words of the Russian Korea expert Andrei Lankov from Kookmin University in Seoul, Shtykov was "the real supreme ruler" in North Korea from 1945 to 1948.[3] It was Chistiakov who chose the city of Pyongyang as the capital of North Korea by locating the headquarters of the 25th Army there.

The occupation of the northern part of the Korean Peninsula presented the Soviet army with a monumental task. The immediate priority was the provision of food and basic supplies to the population and jump-starting the economy, which had suffered terribly as the retreating Japanese had destroyed most small and medium enterprises in northern Korea. Moreover, most management positions had been occupied by Japanese who were now gone. The Soviets themselves initially engaged to some degree in economic extraction, but not to the same extent as in Europe, and most of the heavy industry that was still intact was left in place. The other major task was the creation of a pro-Soviet Korean government. The United States had proposed that Korea should be administered by a United Nations trus-teeship (involving the Soviet Union, the United States, the United Kingdom, and Nationalist China) for five years. Korea would remain united, but its independence would be delayed. Korean leaders, North and South, opposed this plan bitterly, and as discussions with the Soviet Union about the creation of a national government made no progress, the United States began to distance itself from its own proposal. Historians have reserved judgment as to whether the Soviet Union really supported a trusteeship, and if so, why. Archival sources that have become available since the dissolution of the Soviet Union show quite clearly that the Soviet leadership did not really want a trusteeship. Their support for the proposal was designed to gain time in order to be able to establish a loyal satellite regime in North Korea.[4]

The first candidate to lead a North Korean administration was a nationalist called Cho Man-sik. Cho headed the movement for economic self-development and had formed the South Pyeongan Committee for the Preparation of Independence in the last days of Japanese colonial rule, just before the Soviets entered Korea, to prepare for local self-government. His position of leadership made him an obvious choice. Cho Man-sik was the most popular political figure in Pyongyang, and for this reason the Soviets tried to persuade him to head an administration for North Korea that was to be established. Cho Man-sik disliked communists and mistrusted foreigners, and demanded extensive autonomy as a condition of his cooperation with Soviet authorities. Eventually it was agreed that he would be in charge of the Administrative Committee of Five Provinces,[5] which amounted to the first government of North Korea. This entity, whose establishment was announced on October 8, 1945, did not last for long. Moreover, it was subject to supervision by the Soviet Civil Authority, which was established on October 3, 1945.

The fact that the Soviet authorities did not immediately try to put communists in charge of North Korea does not mean that they did not envision the creation of a communist satellite state such as in Eastern Europe. Generally speaking, the development of "people's democracies" involved an initial stage of a broad coalition of political forces, ultimately resulting in a purely communist government. In North Korea, in particular, communists had very little influence at the time.

Relations between the Soviet authorities and Cho Man-sik proved difficult. He opposed the idea of a UN trusteeship and demanded immediate independence. His policies were often at odds with those of the Soviet authorities, who frequently saw a need to bypass him and forge links with other political forces. As more Korean communists returned, the Soviets increasingly put them in charge. The official line of the Soviet government to support the idea of a multilateral trusteeship to govern Korea resulted in a major split in the North Korean leadership and a breakdown in relations between the Soviet authorities and the nationalists. In January 1946 the Soviet authorities requested the South Pyeongan People's Committee to support the plan for a trusteeship, but its leaders refused. Cho Man-sik declined to sign the declaration and promptly resigned his chairmanship. Subsequently he was arrested (he would be executed in 1950). In February 1946 Cho was removed from the chairmanship of the Democratic Party for having contacts with "South Korea reactionaries and even the Japanese police." He was replaced by a former communist guerrilla Choe Yong-geon.

Pak Hon-yong, the leader of the Korean communists, might have been a suitable replacement to lead North Korea, but he was based in Seoul. The arrival of Kim Il-sung in Pyongyang had been timely and the Soviet authorities decided to appoint him as the leader of North Korea, a decision that was ratified by Soviet authorities in Moscow. On December 18, 1945, it was decided that Kim Il-sung should succeed Kim Yong-beom to become chairman of the North Korean Bureau of the Korean Communist Party. On February 8, 1946, he became chairman of the Interim People's Committee, thereby assuming the highest Korean administrative position in the North.[6]

THE KOREAN WAR

Although by 1948 the division of Korea was complete, it was not accepted by the leaders of either South or North Korea. What precipitated the war is still debated by historians. At the time, Western political leaders saw the Korean War as an expansionist move by Stalin, and this view is evident in the standard historical accounts, such as by David Rees and David Dallin, who asserted that the war was planned and initiated by the Soviet Union.[7] Revisionist historian Bruce Cumings questioned these accounts on the grounds that they exaggerated the Soviet role and even raised doubts as to whether the North or the South initiated hostilities.[8] New evidence from Soviet archives has since shown that neither the traditional nor the revisionist accounts are sustainable.[9] It is true that Rhee Syngman wanted to liberate North Korea, but the military weakness of the Republic of Korea, exacerbated by the refusal of the United States to endorse such a move and give South Korea access to necessary military equipment, precluded an invasion of the North. By June 1949 U.S. forces had completely withdrawn from the Korean Peninsula.

It was Kim Il-sung who asked Stalin in 1949 to support his plan to unite Korea by force. Stalin first refused and did not give the green light until he was convinced that the North Koreans would succeed with only minimal support from the Soviet Union. A crucial factor was the support of Mao Zedong, who Kim went to see in May 1950.[10] The basic assumption of Kim Il-sung's plan was that the United States would not intervene, that North Korean forces were so superior that they would overwhelm the South within three days, and that guerrillas in the South would support Northern troops. But Kim and his supporters in Beijing and Moscow miscalculated badly. Although the forces of the South did indeed prove no match for the well-equipped troops of the North, the United States did intervene, commanding an allied intervention force mandated by the United Nations Security Council. The expected uprising in the South and the guerrilla campaign failed to materialize. Although the North Korean forces occupied most of the peninsula, they were eventually beaten back and had to rely on massive Chinese intervention. The UN involvement could have ultimately liberated the whole of Korea, but President Truman vetoed any attempt to reoccupy North Korea or attack China. The armistice restored more or less the status quo ante (except that the city of Gaesong was now part of North Korea).

The human toll of the Korean War was very high: counting all soldiers and civilians, about two million Koreans (North and South) perished. According to U.S. official data, 54,246 Americans died, 103,284 were wounded, and 8,177 were missing in action. The People's Republic of China did not publish any figures, but some estimates put the Chinese death toll at 900,000 (including Mao Zedong's own son).[11]

For Kim Il-sung, the war turned out to be a disastrous enterprise. He very nearly lost the country completely, and allied bombing devastated North Korea. It took massive economic support from the Soviet Union and China to rebuild the country and save it from the brink of catastrophe. The end result was military stalemate, a stable and yet precarious state of deterrence that prevails to the present day.

THE PATH TO DICTATORSHIP

In the aftermath of the Korean War, North Korea was heavily dependent on the Soviet Union and China to prevent large-scale starvation and rebuild the country. Kim Il-sung was vulnerable, having led the country into a catastrophic and unsuccessful war, even though the myth of the victorious fight against the attack by the United States and her South Korean puppets became a central element of the official narrative of the history of the war. The North Korean communists comprised several factions: the Southern communists (also described as the domestic faction), the so-called Yan'an faction (composed of Korean communists exiled to China's Shaanxi Province during World War II and who became members of the Chinese communist party), the Soviet faction, and the Manchurian guerrilla faction. Kim

Il-sung belonged to the latter. The Southern communists were blamed for the failure to organize an uprising against the South Korean government during the Korean War. They had no external backer and were therefore more vulnerable to a purge. Yi Seong-yeop, minister of State Control and a leading member of the domestic faction, was arrested on the absurd charge of spying for the United States. The leader of the domestic faction, Pak Hon-yong, also lost his position of foreign minister. They and various other leading figures in the domestic faction were tried and sentenced to death.

Kim Il-sung did not attend the 20th Party Congress of the Soviet Communist Party (February 1956), at which the Soviet premier Nikita Khrushchev denounced Stalin and announced a program of liberalization, sending shockwaves through the communist world. This was a difficult time for Kim, who was trying to assert his leadership over the competing factions and was still wedded to Stalinism as the fundamental guiding principle to the development of the country. The fight against the Yan'an and Soviet factions was related to Kim's efforts to free the DPRK from Soviet and Chinese influence, as well as promote his own cult of personality. At the same time, he wanted to shield North Korea against the wave of de-Stalinization that ran through the communist world. In the summer of 1956 Kim Il-sung went on a foreign trip that lasted almost seven weeks, during which he visited Moscow twice, where he was given strong admonitions by Khrushchev regarding his attitude to the Soviet faction in particular. Meanwhile, during his prolonged absence, the storm clouds of rebellion were gathering in Pyongyang. Leading members of the Soviet and Yan'an factions were preparing to stage a coup against Kim during the plenum of the Central Committee of the Korean Workers' Party. Kim delayed the plenum by almost a month and launched a counterattack in the form of a stage-managed response to the attacks that were launched against him by members of the Yan'an faction, Choe Chang-ik and Yun Kong-heum, when the plenum opened on August 30, 1956.[12] A majority of the Central Committee voted in favor of Kim Il-sung, and Choe and Yun, among others in the so-called anti-party group, were expelled from the Central Committee. The plenum was followed by a purge of the other factions. Many members of the Yan'an faction fled to China; many others from both factions were arrested or left the country. Kim Tu-bong, the leader of the Yan'an faction and the nominal head of state, apparently sympathized with the move against Kim Il-sung but did not take an active part in what has come to be known as the August incident.[13] Kim was later purged and most likely died in 1957. The leader of the Soviet faction, Aleksei Ivanovich Hegay (a Russian born in Khabarovsk in 1908 and known as Heo Ga-i in Korea) committed suicide on June 2, 1953, because of the attacks against his group; his successor, Pak Chang-ok, was purged after the plenum in 1956. In September 1956 the Soviet Union and China sent a joint delegation to Pyongyang in order to demand the reversal of the purges. Kim Il-sung temporarily complied, but a year later the purges resumed, demonstrating that neither Moscow nor Beijing had the determination to enforce their will on the North Korean leadership. By 1961 the factionalism in the Korean Workers' Party had been practically eliminated and Kim Il-sung emerged as the undisputed leader of the DPRK.[14]

Kim Il-sung was not an intellectual and did not develop an ideology of his own. His commitment to socialism was based on the concept that Korea had to develop its own national approach to communism based on the tradition, culture, and circumstances of the country, rather than simply copy the model and ideology of other countries. He did want the DPRK to become another state controlled by Moscow like the East European countries. When he addressed a meeting of Korean Workers' Party propaganda and agitation workers on December 28, 1955, he introduced the concept of *juche*, which referred to a sense of sovereignty and independence. It was not until much later (1972) that *juche* became central to a North Korean ideological approach to Marxism-Leninism that was articulated by Hwang Jang-yeop (who would become North Korea's most prominent defector). The word *juche* is often translated as self-reliance, but its broader meanings have never been fully clarified. Hwang explained it in the following terms:

> Establishing the subject *juche* means approaching revolution and construction with the attitude of a master. Because the masses are the master of revolution and construction, they must assume a master's attitude in regard to revolution and construction. A master's attitude is expressed in an independent position and a creative position. Revolution and construction are endeavours for the sake of the masses, and endeavours that the masses themselves must carry out. Therefore, in reshaping nature and society an independent position and a creative position are called for.[15]

B. R. Myers, in his path-breaking study of North Korean political thought, characterizes it as follows:

The pseudo-doctrine of Juche continues to serve its purpose all the same. It enables the regime to lionize Kim Il Sung as a great thinker, provides an impressive label for whatever policies it considers expedient, and prevents dissidents from judging policy on the government's own ostensible terms. Just as importantly, it decoys outsiders away from the true dominant ideology. Instead of an implacably xenophobic, race-based worldview derived largely from fascist Japanese myth, the world sees a reassuringly dull state-nationalism conceived by post-colonial Koreans, rooted in humanist principles, and evincing an understandable if unfortunate preoccupation with autonomy and self-reliance.[16]

The political institutions of the DPRK were similar to other "people's democracies" in the communist world. The Korean Workers' Party (*Choson Rodong-dang*), or KWP, controlled the government and the army, although as time went on, the role of the party diminished and eventually the leadership governed through the National Defense Commission. Other legal parties are the Korean Social Democratic Party and the Chondoist Chongu Party. These parties are a remnant of political movements at the time of the creation of the DPRK and are allied and subservient to the KWP. There is no legal opposition in North Korea.

The Supreme People's Assembly (SPA) is North Korea's unicameral legislature. It has 687 members formally "elected" (albeit in practice appointed) for five-year terms. Its main task is to approve the state budget. The head of the Presidium of the SPA is formally designated as the head of state. Although he has no real political power, he carries out the appropriate diplomatic functions abroad. There is a cabinet of ministers led by the prime minister, which formally constitutes the government. However, the cabinet does not make any real decisions, but carries out the policies of the leader. In 1972 Kim Il-sung was named president of the DPRK. After his death he was designated the eternal President, and no other president was appointed.

The structure of the political institutions of the DPRK as such is not significant, as all of the power is concentrated in the top leadership. Kim Il-sung developed sophisticated methods of authoritarian control along the lines practiced in other totalitarian countries, such as keeping control over the economy through central planning and the state budget, and exercising social control through a public ideology based on a cult of personality, enforced by a party structure and severe penalties for any opposition or deviation from the official line. Social control was organized down to the neighborhood level. Even the military could not challenge Kim as a result of the continuous use of patronage and purges to ensure that military officers were loyal to the leader.

THE RISE OF KIM JONG-IL

In the early 1970s it became clear that Kim Il-sung was grooming his oldest son, Kim Jong-il, to be his eventual successor. In 1973 "the dear leader," as Kim Jong-il came to be called, was made party secretary in charge of the Organization and Guidance Department. He was also appointed to the Politburo, thereby becoming part of the top hierarchy, and in February 1974 he was elected to the Political Committee of the Party Central Committee. A nationwide campaign was instigated to promote Kim Jong-il. He himself was engaged in a campaign of ideological mobilization around the ideology of *juche*. He launched the Three Revolution Team Movement to provide political, scientific, and technical guidance and training.

By the early 1980s Kim Jong-il was firmly in charge of the political system in North Korea and increasingly played the leading role in running the country as Kim Il-sung gradually withdrew from the day-to-day activities of government. Formally this transition manifested in Kim Jong-il taking senior positions on the Politburo, the Party Secretariat, and the Military Commission. The final step in 1991 that confirmed his leadership position was his appointment as commander in chief of the armed forces, thus elevating him above the top military leadership. In April 1992 he was also given the rank of marshal, the highest military rank in the North Korean armed forces, despite his lack of actual military experience.[17] By the early 1990s Kim Il-sung was practically retired, although much of the population of North Korea and the outside world were not aware of this situation. He briefly resumed an active role in the course of the crisis with the United States over North Korea's nuclear program in the aftermath of a meeting with former President Jimmy Carter. Not only was there the outline of framework for resolving the crisis, but Kim Il-sung seemed keen to promote North-South reconciliation through a summit meeting with South Korean president Kim Young-sam. This latter ambition did not come to fruition as Kim Il-sung died of a heart attack on July 8, 1994, at the age of eighty-two.[18]

After Kim Il-sung's death a three-year period of mourning was declared. Kim Jong-il did not immediately take up the formal positions of president and general secretary of the Korean Workers' Party, occupied by his father and deemed by some observers to constitute the position of leadership in the country. This resulted in speculation that Kim Jong-il was not yet in full control of the country and that he had yet to convince the Pyongyang elite and in particular the military leadership that he should succeed his father. However, there was no evidence of an internal power struggle (such as large-scale purges or demotions of senior officials), and the transition seemed to go smoothly as the media began to exalt Kim's authority. In fact, this moment marked the completion of a transition of power that had already been taking place over an extended period of time.

There was a notable emphasis in public propaganda on the Korean People's Armed Forces. This heralded a transformation of the structure of governmental organization whereby the Korean Workers' Party and the institutions of government were robbed of their authority as Kim Jong-il concentrated all power in himself as leader of the armed forces. This was in contrast to his father's policy of "civilianizing" the leadership, by not appointing any military officer to full membership of the Politburo and preventing the establishment of an independent power base by military leaders.[19] On October 8, 1997, Kim Jong-il was confirmed as chairman of the National Defense Commission (NDC) and General Secretary of the Korean Workers' Party.

In 1998 the constitution of the DPRK was revised significantly. The NDC was designated the supreme organ of government. Its chairmanship became "the highest office of state," the institution through which Kim Jong-il exercised his power. The cabinet of ministers, headed by the premier, has no real authority but implements the directives of the NDC. The Supreme People's Assembly now functions as a rubber stamp for decisions by the leadership and convenes rarely. Most of its members belong to the Korean Workers' Party. (The Korean Social Democratic Party and the Chondoist Chongu Party still survive, and are still allied and subservient to the KWP). The chairman of the presidium of the Supreme People's Assembly, a mostly ceremonial role, is the titular head of state. He signs treaties, accepts the credentials of ambassadors, and represents North Korea on state visits and at summits. The position of president was practically abolished by a constitutional change that proclaimed Kim Il-sung to be the eternal president.

The core of Kim Jong-il's approach to the governance of the DPRK was the military-first policy (*seongun jeongchi*). It meant that power in the country would be located in the institutions of the Korean People's Army, superseding those of the government and the party. The armed forces, military industry, and other economic entities related to the armed forces would receive priority treatment in the allocation of resources. In fact military-related entities developed in a "second economy" that has flourished, by contrast with the rest of the economy, which was starved of resources and relatively neglected. The goal of this approach was to consolidate Kim Jong-il's control over the country. But it also served the purpose of mobilizing the entire country, exhorting every North Korean citizen to think as a soldier in the effort to build a "strong and prosperous nation" (*gangseong daeguk*).[20]

There is some debate in the academic literature about the existence of different power centers and reformers versus hard-liners in the North Korean political elite. Following the example of Kremlin watchers of the Soviet leadership during the Cold War, Joel S. Wit and Robert L. Carlin traced what they describe as a debate between proponents and opponents of economic reform by contrasting articles in the newspaper *Rodong Shinmun* with those in an economic quarterly, *Kyongje Yongu*. The reformists are associated with the premier and the cabinet. Such a distinction has been encouraged by North Korean diplomats, who refer to opposition by the military to this or that proposal, and by North Korea experts in Seoul, who have perceived a difference of views between the diplomats and the military. The failure to implement various agreements, such as the reestablishment of a railway link between North and South, is blamed on the opposition of the military. However, Carlin and Wit's thesis suffers from serious defects. First of all, except for a general reference to the premier and the cabinet, they do not provide any detailed analysis of the North Korean leadership, so it remains unclear which members of the alleged reformists have any degree of power. The cabinet is not the locus of power and cannot implement any policy not approved by the National Defense Commission, so even if the cabinet were to be in the reformist camp, its influence would remain limited. Second, as will be discussed in more detail later in this chapter, the notion that either Kim Jong-il or anyone of real influence in the North Korean power hierarchy is pushing for serious reform is not supported by the evidence. Kim has rejected serious reforms in order to maintain strict central control over the economy.

A more sophisticated attempt to conceptualize the emergence of different coalitions in an authoritarian state like North Korea was developed by Etel Solingen. This approach posits that the challenge of globalization leads to the formation of competing coalitions, which advocate opposing strategies to deal with this challenge, an "internationalist" coalition and a "statist-national-confessionist" coalition. In most cases this competition ultimately results in a path toward greater international integration and domestic reform, but in some cases the outcome is greater retrenchment and efforts to limit the effects of globalization. Solingen identified several members of the political elite in North Korea as members of the internationalist coalition, such as Kim Jong-u, former chairman of the Committee on Promotion of Cooperation with Foreign Countries; Kim Dal-hyon, a former vice premier; and the former vice chairman of the External Economic Affairs Committee, Kim Mun-song.

The defector Hwang Jang-yeop, who himself was in the inner circle of the North Korean leadership, has rejected the notion of alternative centers of power in North Korea:

Who is in charge? No one has real power. You should know that clearly. Suppose a person comes to the fore in the diplomatic field. This does not mean he has real power. As for the chuche idea, I had given guidance to the overall work for the chuche idea for almost 20 years. However, I did not have real power. We should know the North Korean structure. Only Kim Chong-il has real power.[21]

This level of control is maintained by an extensive network of patronage that has been established and developed over many decades. As well as material rewards, it also includes severe punishment: the radical purging of individuals close to Kim (including executions) is not uncommon. Indeed, those individuals identified by Solingen were all purged, and Kim Mun-song was reported to have been executed.[22] Although the authoritarian instruments of government enable Kim Jong-il to maintain control over the armed forces and political elite and even over the population down to the neighborhood level through a system of mutual surveillance and harsh punishments, the authority exercised by the regime has become weaker over the last fifteen years. As will be discussed in more detail, in the 1990s the DPRK suffered a severe economic decline and a catastrophic shortage of food. Although the collapse of the country expected by many observers did not materialize, the crisis and the lack of resources at the disposal of the government (as manifested by the collapse of the public distribution system that lasted for some time and has not fully recovered) has weakened the capacity of the institutions of state to control social and economic processes in all parts of the country. Individual North Koreans developed mechanisms for their own survival, leading to the growth of markets and monetization outside the officially sanctioned economy. Black marketeering and smuggling became very popular and in fact necessary, given the failure of the public distribution system to provide for the basic needs of the population. It is illegal to sell goods at a price higher than that of purchase or to lend money for interest, so all the basic functions of private economic activity are prohibited, and yet they are ubiquitous. Theft and embezzlement are endemic in state enterprises and the managers engage in the illegal trade of state property in order to be able to provide for their employees and line their own pockets. Members of the security services are not outside this illegal structure.[23] Likewise the border between the DPRK and China has become quite porous, resulting in a flow of illegal border crossings by refugees, migrant workers, and illicit traders. The ability of the North Korean government to shield the country from all outside information by the total control of the media (including the Internet) is also challenged by access to Chinese cell phones, radios, and South Korean media (including DVDs of South Korean soap operas and movies).

THE ECONOMY AND MARKET REFORM

North Korea's economy is a central command economy that is largely isolated from the rest of the world economy and the global financial system. In the 1950s and 1960s, even as the Soviet Union engaged in economic reforms, Kim Il-sung had insisted on industrial development on the basis of a Stalinist model, where the state owns all the means of production (including agriculture) while the basic requirements for a market economy (freedom of movement, access to information, the right to engage in commerce and earn a profit) are absent. The general population receives food through the Public Distribution System.

Between 1953 and 1985 the North Korean economy grew substantially, as aid from the Soviet Union and China helped to rebuild the country that was devastated in the Korean War. Back then, North Korea looked like a relative success story, at least on the surface. Its gross domestic product was greater than that of the South, which had been in a rather poor state of development after the Korean War. Ordinary citizens could have a reasonable lifestyle in urban North Korea in the 1960s. But the North Korean economic miracle, such as it was, could not last. The six-year plan that started in 1971 sought to rebalance the distorted economic structure somewhat by dealing with the bottlenecks in the supply of raw materials, electric power, and fuel, giving more emphasis to technical modernization and light industry. In 1972–1974 the DPRK invested heavily in foreign industrial machinery and infrastructure, such as a cement plant, textile factories, and steel-making equipment from Japan, a French petrochemical plant, a large fertilizer plant, and so on, to the tune of $500 million. This meant incurring significant external debt, which was to be paid back by increased exports. The assumptions on which this strategy was based turned out to be unrealistic. North Korea's industry had serious difficulties in absorbing the Western equipment and making proper use of it. Some of the plants never became operable. Thus the increased export earnings were hard to realize. In addition there was the oil crisis of 1973, which caused a huge increase in the international price of oil. North Korea was unable to service the debts and began to default in 1974. As a result the DPRK was virtually cut off from access to Western technology. Foreign debt payments were stretched out and almost completely halted in 1985, when they amounted to $5.2 billion. The government had practically no hard currency reserves. This fact, the limited export potential of North Korean industry, and the inadequacies of its transport infrastructure (especially shipping) severely restricted the DPRK's capacity to trade.

The end of the 1980s marked a significant transition point for the North Korean economy. The subsidies and investments from the Soviet Union had mitigated to some extent the failure of economic management in the DPRK, but after 1990 all of that ended and the economy began to shrink. The contrast with the Republic of Korea was striking: In 1990 South Korea's GDP was ten-fold that of the DPRK, and its annual increase in GDP exceeded the total of the North. In the period from 1990 to 1997 the economy as a whole decreased by 42.2 percent, a decline of catastrophic proportions.

The gross national product of North Korea in purchasing power parity prices (PPP) in 2008 was estimated by the CIA to amount to a total of $40 billion. The Bank of Korea estimated the GDP of the DPRK in market prices at $26.7 billion ($1,233 per capita), but Lee Jong-seok, South Korean minister of unification in the Roh Moo-hyun government, told the author that the Bank of Korea vastly overestimated North Korea's GDP and that the real figure was about $15 billion.[24] In any case, North Korea is clearly one of the poorest countries in the world.

Agricultural products are mainly rice, corn, apples, soybeans, potatoes, pork, and eggs. Manufacturing is concentrated in military industries, machine building, chemicals, and textiles. North Korea has rich mineral deposits (coal, gold, iron ore, uranium ore). Major trading partners are China, South Korea, Singapore, India, and Russia. Analysis of trade statistics from its main trading partners reveals a persistent trade deficit ($1.52 billion in 2008). Main exports are minerals, nonferrous metals, precious metals, clothes, chemicals, wood products, and animal products. North Korea is also believed to engage in the sale of narcotics, counterfeit drugs, cigarettes, counterfeit currencies, the sale of missiles and other weapons systems, and various illicit activities.

In the absence of DPRK government statistics, the U.S. government and independent experts have used various methods to assess the state of the North Korean economy. For example, aerial photography has been used to determine the rate at which factories are operating (observing the smoke from chimneys and counting the people going to work). On the basis of such methods, it has been concluded that since the mid-1990s only 25 percent of factories in North Korea have been operating. There appears to be virtually no production of civilian goods; only the production of armaments is still ongoing, while markets are selling cheap Chinese consumer goods. The reasons for this parlous state of industry are manifold: lack of investment, technological obsolescence, breakdown of equipment, scarcity of funds for wages, and unreliable supplies of electricity. Transportation is in a catastrophic state—North Korea has a very low mileage of paved road, and most trunk roads connecting cities are not paved. Private travel between cities requires special permission. The roads are virtually empty, as few outside the elite have motor vehicles. In Pyongyang most people use buses and the subway system, and bicycles are ubiquitous. Trains travel at twenty miles an hour. The scarcity of gasoline has meant that many trucks have been converted to use charcoal burners. The use of cattle and horses to transport goods is commonplace.

Agriculture is similarly a disaster story. North Korea does not have enough arable land, but the inefficiency of collectivized agriculture has made matters even worse, which means the country is unable to feed its population. National disasters contributed to a major famine in 1995–1996. The government does not allocate a sufficient portion of its scarce foreign currency reserves to make up for the shortfall. For example, in 2008 and 2009 the total food production in the DPRK was estimated to amount to 4.21 million tons. The deficit in grain production amounted to 836,000 tons, despite imports of 500,000 tons. (The UN World Food Program reported that chronic malnourishment among children amounted to 62 percent in 1998 and fell to about 37 percent in 2004 as result of help by the WFP and other external donors. Roughly a third of all mothers were considered to be malnourished.) One manifestation of the scarcity of food is that North Koreans are on average shorter than people from other East Asian nations.

The dismal situation in agriculture had a range of systemic causes. Some of these were a consequence of the general state of the economy. There was a shortage of electricity for irrigation, agricultural machinery, and various other required supplies. Dense planting and continuous cropping resulted in soil depletion, and the overuse of chemical fertilizers caused soil erosion, which became exacerbated as more and more marginal lands were brought into use. At the same time the lack of fertilizer and poor storage and transportation practices contributed to the problems that were dramatically exacerbated by natural disasters in the mid-1990s. Torrential flooding alternated by severe droughts exacerbated the crisis, which reached literally catastrophic proportions. About 16 percent of arable land became unusable. From 1990 to 2000 grain production fell from 9.1 million tons to 3.2 million tons. From 1994 to 1996 there was a precipitous drop in production, from 7 million tons to 2.5 million tons, according to official North Korean statistics. In 1995 the availability of grain was around 3 million tons short of minimum requirements. Already in 1994 North Korean radio had admitted the existence of a famine.

There is no doubt that the famine of the 1990s resulted in widespread malnutrition and a large number of premature deaths from hunger (estimates range from 250,000 to 3.5 million). In 1996 foreign donors provided about 900,000 tons of food. These included the Republic of Korea, the United States, China, the European Union, and Japan. In 1997 foreign food aid amounted to 1.2 million tons; in 1998 it reached 1.3 million tons. It certainly saved many lives but did not bridge the total shortfall. Moreover, the North Korean government interfered with the distribution and monitoring of food aid and placed serious restrictions on donor agencies. While the threat of famine has receded, whole sections of the population, especially outside Pyongyang, still do not have adequate access to food, resulting in a lower than sufficient intake of calories on a daily basis.

The difficulties encountered by the North Korean economy forced the North Korean government to introduce some reforms through changes in the constitution and the reorganization of the government. Outside the country this was seen as a positive sign that gradual reform might actually happen in North Korea. In July 2002 the North Korean government announced various measures as part of an economic adjustment policy that outside observes hoped would herald the beginning of the end of the Stalinist-type planned economy and a movement toward a greater role for markets. The key features of these reforms were the termination of the rationing system for commodities (except for food) and substantial wage and price hikes. The foreign exchange coupon system was abolished, markets could establish themselves, and some foreign investment was to be permitted. Enterprises were to be given more autonomy to trade some of their production and materials among themselves, but now had to cover their own costs. They were also encouraged to reduce the number of workers.[25] Centralized price control was retained, but the government attempted to capture the business of the black markets by raising prices to similar levels (by 10 to 20 times). Some price hikes were much steeper; the price of rice rose by 550 times, electricity 60 times, and diesel oil 38 times.[26] Wages were also raised substantially (by 18 times for workers and 20 times for managers), but nowhere near enough to compensate for price increases. In effect the reforms amounted to enormous inflation, leaving many households worse off than before.

In 1998 the constitution was revised to permit individuals to keep profit earned through commercial activities. Small farmers' markets were not legal until June 2003, but once permitted, markets and shops selling goods for cash rather than coupons spread and in Pyongyang a three-story building was erected to house the Pyongyang Central Market.

On the whole, the confidence that Kim Jong-il would promote meaningful economic reform in North Korea, however, has turned out to be misplaced. The reforms that were introduced were relatively modest and soon the government tried to reassert its control. In October 2005, private sales of grains were forbidden and the centralized food rationing system was reestablished. By December 2005, most international humanitarian assistance operations in North Korea were terminated. The activities of nongovernmental aid organizations such as the World Food Program were severely restricted.

By 2007 the success of the markets that supplied its customers with clothes, fruit, watches, TV sets, and liquor from abroad began to alarm the authorities. On August 26, 2007, Kim Jong-il characterized the markets as anti-socialist, Western-style markets. Subsequently the government has cracked down on markets with various new regulations such as banning women under forty from working in markets (given that most men work in enterprises, this rule significantly reduced market activity) and forbidding various nonsocialist (especially foreign) goods from being traded. Efforts have also been made to inhibit the activities by merchants to procure goods from abroad or other parts of the country.[27] In May 2008, 500,000 metric tons of food to North Korea were made available by the U.S. government through nongovernmental organizations (NGOs) and the World Food Program. Initially these shipments were received, but additional shipments were rejected by the North Korean government starting in March 2009.[28] Favorable climate condition and energy assistance as a result of the Six-Party Talks agreement led to economic growth in 2009. In December 2009, the North Korean government embarked on a currency reform, limiting the amount of money that could be exchanged, and prohibiting the possession of foreign currency once again. This amounted to a large-scale confiscation of savings of ordinary people and the collapse of virtually all market activity. The reform resulted in unprecedented public protests and the government was forced to partially reverse course and issue a public apology. The official in charge of the currency reform was executed.[29] Nevertheless, these actions amount to a virtual closing down of the nonstate sector, thereby causing economic activity to contract severely. This is exacerbated by the virtual cessation of foreign aid (except from China). In 2009 the U.S. Congress severely curtailed funding for aid to North Korea. By 2010 U.S. aid had practically ceased, except for some minor medical assistance. Aid from South Korea also declined in response to the *Cheonan* incident in March 2010, when North Korean mini-submarines were used to sink a South Korean frigate. The South Korean government cut off all economic assistance to North Korea (excluding the Gaesong Industrial Complex). In sum, the outlook is bleak. Due to decades of underinvestment and neglect, industrial capital stock is nearly beyond repair, and the country cannot generate enough electricity. No prospect of economic recovery is in sight, while the military continues to draw resources needed for investment and civilian goods.

The establishment of free economic and trading zones is another strand of economic reform. The first of these was created in the Rajin-Sonbong area in the northeast corner of the country in 1991. It failed to attract investment due to its remote location, poor infrastructure, bureaucratic administration, and interference in its running by party officials. The only major investment was a hotel casino that became the focus for illicit activities. Another special economic zone was established in the northeastern city of Sinuiji, also near the Chinese border. This project was given remarkable autonomy, with the power to issue its own passports and its own legal system. It was supposed to be run by Yang Bin, a Chinese businessman with Dutch citizenship. This plan was scotched when Yang Bin was arrested in China on tax evasion charges. It still remains to be seen whether the Sinuiji project will generate much investment. More promising is the industrial park at Gaesong (or Kaesong) near the DMZ, where the South Korean government is committed to support major investments. Forty thousand North Koreans are employed in South Korean businesses in Gaesong. A joint tourist venture at Mount Geumgang has been closed down after a South Korean tourist was killed by a North Korean soldier. The Gaesong Industrial Complex remains the last joint North-South venture, but it is still at risk from the deteriorating atmosphere in relations between the two countries.

TOWARD ANOTHER SUCCESSION—THE END OF THE KIM DYNASTY?

Periodically there is some speculation of disagreements among the governing elite and of challenges to Kim Jong-il's rule. On April 22, 2004, there was a major explosion in Rongjon near the Chinese borders involving a train with explosives for construction just nine hours after a train taking Kim Jong-il back from a visit to China. This coincidence inevitably gave rise to speculation that the explosion was a failed assassination attempt. The finger of suspicion was pointed at Jang Song-taek, Kim's brother-in-law and a feared and powerful figure in the DPRK. This seemed to be confirmed by the fact that Jang apparently fell from grace in late 2004 and was under house arrest for a while.[30] However, Jang was subsequently rehabilitated, so the incident may have been an accident after all. In early 2005 there was a lot of speculation about a possible coup as Kim Jong-il's portraits disappeared from public view and there were indications of serious discontent among sections of the military. While no clear explanation for these occurrences have ever emerged, Kim appeared to have strengthened his position by promoting younger cadres to official positions in the government and the military.

Although Kim Jong-il seemed to remain in complete control over the government and the armed forces of North Korea, and there was no prospect for any kind of organized uprising against the leadership from below, the problem of succession became increasingly a factor of uncertainty. There was increasing speculation about Kim's health and there were persistent reports that he was suffering from heart, liver, and kidney problems as well as diabetes. Unlike his father, Kim Jong-il had not spent two decades grooming a successor. His son Kim Jong-nam, who now lives in Beijing, was at one time considered the most likely candidate, but seemed to fall out of favor after attempting to enter Japan on a forged Dominican Republic passport in 2001. The incident caused Kim Jong-il to cancel a trip to China to avoid embarrassment.

In August 2008 Kim Jong-il suffered a severe stroke that resulted in partial paralysis in an arm and a leg. During the time when Kim was incapacitated, it appears that a small group consisting of top figures in the KWP and the armed forces was running the country on a day-to-day basis. The key figure in this group was, according to various reports, Kim's brother-in-law Jang Song-taek. When Kim first reappeared in public, he was looking very gaunt, giving the appearance of someone who had suffered a serious illness. Reports from China surfaced that he was suffering from pancreatic cancer, and other reports claimed he was receiving kidney dialysis. The urgency of dealing with the succession issue sooner rather than later became clear. In 2009 it was reported that Kim's youngest son Kim Jong-eun had been designated to succeed his father in 2012.

The period after the stroke has been characterized by increased international tension, greater restrictions of access to North Korea by outsiders, as well as efforts to limit the unapproved border trade with China and the activity of markets in North Korea. In April 2009 the National Defense Commission was expanded, a move that was interpreted as an assertion of the military and the hard-liners while the succession process was gathering momentum. At the same time the military was taking a more visible role in the governance of the country. Both in the negotiations with the Americans about the nuclear program and in the North-South dealings relating to the Gaesong Industrial Complex, the North Korean side was represented by military officers. On April 18, 2009, a statement by the North Korean General Staff indicated that the military had no expectations of the negotiations about the nuclear program and that the military would advance the country's military power, including the nuclear deterrent, in every way in the future, which in turn led to the end of food aid.

The rise of Jang Song-taek in 2009 and 2010 indicates how Kim Jong-il is coping with his diminished capacity to control the country as a consequence of his health problems by relying on close contacts and family to preclude the emergence of other powerful figures. In October 2007 Jang was appointed vice director of KWP. In April 2009 he was elected to the National Defense Commission. This was part of a larger leadership reshuffle that also included the appointment of Choe Yong-rim as premier. Choe was previously the Pyongyang party chief and he replaced Kim Yong-il, who held this position from September 2007. Another close associate of Kim Jong-il's on the NDC, O Kuk-ryol, who is known to have close links with the armed forces, appears to have gained greater influence in the leadership. Others, such as Pak Jaek-yong, the deputy director in charge of propaganda of the General Political Department of the Korean People's Army, were demoted or worse: Ri Je-gang, first deputy director of the Workers' Party's Organization and Guidance Department (the institutional base for Kim Jong-eun), mysteriously died in a car accident.[31] In June 2010 Jang was promoted to the role of vice chairman of the NDC, thereby putting him in the second most powerful position in the country. He replaced Jo Myung-rok, until then North Korea's top military commander. His future role to assist Kim Jong-eun in establishing a power base as successor to the leadership vis-à-vis possible rivals in the military was formally confirmed in August 2010.[32] At a congress of the Korean Workers' Party, the first such gathering in thirty years, on September 28, 2010, Kim Jong-eun's position as the successor to the leadership was formalized. He was made a four-star general to give him a high military rank. He was also given membership of the Central Committee of the party and appointed vice chairman of its central military commission. Kim Jong-il's sister Kim Kyong-hui became the first woman in North Korea to be made a four-star general. She is the wife of Jan Seong-taek, meaning that Kim and Jang are to protect Kim Jong-eun's position in the event that Kim Jong-il is incapacitated.[33] Thus North Korea has entered a period of transition with an uncertain outcome.

4

The South Korean Security Dilemma
Between Confrontation and Unification

From its very inception as a state, the Republic of Korea faced fundamental challenges to its national security and to its very identity as a country. It was at one of the fault lines in the Cold War between East and West, where the outbreak of war was an ever present possibility, given the intention of Kim Il-sung to reunite the Korean nation by force. Indeed, a devastating war did break out in 1950, and even though the North was defeated through the U.S.-led intervention, the threat of renewed conflict persisted. At the same time the South itself wanted to achieve the unification of the peninsula.

The end of the Cold War and the transition from an authoritarian government to a democracy in the South bolstered the claim of the Republic of Korea to be the only legitimate representative of the Korean nation. However, although the threat from the struggling DPRK has changed, South Korea continues to face a dilemma as North Korea continues to revert to military threats and the South is caught between the desire to engage the North diplomatically while resisting its diplomatic and military pressure.

POLITICAL HISTORY OF SOUTH KOREA

The Republic of Korea was formally established on August 15, 1948, and recognized as the sole legal government of Korea by the United Nations General Assembly on December 12, 1848. The first president of South Korea was Rhee Syngman, who instituted an authoritarian rule based on anti-communist rhetoric. His main political aims, apart from consolidating his rule and stabilizing the Republic of Korea, were to maintain the support of the United States and reunify the Korean Peninsula by force. Opponents of the regime, and in particular suspected communists and North Korean agents, were detained without due process and tortured or killed. Uprisings in Yeosu, Suncheon, and on Jeju Island were brutally put down. In 1951 Rhee founded the Liberal Party, but lacking a base of support in the National Assembly he sought to perpetuate his rule by an amendment of the constitution whereby the president would be directly elected. This failed, but Rhee stayed in office during the Korean War by declaring martial law when he was based in Busan in 1952. Subsequently he pushed through the changes in the constitution and was reelected to the presidency. In 1954 he finally gained control of the National Assembly and further changes to the constitution were enacted to eliminate the eight-year term limit for the presidency. On March 15, 1960, Rhee, whose repressive rule created very deep resentment in the population, was reelected to office through a rigged presidential poll. This blatant manipulation of the elections resulted in major student protests and widespread public outrage after the body of a student was found floating in the harbor of Masan. The violent response by the police resulted in the deaths of 142 students. In the course of what became known as the April Revolution, Rhee was forced to resign and flee the country.[1]

Rhee's departure left South Korea under the leadership of President Yoon Bonseon and Prime Minister Chang Myon, and the country experienced a period of intense political turmoil and instability until a military coup led by Major General Park Chung-hee on May 16, 1961. Park was supported by a group of military officers who wanted to save the Republic of Korea from collapsing and being taken over by communists. The main focus was on restoring political stability and modernizing the economy through industrialization and export-led growth. Central to Park's foreign policy was a close alliance with the United States and normalization of relations with Japan. The United States not only guaranteed South Korea's security against North Korean aggression, but also was a major source of foreign aid as well as foreign direct investment. Normalization of relations with Japan in 1965 brought loans, foreign direct investment, and compensation for Japanese actions in the colonial period.

In order to pacify U.S. criticism of military rule, South Korea returned to nominal civilian government and Park held presidential elections. He was elected president in 1963 and again in 1967. To permit him to run for a third term in 1971, the constitution had to be changed, and he narrowly prevailed against the opposition leader Kim Dae-jung. On November 21, 1972, more far-reaching constitutional changes took place. The Yushin (revitalization) Constitution was adopted, which involved the temporary dissolution of the National Assembly (it was reconstituted with a significant proportion of members appointed by the President), putting the legislative and judiciary branches under government control, and the abolition of direct presidential elections, enabling Park's term to be extended in perpetuity through indirect elections by a national convention.

Park gave priority to economic development over Korean unification. The export-based industrialization policy remained at the core of Park's political agenda. The chaebols, or multinational conglomerates, were key instruments of the strategy for economic development. As the North Korean threat persisted, a close alliance with the United States remained a cornerstone of foreign and security policy. During the conflict in Vietnam, Park sent 25,000 Korean troops to support the U.S. efforts there, but the Vietnam War and the rapprochement with China stirred up anxieties with regard to U.S. policy and the reliability of the U.S. commitment to the security of the Republic of Korea, exacerbated by the withdrawal of the Seventh Division of the Eighth Army from Korea in 1971.

The authoritarian government sustained itself politically with a discourse emphasizing the struggle against communism and the North Korean threat. But that was not enough to generate a national consensus. Instead there was growing unrest that did not remain confined to students, but included a growing number of union workers, intellectuals, and religious leaders; efforts to suppress dissent by jailing members of the opposition only stimulated political turmoil. By 1979 mass demonstrations took place throughout the country, as labor unrest came to a head. In a police raid involving 1,000 riot police on the headquarters of the New Democratic Party (NDP)—where 180 women employees of the YH Industrial Company and 30 members of the NDP were staging a sit-in to protest the closure of the company—many people were badly beaten and one woman died. The chairman of the NDP, Kim Young-sam, was expelled from the National Assembly, an action which in turn sparked large demonstrations by workers and students in Busan, the area in which Kim's political base was, and the unrest spread further afield. A few days later there was a bizarre incident at a safe house of the Korea Central Intelligence Agency (KCIA) near the presidential compound (known as the Cheong Wa Dae, or "Blue

House") when the director of the KCIA, Kim Jae-gyu, shot President Park's security chief Cha Chi-chul for berating him and blaming him for the failure to stop the protests. After that Kim fired at and killed President Park himself. Kim claimed that he acted in order to end the Yushin system and bring about democracy, although after the shooting he attempted to persuade Army Chief of Staff Jung Seug-hwa to declare martial law and take control of the country.[2] Within a few days there was a military coup led by Chun Doo-hwan, the commander of the Korean Defense Security Command. Chun became de facto leader of South Korea under the nominal president Choi Kyu-ha (previously the prime minister). Opposition leaders Kim Dae-jung and Kim Jong-pil were arrested, while Kim Young-sam was kept under house arrest.

The Park assassination raised hopes for change in the Republic of Korea and stimulated further nationwide demonstrations promoting democracy, press freedom, an end to martial law, and various other demands. However, the government was determined to suppress the demonstrations. Political activities were banned and universities were closed, while more opposition leaders were arrested. The government managed to calm the situation by promising a move toward democratic government by May 17, but instead there was the extension of martial law to include the entire territory of the country (including Jeju Island) justified by a North Korean threat that was later proven to have been an invention.[3]

The arrest of Kim Dae-jung provoked a revolt in the city of Gwangju, which started on May 18, 1980, when students gathered at Chonnam University in defiance of its closure by the authorities. Initially soldiers attacked students and bystanders with clubs as students threw rocks at the soldiers. A twenty-nine-year-old deaf man was clubbed to death. The conflict escalated and spread to the city center. By May 20 the number of protesters exceeded a hundred thousand. The army began to fire live ammunition at the protesters, resulting in a significant number of casualties near Gwangju Station. In response to the soldiers' actions some protestors broke into armories and police stations and acquired weapons, which then were used by spontaneously formed militias. Security forces were beaten back and were forced to withdraw to the outskirts of the city. For a few days the city was blockaded while reinforcements arrived.

The news from Gwangju sparked protests in other nearby areas. The uprising ended on May 27 when the 20th Infantry Division of the army together with special forces entered the city in large numbers and the militias were defeated. The official death toll was 144 civilians, 22 troops, and 4 police officers, but a review carried out in 1995 concluded that 240 people died when Gwangju was taken and the real figures may have been over a thousand. Most of the troops were killed shooting at each other by mistake during an incident in Songam-dong. In the aftermath of the Gwangju incident, Kim Dae-jung and six others were sentenced to death for their alleged role in the uprising. Many others were indicted.[4] Shortly thereafter, Chun forced the resignation of President Choi, claiming the office for himself.

The Gwangju uprising had a permanent effect on South Korean political culture. Not only did it become the major milestone in the struggle against authoritarian rule, but it also gave rise to significant and long-lasting anti-American sentiments in the new generation.[5] Not only did the United States fail to come to the aid of the pro-democracy demonstrators, but it was widely perceived as supporting Chun and the crackdown in Gwangju.[6] In particular it was believed that the United States had given permission for the 20th Division to be released from the Central Forces Command and for the use of special forces. Although their approval wasn't required, the U.S. commander John Wickham and U.S. ambassador William H. Gleysteen did approve the use of the army to restore order. However, the United States strongly disapproved of the violent attacks against the demonstrators and the South Korean government's handling of the Gwangju uprising. Indeed, the event resulted in a very considerable cooling of relations between the two governments.

The death sentence imposed on Kim Dae-jung became a major bone of contention between the U.S. and the South Korean leadership. After Ronald Reagan assumed the presidency of the United States, Kim's sentence was commuted in return for normalization of U.S.-ROK relations. Reagan cancelled plans for the reductions of U.S. forces in Korea, increasing the number of troops to 43,000 and completing a previously negotiated sale of F-16 fighter planes. Various events contributed to the strengthening of relations between the South Korean government and the Reagan administration. For example, on September 1, 1983, Soviet interceptors shot down a South Korean airliner KAL-007 over the East Sea (269 lives were lost in the tragedy). The Korean airliner had strayed over Soviet airspace due to a navigational error. This became a major incident in the Cold War leading to heightened tensions between the superpowers. The years 1983–1992 saw increased North Korean terrorism against South Korea, including various infiltration attempts and some major provocations.

In particular, on October 9 there was an attempt to assassinate President Chun during a state visit to Burma. A bomb was detonated in the Martyrs' Mausoleum in Rangoon by North Korean agents. The attack killed twenty-one people, including four cabinet ministers. Chun escaped because his car arrived late at the location. Other examples included a bomb that detonated at Gimpo International Airport in September 1986, killing five people. On November 29, 1987, two North Korean agents planted and detonated a bomb on a Korean Air flight to Bangkok from Abu Dhabi. All one hundred and fifteen passengers died. One of the agents, a woman by the name of Kim Hyon-hui, was arrested.[7]

Shortly after he assumed the highest political office in South Korea, Chun had declared that he would limit himself to one presidential term. During this time the pressure for constitutional reform continued unabated. Chun's designated successor, Roh Tae-woo, who was nominated as the presidential candidate for the ruling Democratic Justice Party (DJP), negotiated an agreement on constitutional change with the opposition groups that was finally approved by the National Assembly on October 12, 1987, and subsequently confirmed in a national referendum.[8] The new constitution envisaged direct presidential elections, more powers for the National Assembly, and a safeguarding of the rights of individuals. It also limited the presidency to a single term.

Although in the mind of the population Roh represented the old regime, he won the elections in December 1987 because the opposition vote split between the leading candidates Kim Young-sam and Kim Dae-jung. The new constitution limited the power of the presidency and also separated the executive clearly from the unicameral legislative. The DJP failed to win an outright majority in the parliamentary elections on April 26, 1988, in which the seats conformed to a distribution of political support along regional lines. Consequently the three main parties (the DJP; the Reunification Democratic Party, led by Kim Young-sam; and the New Democratic Republican Party, led by Kim Jong-pil) merged to form the Democratic Liberal Party. This provided a platform for the presidential campaign of Kim Young-sam in December 1992, when he was elected as the first democratically elected civilian president of the Republic of Korea.

The transition to democracy in the Republic of Korea occurred at a time of monumental changes in the international system as the Cold War came to an end. President Roh Tae-woo initiated his so-called Nordpolitik[9] to improve relations with former communist countries and reduce tensions with North Korea. As China decided to shift to a "two-Korea" policy, full diplomatic relations between China and the Republic of Korea were established in August 1992, much to the dismay of the North Korean leadership. In November 1992 ROK also established diplomatic relations with the Russian Federation. Roh Tae-woo hoped the close relationship with China would prompt Beijing to put significant pressure on Pyongyang to change inter-Korean relations. This hope turned out to have been illusory, but in the changed international environment inter-Korean dialogue did make some progress. After several rounds of talks, an "Agreement on Reconciliation, Nonaggression, and Exchanges and Cooperation between the South and North" was concluded in December 1991. This agreement codified a form of peaceful coexistence. In 1992 the "Joint Declaration of South and North Korea on the Denuclearization of the Korean Peninsula" effectively amounted to a commitment by North Korea not to develop nuclear weapons.[10]

The Kim Young-sam government also sought to achieve further progress in the North-South dialogue by proposing four-party talks with North Korea, despite some division of opinion within Kim's administration (unification minister Han Wan-sang and foreign minister Han Sang-joo favoring increased bilateral negotiation with North Korea). In the presidential inaugural address on February 24, 1993, Kim Young-sam offered to meet Kim Il-sung any time, any place. The North Korean leader did accept this offer, following a visit by former U.S. President Jimmy Carter to resolve the nuclear crisis. However, the idea of a summit was relegated to the backburner after Kim Il-sung's death in 1994.

When North Korea plunged into famine soon thereafter and asked South Korea for help, President Kim ordered the provision of 150,000 tons of rice. But the inter-Korean dialogue would become hostage to the stand-off with the United States over the nuclear program, with the result that the ROK lost control over a process that was now managed by direct U.S. talks with Pyongyang. The manner in which this issue was resolved through the Agreed Framework increased tension in U.S.-ROK relations; understandably, Seoul felt excluded and unable to represent its national interests in this process, which required a very substantial financial contribution from South Korea. Consequently the hard-liners in the Kim government gained ascendance: Han Sung-joo was replaced by Gong Ro-myung, and Kim Deok, head of the KCIA, replaced Han Wan-sang. There was a belief in the Kim administration that North Korea was close to collapse and that dampened any enthusiasm for further dialogue or deals. The situation became more complex for the Kim Young-sam government in the mid-1990s as the financial crisis swept through Asia, leading to a collapse of South Korea's currency and profoundly affecting the South Korean economy, thus reducing its leverage in the international community.[11]

SUNSHINE POLICY

In 1997 Kim Dae-jung, the hero of the struggle for democracy, who had been relentlessly persecuted by the authoritarian military leaders of the past, was finally elected president of the Republic of Korea. This was significant in many ways, in particular with regard to strengthening the hold of democracy and eliminating the last vestiges of military rule and its authoritarian practices. Kim proposed a radical departure in unification policy. The new policy became known as the Sunshine Policy, in reference to one of Aesop's fables, and was comprised of "three principles" and involved "three stages." The three principles were peaceful coexistence, peaceful exchange, and peaceful unification (he explicitly excluded the notion of "unification by absorption"). The three stages were union of the republic, federalism, and finally full unification. The underlying principle of relations with the North was that of engagement. While rejecting any provocations by the North, which required maintaining a robust defense capability based on the U.S.-ROK alliance, South Korea would practice political dialogue and economic engagement. This was to be based on the separation of politics and economics, so that economic engagement would not be derailed by the ups and downs of political relations.

There were two assumptions underlying the Sunshine Policy. The first was that a continuing policy of confrontation was dangerous and would not change North Korean behavior or bring unification any closer. North Korea's aggressive conduct was fundamentally a survival strategy, and responding to it with military pressure would only exacerbate the situation. The second was that a policy of economic engagement to promote reconciliation and cooperation could persuade North Korea to give up its policy of hostility and isolation. If North Korea no longer feared that outside powers were seeking regime change, but instead there was a prospect of economic support, significant changes were possible. This would require a sustained process of assurances and increasing economic interaction, which would induce the North Korean leadership to open the country up to the world and create a dependence on its relations with South Korea.[12]

The process of engagement envisaged by Kim Dae-jung was not totally uncon-ditional, and North Korea was expected to reciprocate. But such reciprocation did not need to be immediate, and could come at a later stage. In other words, it was not based on inducements so that North Korea would take certain kind of actions, but was rather intended to change North Korean behavior in the longer term.[13] In this sense the Sunshine Policy was fundamentally different from the kind of "carrot and stick" approach to engagement practiced by the U.S. government at various times.

The Sunshine Policy was a hard sell at home and abroad. Many conservatives voiced their skepticism that the plan would work. Worse, the government bureau-cracy put in charge of implementing the new policy was still wedded to attitudes from the past. Kang In-duk, the new minister of unification, previously occupied a senior position in the KCIA, which implemented the previous government's hostile policy toward the North. The most important figure in the North Korea policy of Kim Dae-jung was Lim Dong-won. Critics in South Korea voiced their doubts that North Korea would respond to what seemed to amount to an unconditional policy of providing economic support, and the lack of conditionality meant that these re-sources could be used to support North Korea's threatening military developments. In the United States the Clinton administration was pursuing its own engagement policy with North Korea, but this encountered significant opposition in Congress. Thus efforts by Kim Dae-jung to persuade the United States to lift sanctions against North Korea faced significant obstacles. The North Koreans, on the other hand, were not convinced that Kim Dae-jung was any different from his predecessors.[14]

The presidency of Kim Dae-jung faced very significant challenges. The first of these challenges was to consolidate the transformation of the country into a modern democracy by ensuring that the government bureaucracy, which had previously been an instrument of authoritarian military rule, did in fact implement the policy agen-da of the democratically elected government, and that civil-military relations were adapted to the conditions of a modern democratic society. The second challenge was dealing with the aftermath of the mid-1990s financial crisis that had swept through Asia. This involved bringing both the industrial conglomerates and the labor unions in line. The third challenge was the policy of engaging North Korea.

Kim Dae-jung persisted in his efforts, even though there were continuing provo-cations from North Korea, in particular the launch of the Paektusan-1 (Taepodong-1) missile that came down in the Sea of Japan on August 31, 1998. Of course, South

Korea was already providing substantial financial assistance to North Korea through the financing of the construction of two light-water reactors as part of the U.S.-DPRK Agreed Framework that would freeze the nuclear program in North Korea.

A review of North Korea policy by the U.S. government resulted in a report by Defense Secretary Bill Perry that broadly supported a policy of engagement with North Korea in order to achieve cooperation on implementing the Agreed Framework, eliminating any nuclear weapons capabilities in the DPRK as well as terminating the long-range missile programs. The so-called Perry Report advocated a dual-track policy. If North Korean cooperation was forthcoming, there could be engagement with North Korea; if not, the United States would shift to a policy of containment.[15]

The two showcases for South Korea's engagement policy were the Mount Geumgang tourist resort and the Gaesong Industrial Complex. The idea of developing Mount Geumgang into a tourist resort goes back to 1981, when Kim Il-sung was inspired by Fidel Castro's success in attracting tourists who brought hard currency earnings to Cuba. The Kumgangsan International Tourism Company, set up in 1988, failed to attract significant numbers of tourists. It did not have any international partners and was unable to build the proper facilities and organize tours that could be easily accessed by potential South Korean tourists. Chung Ju-kyun, the founder of the Hyundai Corporation, was a business leader with political interests and ambitions. In the Geumgang project Chung saw a great opportunity, but he was unable to make any deal with the North Koreans in the unfavorable political climate that prevailed during the Kim Young-sam administration. As the political climate became more favorable with Kim Dae-jung's Sunshine Policy and the reduction of tensions with the United States due to the Agreed Framework, the project had a chance. Chung's leadership and entrepreneurship afforded him a central role in the inter-Korean dialogue. On June 16, 1998, Chung traveled to North Korea with a convoy that included a gift of five hundred cows and the fifty trucks that were carrying them. A contract was signed between the Hyundai Corporation and the Korean Asia-Pacific Peace Committee in North Korea in October 1998 that permitted the first South Korean tourists to travel to Mount Geumgang one month later. On February 5, 1999, the Hyundai Asan Corporation was established to manage inter-Korean cooperation projects such as tourism, cultural exchanges, and the building of an industrial park. The Hyundai Corporation pledged to pay $942 million for the rights to operate the tours to Mount Geumgang for thirty years. The funds were to be transferred in various monthly installments until 2005.[16] The tours were very popular; by April 2000 more than 190,000 South Koreans had visited the resort, but this did not come even close to the break-even point, and in view of mounting losses the Hyundai Corporation sought and received financial support from the South Korean government.[17]

The other great project of North-South cooperation was the Gaesong Industrial Complex. The Gaesong Industrial Region was established in 2002 and the industrial park opened in 2004. South Korean companies were encouraged to invest in production facilities in Gaesong and hire North Korean workers. In the initial phase, fifteen South Korean companies were to construct factories in the region. Eventually 110 factories were operating in the region, employing about 42,000 North Korean staff. South Korea supplied electricity, telephone services, as well as the buildings and general infrastructure. Several hundred South Korean citizens were also working in Gaesong. The project is considered by its supporters as the most promising example of North-South economic cooperation and a pilot for a policy of engagement that would eventually integrate the North and South Korean economies.[18]

An important part of Kim Dae-jung's strategy of engagement was to orchestrate a summit meeting with North Korean leader Kim Jong-il. In 1994, when ROK was still headed by President Kim Young-sam, a North-South summit was supposed to have taken place in Seoul, but after the death of the Great Leader it had been postponed indefinitely. On January 20, 2000, Kim Dae-jung proposed a meeting with Kim Jong-il.

On March 9, 2000, Kim Dae-jung made the "Berlin Declaration" during a speech at the Free University in Berlin, promising that South Korea would provide the North with the infrastructure needed to jumpstart its economy. This was part of an effort to solicit substantial and wide-ranging support from European countries in preparation of what was expected to be a new era of North-South relations as arrangements for a summit were progressing.

After secret meetings held in China, an agreement to hold a summit in Pyongyang was announced on April 10, 2000. Lim Dong-won, now director of the National Intelligence Service, was in charge of working out the details with the North Koreans.

The summit began on June 13, 2000, when President Kim arrived in Pyongyang with a large entourage, consisting of 130 officials, political experts, and business leaders, as well as 50 journalists. The two leaders spent three days discussing the whole panoply of inter-Korean relations, including cultural exchanges, reuniting divided families, the U.S.-ROK alliance, and practical steps toward unification, of which a confederation along the lines of a "Korean commonwealth" would be the first step. After the summit there were some stories that Kim Jong-il had told Kim Dae-jung he did not object to the presence of U.S. troops in South Korea during the period of confederation. But according to Lim Dong-won, who sat through various meetings between the two leaders, this referred to a token presence on the assumption that the United States did not pose a threat to North Korea.[19]

The joint statement at the end of the summit, now known as the June 15 Declaration, set out far-reaching proposals:

1. The South and the North have agreed to resolve the question of reunification on their own initiative and through the joint efforts of the Korean people, who are the masters of the country.

2. Acknowledging that there are common elements in the South's proposal for a confederation and the North's proposal for a federation of lower stage as the formulae for achieving reunification, the South and the North agreed to promote reunification in that direction.

3. The South and the North have agreed to promptly resolve humanitarian issues such as exchange visits by separated family members and relatives on the occasion of the August 15 National Liberation Day and the question of former long-term prisoners who had refused to renounce communism.

4. The South and the North have agreed to consolidate mutual trust by promoting balanced development of the national economy through economic cooperation and by stimulating cooperation and exchanges in civic, cultural, sports, public health, environmental and all other fields.

5. The South and the North have agreed to hold a dialogue between relevant authorities in the near future to implement the above agreement expeditiously.

6. President Kim Dae-jung cordially invited National Defense Commission chairman Kim Jong-il to visit Seoul, and Kim Jong-il decided to visit Seoul at an appropriate time.[20]

It is not surprising that reaction to the summit in South Korea was rather mixed. Conservatives demurred that the June 15 Declaration did not address the problem of reducing political and military tension between the two Koreas, and that there was a lack of transparency regarding economic aid, while it remained vague to what extent North Korea would respond with reciprocal economic and political concessions. It soon became evident that although the summit sparked various rounds of inter-Korean dialogue, not much progress was made in implementing the joint declaration. In fact, there was little reason to believe that Kim Jong-il was serious either about opening up the country or moving toward any form of confederation. Nevertheless, at that time the mood was positive. The Agreed Framework, the visit of Vice Marshal Jo Myong-nok to the United States, and the visit of Secretary of State Madeleine Albright for a summit with Kim Jong-il in Pyongyang was widely seen as preparing the way for a new relationship between the United States and the DPRK. Kim Dae-jung's achievement was recognized when he was awarded the 2000 Nobel Peace Prize for his work for democracy and human rights in South and for peace and reconciliation with North Korea.

The mood turned sour when it later became evident that $450 million dollars had been transferred to North Korea in an elaborate scheme involving the presidential office, the National Intelligence Service, financial institutions (such as the Korea Development Bank), and the Hyundai Corporation. In 2003 various leading figures from the Kim administration were indicted for violating the Law on South-North Exchanges and Cooperation as well as the Law on Foreign Exchange Transactions. Although it was evident that President Kim had been aware of these transactions, he was not indicted himself.[21] Apart from generating an impression of corrupt government, it seemed that the summit had been more the result of a pay-off rather than a diplomatic breakthrough, and thus tarnished both the image and achievements of Kim Dae-jung.

The implementation of the Sunshine Policy became more difficult as a result of shift in U.S. policy after the Bush administration assumed office in 2001. President Bush was adamantly opposed to a policy of engagement, which he perceived as futile and naive. During a U.S.-ROK summit in 2001 the disagreements about policy toward North Korea became evident. There was also a backlash in South Korea as Kim Jong-pil, the leader of the conservative United Liberal Democrats (ULD) withdrew from the governing coalition because of the Sunshine Policy (as will be discussed later). The forced resignation of the cabinet and the loss of the majority in the National Assembly made it much more difficult for the president to implement his policies. On the other hand, it became evident that the summit was a watershed in public attitudes toward North Korea. Since then, many South Koreans no longer regard North Korea as a threat, despite the various provocations that followed. This legacy of the Sunshine Policy persists, even though the promises of engagement have not yet been fulfilled.

PEACE AND PROSPERITY: SOUTH KOREAN NATIONAL SECURITY POLICY AT THE CROSSROADS

The fate of South Korea's policy of engagement hinged also on the presidential elections as Kim Dae-jung's term in office came to an end in 2002. To the surprise of many observers, the candidate of the Millennium Democratic Party (MDP) Roh Moo-hyun defeated the conservative Lee Hoi-chang in the presidential elections.

Roh's success can be explained, in part, by his anti-American rhetoric. Right around election time, the rising tide of anti-Americanism was worsened after an incident involving two school girls killed in an accident by two American soldiers on a training mission (the soldiers were subsequently acquitted under U.S. jurisdiction). In response, South Koreans organized mass protests and candlelight vigils, calling for a change in the Status of Forces Agreement (SOFA), giving a decisive boost to Roh's campaign.

Roh Moo-hyun was steeped in the liberal tradition represented by his predecessor. He was supported by the "386 generation," emerging South Korean leaders whose political views were forged in the struggle against the authoritarian military rule in South Korea, and they became leading officials in the Roh administration. The "386 generation" were socially liberal, and they did not accept the previous axioms about Korea's role in the world or its geopolitical alignments, including the alliance with the United States.

After his election Roh Moo-hyun abandoned the MDP because its leading members were too conservative and still linked to Kim Dae-jung, and instead founded the Uri Party, which became the largest party for a time in the National Assembly after the Grand National Party (GNP) had voted to impeach Roh (this impeachment was overturned by the Constitutional Court). The Uri Party, many of whose leading members were freshmen from the "386 generation," was more of a reformist rather than a socialist party and reflected the agenda of the president.

The national security agenda of the Roh administration was articulated in an intellectual climate that reflected the changed mood in many parts of the country. The anti-communist public discourse, which had served to legitimize the military dictatorship, had been replaced by a different kind of discourse, one that emphasized the democratic process. In any case, the end of the Soviet empire rendered the anti-communist discourse less plausible. In the 1990s democratization was accompanied by changes in the perception of the North Korean threat by the wider public. Instead of a powerful and menacing neighbor, North Korea was perceived as a country in crisis, a weak state that could not feed its own population and required food aid from the South to survive. The 2000 summit changed the image of the North in the minds of many South Korean people, especially those in the younger generation for whom the defining political event of their life was the Gwangju massacre and the struggle against dictatorship, not the Korean War.

The flip side of this coin was increasing anti-Americanism. There was a widespread belief that the United States was complicit in the Gwangju massacre, and the U.S.-ROK alliance was identified in the minds of many with the authoritarian past of the country. Many also believed that it was the hard-line policy of the United States toward North Korea that was the fundamental cause of the security crisis on the Korean Peninsula.

Once Roh became president, it became clear to him that the Republic of Korea could not afford to abandon the U.S.-ROK alliance. The overarching theme of his national security policy was "independence" and "self-reliance," envisaging a restructuring of the alliance that would make the United States and the Republic of Korea equal partners, while preserving the American security guarantee. Underlying this approach were different conceptions about the identity of the Korean nation, North and South. Instead of the axiomatic identification of South Korea as being located in the Western camp, Roh's conception (which was never fully articulated) was based on the notion of Korea as an independent nation, a balancer between the great powers. The U.S.-ROK alliance in this perspective is not an alliance based on common values and shared identities. Instead Korea is to play a more neutral role in the regional international system and the U.S.-ROK alliance is based instead on necessity. But given South Korea's status as a highly industrialized and democratic country, it is only appropriate that the Republic of Korea should be in an alliance that is a partnership of equals, and not one based on a hierarchical structure. North Korea, on the other hand, is not to be viewed as a rogue state and a source of insecurity that needs to be contained. Rather, North Korea is a weak state that faces multiple threats to its security and that needs to be engaged so that these threats are mitigated and that a process of transformation can be embarked upon that will ultimately end in Korean unification. One clear indication of the changed perception of North Korea was the removal of the designation of North Korea as the main enemy of the Republic of Korea from South Korea's official defense policy.

One of Roh's key advisors in formulating national security policy was Lee Jong-seok (initially deputy national security advisor and later unification minister, until he resigned in the aftermath of North Korea's nuclear test in 2006).[22] Lee, a specialist in North Korea affairs from the Sejong Institute, promoted an unswerving belief in constructive engagement and restructuring the U.S.-ROK alliance. It was essentially a continuation of the Sunshine Policy, now dubbed "policy for peace and prosperity" by the "participatory government."

Unfortunately, South Korean national security policy under the Roh administration was based on fundamental misconceptions. The first was that the conceptualization of the nature of the North Korean regime and the policy of engagement that was based on it turned out to be illusory. Contrary to expectations, engagement did not alter North Korea's aggressive foreign policy behavior. The nadir came in 2006 when North Korea detonated a nuclear device, symbolizing the culmination of the false expectations invested in the policy. The fact that significant sectors of the South Korean population no longer considered North Korea a threat did not alter the realities of the North Korean regime or its actions, which were designed to limit the options for engagement and ensure that it did not weaken the hold of the regime over the country. As time went on, the Roh government came under increasing criticism from conservatives for taking too soft a line toward North Korea, enduring its provocations while continuing to provide aid.

The second misconception related to the U.S.-ROK alliance and the role of the Republic of Korea and the geopolitics of the region. The idea that South Korea could be a "balancer" between the great powers in the region was patently absurd, given that it was a frontline state faced with the potential for a massive military conflagration and relying on the United States for its security. There was no realistic option for neutrality or alternative alliance arrangements. This reality was brought home by a dispute in 2004 over China's Northeast Project, which challenged the narrative that the historical Koguryo kingdom belongs to Korea's national past. Whereas prior to this controversy the majority of Uri Party members in the National Assembly favored a reorientation toward China, many leading members of the "386 generation" became disillusioned with the idea of strategic partnership with China.[23] Officials whose job it was to draft the document on the "balancer" concept for the Roh government were aghast at the idea.[24] Not only is the political culture in South Korea incompatible with that of the People's Republic of China, but China's policy toward the Korean Peninsula is contrary to the vital interests of the Republic of Korea (see chapter 7).

With regard to the United States, the Roh government mistakenly believed that the threat of entrapment in a conflict with North Korea was greater than the risk of abandonment. In fact, it was the other way around. The Bush administration was less firmly committed to South Korea and more willing to shed its responsibilities than the South Koreans realized. On the other hand, the risk of U.S. military action against North Korea was far more remote than Roh and his aides believed, as U.S. policymakers had become acutely aware of the risks of escalation during the first nuclear crisis in 1994. Another misconception was that through its policy of engagement South Korea could take over the lead role in dealing with North Korea. Instead the United States remained firmly in command with regard to the North Korean security issues, notwithstanding efforts to extricate itself through the Six-Party process, as a result of North Korean proclivities. Despite various high points of the inter-Korean dialogue, including a summit toward the end of the Roh presidency, the only progress achieved in relation to the security issues was in dialogue with the United States.

The Roh government generally opposed putting pressure on North Korea; not only was it unsupportive of U.S. efforts to put sanctions on the North, but it adamantly refused to cut aid or take any form of punitive measure against Pyongyang. The South Korean government even discouraged defections from North Korea in order not to upset the North Korean government, and muted any criticism of the humanitarian situation in the DPRK. This is not to say that Roh or Lee did not appreciate the seriousness of the nuclear issue. But they were frustrated by the policy of the Bush administration that (at least in the first term) rejected any form of engagement—even including a sustained U.S.-DPRK dialogue, in firm opposition to the policy of the Roh government—and that in fact seemed to block any progress.

Consequently the South Koreans mounted a sustained effort to persuade the U.S. government to change its policy and use the Six-Party Talks as a mechanism to engage in direct negotiations with the North Koreans, a policy that ultimately yielded some results in the second Bush administration, when the United States became involved in very intense direct negotiations with Pyongyang (see chapter 6).

It would not be correct to say the Roh government was anti-American, as such. The centrality of the U.S.-ROK alliance to the national interest of the Republic of Korea became increasingly clear during Roh's term of office. But rebalancing the alliance in order to move from a hierarchical structure to an equal partnership was central to its national security strategy. The purpose was to secure South Korea's independence and regain aspects of national sovereignty that had been lost as a consequence of the Korean War. This policy had three different planks: the "peace and prosperity" policy of engaging North Korea, moving toward "self-reliance" in national defense, and moving away from the existing command structure, in which an American general would be in charge of U.S. and South Korean forces in the event of war.

Roh Moo-hyun and Lee Jong-seok were keenly aware of the centrality of the alliance of the United States for South Korean security. This was indicated by the fact that South Korea provided 3,000 troops for noncombat roles in Iraq, despite public opposition to this move. The Roh administration tried to create a linkage between the provision of South Korean troops and greater flexibility from Washington in relation to North Korea. This produced much irritation in Washington and a vague promise by President Bush to offer North Korea some security assurances. Seoul dispatched the minimum level of troops the government believed the United States would accept, but Lee Jong-seok insisted that these troops should not be combat troops, but rather be deployed for peaceful reconstruction in an area where there was no fighting.[25] Lee wanted to put the alliance on a different footing. In April 2003 the two governments engaged in an exercise called the Future of the Alliance (FOTA). There were a number of critical issues which engendered the impression in Washington that the Republic of Korea's support for the alliance was diminishing, while the ROK began to sense the possibility of abandonment by the United States. The first issue was the relocation of the Yongsan garrison of the United States Army from downtown Seoul to Pyeongtaek. This was a response to public discontent with the presence of the U.S. forces in a central location of Seoul. But the United States also proposed the relocation of the 2nd Division of the U.S. Army from its position along the DMZ to south of Seoul. This would significantly change the role of the U.S. Army, which until then had functioned as a tripwire for the reinforcement of U.S. forces in the event of a war. The ROK government suspected that the United States wanted it to fund the costs of this relocation and moreover feared that these changes would be accompanied by actual force reductions. President Roh and his advisors were also concerned about the aggressive language used by the Bush administration toward North Korea and that the relocation of U.S. forces was partly designed to facilitate air strikes on North Korea. Bush reassured Roh that he had no plan to attack North Korea, and it soon became evident that the relocation was part of Defense Secretary Rumsfeld's "revolution in military affairs," which involved more flexible forces at a lower level (i.e., troop reductions).

The decision to relocate the 2nd Army Division to Iraq hit the South Korean policymakers like a bombshell. They were also concerned about the notion that South Korea would essentially become a hub from which U.S. forces could be dispatched anywhere in the region when needed. This new concept raised concerns about entrapment and abandonment simultaneously, because it might mean that U.S. forces in Korea could be used in contingencies in Taiwan, which would reduce the protection of the ROK and embroil it in a potential conflict with China.

The national security dialogue between Seoul and Washington was confusing because the South Koreans wanted to prevent a weakening of the alliance while at the same time seeking emancipation in a manner that could easily be seen as South Korea distancing itself from the United States. For instance, the ROK advocated "self-reliance" in national defense and informed the United States that it wanted to take over "wartime command" of Korean forces from the U.S. Army. President Roh Moo-hyun explained his commitment to "self-reliant defense":

> In order to achieve firm national security, first we should achieve self-reliant national defense within the next 10 years. During my term in office, I intended to lay the foundation for such self-defensive capabilities. It is beyond question that as an independent, a nation should have enough strength to defend itself on its own.[26]

While the South Korean armed forces were now superior to those of the North, the question was whether South Korea alone could convincingly deter a North

Korean attack. True self-reliance was not achievable because of North Korea's unconventional forces (also described as asymmetrical threats), such as chemical weapons, ballistic missiles, and nuclear devices. Indeed the nuclear test of 2006 made it abundantly clear that South Korea needed to rely on the U.S. security guarantee to deter North Korea.

In 2005 a military reform plan for the South Korean armed forces was announced. The plan envisaged a reduction in active military personnel from 680,000 to 500,000 by 2020, and a reduction of reserve forces from 3.04 to 1 million. There would be a shift of greater reliance from conscripts to volunteers by reducing the length of military service. The size of the army was to be reduced from 550,000 to 350,000, with a major reduction in senior positions. The 13 army corps were to be reduced to 6 and the 47 divisions reduced by about 20. Troops currently deployed at the border were to be replaced by brigades especially trained for guard duty, and coast guard duty would be transferred from the military to the police. The underlying principle of the reform was to make the armed forces leaner, and yet more capable, by spending $195 billion on new weapons, including unmanned spy aircraft, attack helicopter, armored vehicles, and self-propelled artillery. The air force was also to undergo a transformation, with more advanced fighter aircraft and airborne early warning systems. Defense expenditure was supposed to reach a level of 3 percent of GDP by 2015, although it remained unclear as to where the funds would come from.

Whether the Republic of Korea can bring the level of its fighting capability up to that of the United States armed forces remains to be seen, even if it could generate these unrealistic defense budgets. Particular gaps in ROK military capabilities are in air power, airlift capacity, and C4I (command, control, communications, computers, and intelligence). The United States deploys space-based assets which the ROK will be unable to emulate in the foreseeable future, and the South Korean armed forces lack the sensors and target acquisition capabilities, meaning that they rely on the United States for strategic and tactical battlefield information, which is unlikely to change. Finally, the ROK currently lacks the capacity for large-scale amphibious landing operations.[27]

All of this means that ambitions for the Republic of Korea to become self-reliant in defense remain illusory. The Roh administration also was oblivious of the lessons to be learned from the experience of the NATO alliance during the Cold War. European defense expenditures by the key members of the Alliance (the United

Kingdom and West Germany) were constrained by domestic political factors, and thus failed to meet the expectations of U.S. governments. This led to various efforts by members of Congress to reduce U.S. troop levels in Europe. The Europeans found themselves on a spectrum between doing too much and too little. If the Europeans were to fill all the gaps in their capabilities, apart from facing unsustainable expenditures they would run the risk that the United States might be induced to reduce its costs and draw down its forces. This became a greater fear in the aftermath of the Cold War, after the military confrontation in Central Europe had come to an end. If the Europeans did too little, Congress would complain that the Europeans weren't doing enough for their own defense.[28] But the Roh government seems to have been oblivious to the effect that their plans might have had in Washington. Instead Roh was seeking to rebuild the national image of the Republic to Korea without any due regard about how it was viewed elsewhere. The problem was that this had potentially serious consequences for the national security of the country.

The second element of Roh's effort to restructure the U.S.-ROK alliance to regain South Korea's national sovereignty was the change in wartime operational control of the South Korean armed forces. According to an agreement concluded in 1994, South Korea has operational control over its forces in peacetime. In wartime designated ROK forces will be assigned to the Central Forces Command (CFC), which is headed by a U.S. commander who will control those as well as all U.S. forces. The units to be assigned will depend on the precise nature of the contingency, but in the event of full-scale war would constitute the bulk of ROK forces, with the expectation that CFC would receive large-scale reinforcements of U.S. troops and matériel. In this situation the U.S. commander in Korea would be answerable both to the U.S. president and the president of the Republic of Korea. Political decisions would be passed through a Military Committee that would issue orders to the military command.

In 2006 President Roh announced that wartime command (operational control) of the armed forces of the Republic of Korea should be transferred to South Korea. As Lee Jong-seok explained to me in a two-hour interview, this was a point of high principle for him related to the national sovereignty of the Republic of Korea.[29] It was bitterly opposed by South Korea's military leaders (including many former defense ministers), but in Washington Lee was pushing against an open door. Rumsfeld made remarks that indicated his willingness to leave the Korean Peninsula entirely, and the United States wanted to move toward the transfer of wartime command even faster than the South Korean government. On October 20, 2006, at the 38th Security Consultative Meeting (SCM), a biannual meeting of U.S. and South Korean defense ministers and officials, it was agreed that wartime operational control should be transferred to South Korea after October 15, 2009 (the date preferred by Rumsfeld), and no later than March 15, 2012. The "Strategic Transition Plan for the transition of Operation Control over Korean forces during wartime from the United States to South Korea" was signed on June 28, 2007, by the Joint Chiefs of Staff (JCS) chairman Gen. Kim Kwan-jin and CFC commander Gen. B. B. Bell. Rumsfeld's successor at the Pentagon, Robert Gates, signed an agreement with ROK minister of defense Kim Chang-soo to dissolve the CFC on April 17, 2012.

However, many questions remained unanswered. How would ROK and U.S. forces be coordinated in the absence of a joint command? Would the ROK acquire the capabilities needed to take over wartime operational control? Military and leading conservative politicians were deeply concerned, and when Lee Myung-bak from the GNP campaigned to become Roh Moo-hyun's successor, his policy team advocated rescinding the decision to transfer wartime operational control. Once Lee was elected, the United States and South Korea agreed to postpone the transfer and left the door open to the possibility of abandoning it altogether.

Another point of contention between Roh's administration in Seoul and Washington was about revisions to the Operational Plan (OPLAN) 5029, which deals with the contingencies in the event of a North Korean collapse. Lee Jong-seok insisted that South Korea could not accept the revised version proposed toward the end of 2004 because it interfered with the sovereign rights of Korea. He insisted that 5029 should be a Conceptual Operational Plan (CONPLAN) rather than an OPLAN and that in the event of such instability in the North, South Korean forces should be the first to respond, with Americans joining in if asked. This issue, and the U.S. insistence on the strategic flexibility of their forces, was not fully resolved during the period of the Roh government.[30]

Criticism of the national security policy in the Kim Dae-jung and Roh Moo-hyun governments often focuses on the policy's tactics, claiming it was simply ineffective in countering the North Korea regime. But conservatives in South Korea pointed to a much deeper underlying problem, namely that the Sunshine Policy was based on a false understanding about the nature of the North Korea regime and its ultimate objectives. It was not just a different philosophy of social organization, or that the current situation was the result of a bitter civil war that had divided the country for more than half a century. At the core of the continuing division of the two Koreas was the fact that the DPRK was ruled by the Kim dynasty, which was unwilling to relinquish power under any circumstances. While it was true that the regime was under very severe pressure due to its failing economy, the very fact that it survived even the consequences of a severe famine in which over a million people died demonstrated the extreme lengths it was prepared to go to ensure its survival. It showed how tight its grip was on the population and that as long as the livelihood of the political elite and the army was guaranteed (although even soldiers were not entirely immune from the problems of food scarcity) there was no hope of an indigenous uprising. This understanding of the nature of the North Korean regime has important implications for the prospects of alternative arrangements on the Korean Peninsula, such as a confederation offered by Kim Jong-il or even unification. It implies that from the Northern perspective any arrangement that brings the Koreas closer means greater influence for the North over the South (while keeping the North closed to influence from the South) and unification means extending the rule of the Kim dynasty over the entire Korean Peninsula. This means there can be no real rapprochement between North and South without regime change.

Even if the conservative analysis of the situation on the Korean Peninsula is accepted, this does not negate the rationale for a policy of engagement entirely. First of all there is a general consensus in the Republic of Korea that a sudden collapse of North Korea is not desirable. Indeed, the possibility of such an event is the most serious threat that South Korea faces. The expected flood of refugees would create massive instability in both North and South, jeopardizing both the economic and societal cohesion of the South. The costs of such unification are hard to quantify and depend on the manner in which it occurs, but have been variously put at somewhere between $500 billion to $2 trillion.[31] Moreover, the movement of refugees could occur in both directions, prompting a possible intervention by China. Finally, given the size of the armed forces and their enormous conventional military arsenals, there would be plenty of scope for uncontrolled violence. A sudden unification along the lines of the example of Germany is not viable because the Republic of Korea does not dispose of the resources that West Germany had, and the level of the North Korean economy is very much lower than that of the German Democratic Republic in its final years. The only viable alternative therefore is a "soft landing," a gradual regime change and a long period of economic and political reform in the North that will make unification possible to achieve sometime in the future. The prospects for a soft landing, however, are hampered by the persistence of the Kim regime. There is no doubt that the regime is resisting any efforts by the South to promote political change in the North. This is why the situation on the Korean Peninsula remains so intractable.

Despite its inherent difficulties and the recalcitrance of the North Korean regime, the logic of the policy of engagement remains compelling. At the very least this policy will prevent a catastrophic collapse of the North. Until economic relations were suddenly curtailed in the aftermath of the *Cheonan* incident in 2010, North Korea had been gradually becoming more economically dependent on the South. Trade between the two Koreas grew steadily, to the point where the Republic of Korea had become the DPRK's most important trading partner, getting ahead of China and Japan (the share was 27, 26.9, and 23.3 percent, respectively, in 2002).[32] During the term of Kim Dae-jung's presidency alone, the volume of trade increased from $221 million in 1998 to $641 million in 2002. South Korea is an important source of critical aid for the North, both in terms of cash and the provision of rice, fertilizer, and other essential goods. The Republic of Korea is also providing investment for various projects in the North, the most significant of which is the Gaesong Industrial Complex. The complex is located forty miles north of Seoul and was designed to attract South Korean business with cheap North Korean labor and government loan guarantees of up to $10.5 million per loan. More than 1,300 companies applied to set up production facilities in Gaesong. Yoon Young-kwan, South Korea's foreign and trade minister from 2003 to 2004 and one of Korea's leading experts on international political economy (now at Seoul National University), told the author that he envisaged the Gaesong Industrial Complex to become economically united with the northern region of South Korea. It is better positioned than the Rajin-Sonbong Free Economic Zone, with a hotel and a casino as its main attractions. The attempt to develop the Sinuiju Special Administrative Region near the Chinese border has stalled as Yang Bin, the Chinese businessman who was appointed to run it, was arrested in China on charges of corruption and sentenced to eighteen years in prison.[33]

The theory, then, is that an increase in the density of North-South interactions and greater involvement of the South in the North's economy drive forward a process of economic change, which will ultimately translate into social change. One version of this argument is that North Korea's nuclear program and other threatening activities can be ignored because North Korea is essentially deterred. Ultimately the increasing economic engagement with the South will bring about political reform and regime change, whether the North Korean elite wants it or not. However, it is unclear whether ignoring the security dimension is in the interests of either the Republic of Korea or the region. The events of 2010 support the view that as the DPRK regime weakens it may increase its military provocations as a means of reversing the trend. Moreover, the strategic situation will change as North Korea will increase its capacity to target Japanese forces and American forces based outside the Korean Peninsula (especially if nuclear weapons are involved). Perhaps the most problematic feature of the Sunshine Policy is the ambiguity it has generated both about the direction of the process and the status of the Republic of Korea itself. The precise nature of any "closer association" between North and South has remained unclear. Specific steps on the road of unification have not been elaborated upon, except for the intermediate stage of confederation. Conservatives have been deeply concerned by the fact that this process effectively abandons South Korea's claim to represent the true Korea, since a confederation might ostensibly give equal legitimacy to both Korean states. In other words, critics of the Sunshine Policy have emphasized that any rapprochement between the two Koreas must avoid undermining the integrity and the status of the Republic of Korea.

North Korea's nuclear test in 2006 was a dramatic blow to the peace and prosperity policy. For one thing, it removed any ambiguity about North Korea's nuclear ambitions and capabilities. Up to that point, liberals in South Korea and China could pretend that the threat wasn't real. Even worse, it became evident that the engagement of North Korea had failed to prevent this provocation and could not, after all, moderate North Korea's behavior, which meant that as a policy it was seriously misguided. Unification minister Lee Jong-seok accepted the consequences and resigned. Roh Moo-hyun, although visibly shaken by this turn of events, persevered. His efforts were rewarded by a second North-South summit held in Pyongyang on October 2–4, 2007, not long before the end of Roh's term. The summit produced a range of agreements to intensify inter-Korean dialogue and cooperation and proceed with the implementation of the June 15 Declaration from the previous summit. Conservatives in Seoul derided the summit as a thinly disguised effort by

Kim Jong-il to bolster the chances of the liberals in South Korea in the forthcoming presidential elections. Roh's period in office ended without any consensus on the achievements of the policy of engagement.[34]

BACK TO THE FUTURE: THE COLLAPSE OF
NORTH-SOUTH RELATIONS

The conservatives got their chance when on December 19, 2007, Lee Myung-bak won the presidential elections in a landslide. His national security team was adamantly opposed to the Sunshine Policy. It is not that they rejected engagement with North Korea—there was now a consensus that engaging North Korea was necessary and that a sudden collapse of the North Korean state must be prevented. However, they were determined that there should be a strong conditionality attached to support for North Korea. At the same time, their plan for engaging and transforming North Korea was extremely ambitious. They wanted to double the GDP of the DPRK through a large-scale investment program in infrastructure (conditional on resolving the nuclear issue). This policy had the cumbersome title "Initiative for Denuclearization and Opening Up North Korea to Achieve US$3,000 in Per Capita Income." The ultimate goal was to bring about a socio-political transformation in North Korea, which would eventually result in regime change. President-elect Lee also wanted to rejuvenate the U.S.-ROK alliance and reverse some of Roh's decisions, such as turning over wartime command of allied forces to the Republic of Korea.[35]

At the time of the presidential election, public support for the outgoing president and his party (which had already dissolved twice and reconstituted itself during his time in office) was low. The conditions under which Lee was elected were auspicious in principle because the GNP now controlled both the presidency and the National Assembly. But the contest between Park Geun-hye and Lee Myung-bak about who would be the presidential candidate opened up deep divisions in the party. The failure to unite the party was the first major misstep of the Lee government, which soon acquired a reputation for arrogance. The opposition Democratic Party, whose leader lost a high-profile battle for the Jogno constituency (covering part of central Seoul, Jogno is considered to be the highest-ranking of all constituencies in the country) against the incumbent Park Jin, began a relentless campaign against President Lee (who was called the Bulldozer). Public support for Lee Myung-bak fell rapidly and dramatically. Surprisingly, it was foreign policy that played a major role in the loss of confidence in the nation's leader. The chorus of disapproval in South Korea was almost universal, emanating from all parts of the political spectrum. There were large-scale public protests and candlelight marches in downtown Seoul that demonstrated public dissatisfaction with the government's policies. The issue that resonated most with the Korean public was the Free Trade Agreement (FTA) with the United States. The opposition engaged in what could be described as fearmongering about beef imports from the United States and the risk of mad cow disease. Korean newspapers were full of scathing articles dissecting the failures of the Lee Myung-bak government in tedious detail.

President Lee Myung-bak had moved quite quickly to bring about a substantial shift in South Korean foreign policy. At the core was a rejuvenated alliance with the United States and closer relations with Japan, reaffirming South Korea's position as a pro-Western state. Relations with China were to be cordial but more distant and subordinate to the U.S.-ROK alliance, and Seoul would pursue a harder line toward Pyongyang. But Lee moved without having gained sufficient public support. Moreover, the implementation of foreign policy appeared rather amateurish: the first steps to implement its new policy toward North Korea were maladroit, to say the least. Instead of showing quiet resolve coupled with productive proposals to move forward, the government in Seoul engaged in careless rhetoric, which only served to antagonize the leaders in Pyongyang. Moreover, the Lee government refused to endorse all of the agreements to develop North-South relations reached at the summit toward the end of the Roh administration. The hard-line response from Pyongyang and the widespread criticism in South Korea of the new approach persuaded Lee to soften his stance. He announced the sudden U-turn just as it became known that a tourist had been killed at the Mount Geumgang resort. For many in South Korea this demonstrated an extraordinary lack of basic political skills. Lee's approach toward China was clumsy as well, and the efforts to shore up the U.S.-ROK alliance looked like Lee kowtowing to President Bush.

At the time, critics tended to ignore that many of the problems facing South Korea had to do with a less favorable international environment or were the consequence of the policies of previous governments. Even the Roh government agreed that the ratification of the FTA was in the national interest of the Republic of Korea. The beef issue (exploiting the fear of mad cow disease), which Lee inherited from his predecessor, was an irrelevant sideshow which was being cynically manipulated by the opposition, as there is no doubt that the Korean public is not at risk from U.S. beef. The Lee government continues to maintain that it is imperative that the Republic of Korea reinvigorates its alliance with the United States, an alliance that became strained during the previous two governments (although South Korea was not the only one at fault), because the United States plays an essential role in South Korean national security and is an indispensable partner in dealing with North Korea's nuclear program. Moreover, the political and economic culture of the vibrant Korean democracy is close to the United States, despite the disaffection felt by younger people. The Lee government does not believe that Korea can play the role of balancer or that it can have a similarly close relationship with China. Although China is an important trading partner for South Korea and good relations with China are very important, any strategic partnership with China has limits. Beijing opposes Korean unification, and its strategic goals for dominance in Northeast Asia are not fully compatible with South Korea's interests because it seeks to draw Korea out of the American orbit and into its own. Moreover, China is not a democracy, and its values in domestic and international politics are not those of the modernized South Korea. Similar motivations compel the Lee government to seek a closer relationship with Japan, though the burden of history and the irritating behavior of a weak Japanese government make matters difficult, such as when Japan raised the territorial dispute over the island of Dokdo by asserting its claim in school textbooks. The reaction of South Korea's public to this incident served to derail Lee's policy to forge closer relations with Tokyo. From the South Korean perspective, another problem is the Japanese focus on the abduction of a few of its citizens by North Korea, as this attitude is not contributing constructively to the resolution of the North Korean nuclear issue in the Six-Party Talks.

All of these does not mean that the pragmatic foreign policy is doomed. The goal of strengthening the Northeast Asian community of democratic countries committed to preserving security and resolving the crisis on the Korean Peninsula is central to the Lee government's foreign policy, but it will take time to realize its objectives, especially given the current deadlock in inter-Korean relations.

The Lee administration did succeed in its efforts to revitalize the U.S.-ROK alliance by reestablishing the alliance relationship on the basis of shared values and a common understanding of South Korea's role in Northeast Asian security. By prioritizing a resolution of the North Korean nuclear issue, U.S. and South Korean core foreign policy objectives in the region converged. The unrelenting hostility from the North and its insistence on being recognized as a nuclear state precluded any initiatives that could have given rise to disagreements between Washington and Seoul. The difficulties the Obama administration encountered in engaging China, and the bickering with Japan over basing U.S. forces in Okinawa, were in stark contrast to the congenial relationship with Lee Myung-bak. On June 16, 2009, a U.S.-Korean summit meeting in Washington, D.C., resulted in a joint vision statement on the U.S.-ROK alliance.[36] North Korea's *tongmi bongnam* policy to marginalize the South and use bilateral relations with the United States to gain concessions from the South could gain no traction as North Korean hostility and provocation only strengthened the relations between the United States and South Korea. At the margins of the G20 summit in June 2010 President Obama committed to completing the Korea-U.S. Free Trade Agreement.[37]

The deterioration of relations with North Korea reached a climax in the aftermath of a naval incident. On March 26, 2010, a South Korean navy ship called the *Cheonan* sank off the west coast of the Korean Peninsula, with a loss of forty-six seamen. On May 20, 2010, the results of an investigation carried out by international experts were announced. According to their report, the *Cheonan* had been attacked by a North Korean torpedo (the remains of which had been recovered) fired from a midget submarine. The South Korean government announced the termination of all economic relations with North Korea (with the exception of the Gaesong Industrial Complex) as well as various security-related measures. The latter included a decision for South Korea to become a full-fledged member of the proliferation security initiative (PSI) and joint naval exercises with the U.S. navy that involved the dispatch of an aircraft carrier group to the region.

Washington and Seoul worked very closely in developing a response to the crisis. Obama and Lee made it very clear that they expected China to accept the results of the investigation and North Korea's responsibility for the sinking of the *Cheonan*, but the Chinese and Russians hedged their bets. Consequently the response by the United Nations Security Council was limited to a presidential statement that condemned the attack but did not blame the DPRK specifically. The North Korean leadership interpreted this as a diplomatic victory, but inter-Korean relations had reached their lowest point since the 1980s. It seemed that all the gains of ten years of diplomacy had been lost.

After the sinking of the *Cheonan*, tensions persisted on the Korean Peninsula as the South Korean government made any renewal of engagement, including a restarting of the Six-Party Talks, conditional on an apology for the incident. The North Korean government gave various hints of wanting to restart discussions with Seoul and indicated its willingness to return to the nuclear talks, but since it perceived itself as the winner of this confrontation, it was not prepared to make even a small gesture with respect to the sinking. The situation became even worse as a result of an incident that occurred on November 23, 2010. South Korean armed forces conducted artillery exercises on the island of Yeonpyeong, north of Incheon, close to the Northern Limit Line, which according to the Republic of Korea demarcates the sea border between North and South (it is not recognized by North Korea). North Korean armed forces fired about 170 artillery shells, resulting in four deaths and nineteen injuries. South Korean armed forces shelled the artillery positions in North Korea in response.[38]

This incident occurred at a time period when there were several significant events that were actually not interrelated. The first was the North Korean decision to reveal its uranium enrichment program by inviting U.S. scientist Siegfried Hecker to view some of its facilities. Also in November 2010, U.S. and South Korean armed forces were engaged in a large-scale military drill known as the Hoguk exercise. This is an annual military exercise which in 2010 involved 70,000 South Korean troops from all branches of the armed forces. The U.S. contribution to the exercise involved the 7th Air Force and the 3rd Marine Expeditionary unit.

The live-fire exercise in the waters of Baengnyeong Island and Yeonpyeong Island were not part of the Hoguk exercise (nor was the Hoguk exercise a response to this incident). The North Koreans had warned that they would respond to any shelling of North Korean waters. According to the then South Korean defense minister Kim Tae-young, the routine monthly firing drill on November 23 involved the firing of shells in a southwesterly direction with a range of about 40 km. However, the North Koreans considered the drill to violate their coastal waters and bombarded Yeonpyeong in two different waves using coastal artillery batteries on Mudo, as well as a multiple rocket launcher based on Kaemori. The fire was indiscriminate and hit civilian as well as military targets. In response South Korean artillery fired about eighty shells, first at the command and control structures in Mudo and later at Kaemori. Fighter aircraft were scrambled but did not strike at any North Korean targets. In the aftermath of this incident the public perception of the South Korean military response was generally that it was both weak and revealed a lack of preparedness. Defense Minister Kim, who had already been the focus of criticism after the sinking of the *Cheonan*, resigned after leaders of the government and opposition parties criticized him for a passive response to the attack.

South Korea and the United States considered this to be a very grave confrontation, exceeding even the sinking of *Cheonan*, given that it was an open, undisguised military attack on South Korean territory. Both in South Korea and the United States the incident gave rise to internal debates about how conventional deterrence could be strengthened. In the Pentagon the policy debate was about the paradox that the weaker state (North Korea) was prepared to assume great risks, while South Korea and the United States seemed deterred from taking any action that could result in escalation, even though their capacity to escalate was so much greater.[39] President Lee was under public pressure to prepare for a more forceful response in the event of another provocation.

The assessment in Seoul and Washington was that there were two main reasons for North Korea's aggressive posture.[40] The first was related to the ongoing leadership succession and the efforts to bolster Kim Jong-eun's credentials. Indeed, there were reports that Kim Jong-il and Kim Jong-eun personally ordered and oversaw the attacks. The second reason was the use of military pressure in order to force Seoul and Washington back to the negotiating table of the Six-Party Talks without the preconditions that had been set (i.e., return to the implementation of the agreements negotiated under the Bush administration and some gesture of regret or apology about the sinking of the *Cheonan*). In the aftermath of the Yeonpyeong incident the North Koreans decided to exercise greater restraint and did not implement their threats to launch further attacks, thus reducing tensions in the subsequent months.

The challenge for the South Korean government is how to rebuild a relationship with the North. The response to the *Cheonan* incident may have been an overreaction insofar as it involved an escalation to the highest level short of actual military action. The cutting of economic ties makes North Korea even more dependent on China and reduces South Korean influence to a minimum. It is hard to see how this can be in South Korea's interest. The experience of the efforts to engage North Korea in the Kim Dae-jung, Roh Moo-hyun, and Lee Myung-bak governments has shown that neither conditional nor (almost) unconditional engagement have had significant impact on either the attitudes or the behavior of the North Korean leadership. There are indications that both South Korea and the United States will continue to seek to engage North Korea in order to mitigate tension on the Korean Peninsula and limit China's influence. But the expectations of what can be achieved have been lowered significantly. The Lee government has not yet managed to gain support for its policy among the people of the Republic of Korea. Indeed, no coherent policy emerged after it became evident that North Korea was not interested in Lee's great initiative. Thus the South Korean government faces the twin challenge of reengaging the North and gaining domestic support for its policies.[41] The road to ending the crisis on the Korean Peninsula is still long and arduous.

5

The North Korean Security Dilemma

After the Cold War and the First Nuclear Crisis

The parameters defining North Korea's national security have changed dramatically as a result of long-term political and economic trends that culminated with the end of the Cold War. The collapse of communism in Russia and Eastern Europe was a tremendous blow to Kim Il-sung and the elite of the DPRK. Although North Korea had existed at the margins of the communist world and had maintained a policy of equidistance between the Soviet Union and China, the end of communism in Eastern Europe (and in China in all but name) plunged the country deep into international isolation. Despite its avowed commitment to *juche* (self-reliance), in practice the DPRK had depended on economic support (in particular cheap energy and grain supplies) from the Soviet Union and the People's Republic of China. During the Gorbachev period in the 1980s Soviet interest had shifted toward closer relations with the Republic of Korea. When the Soviet Union put all of its trade with its former allies on a hard currency basis, exports to North Korea declined to almost zero. For example, Soviet/Russian shipments of petroleum-based products fell from one million tons in 1986 to nineteen thousand tons in 1995, and shipments of coking coal ceased entirely with the dissolution of the Soviet Union.[1] Since the end of the Cold War Russia has lost both the incentive and the capacity to provide assistance to North Korea. The terms of assistance forthcoming from China also changed and resulted in a decrease in energy and food exports to the DPRK.

By 1992 both China and Russia had officially recognized the Republic of Korea. Consequently the North Korean economy experienced a dramatic decline with the loss of cheap energy imports, the lack of manufactured goods from Russia, and other aid. In the years 1990–1997 the economy decreased by 42.2 percent. Agriculture was hit by natural disasters in addition to its basic inefficiency, resulting in serious food shortages and starving people leaving North Korea for China. Material conditions of life for ordinary people became almost unbearable.

The situation in the early to mid-nineties was in fact so dire that in the United States as well as in the Republic of Korea there was a widespread expectation that the collapse of the regime was imminent. The situation was particularly problematic in relation to food supplies. As Russian exports to the DPRK collapsed, and domestic food production was inadequate to meet demand, the regime was faced with a difficult set of choices. With the collapse of the barter trade among formerly socialist countries and the poor quality of North Korean goods, it was not feasible to increase exports in order to earn sufficient currency to import food on the required scale. Neither was North Korea able to raise capital due to its previous defaults and constraints imposed by Western countries. Although the gap left by Russia was partially filled by the delivery of oil and food from China, the Chinese soon began to require the North Koreans to pay cash, which constrained the DPRK's capacity to avail itself of Chinese imports. This decision by China and the natural disasters in the mid-nineties were the triggers for the famine in which more than one million North Koreans perished and which caused widespread malnutrition in the country.[2]

Faced with these multiple dilemmas, the focus of the North Korean leadership shifted from its previous ambition to reunite the Korean Peninsula by force to regime survival. North Korea adopted what came to be called "the triple survival strategy" of improving relations with the United States, Japan, and other major capitalist countries, strengthening North Korea's "own way of socialism" in domestic policy, and replacing the previous strategy of the equidistant alliance with Russia and China.

In the 1990s it became very clear that for the DPRK the relationship with the United States was viewed as the central path to regime survival. The main instrument that North Korea had to engage U.S. interest was its nuclear program. However, there is no evidence and it seems rather unlikely that this is how Pyongyang saw its situation at the time. Instead the nuclear program proceeded under its own technological momentum, becoming a critical factor when the United States became aware of North Korea's capability to produce plutonium. When North Korea finally joined the NPT, its activities had to be reconciled with its commitments under the treaty. (NPT membership requires states to submit to safeguards of all their nuclear materials and inspections by the International Atomic Energy Agency, or IAEA.)

For most of the decades since the Korean War, the United States had no direct contact with the DPRK except through the armistice commission. U.S. diplomats were even barred from entering into conversations with North Korean officials. However, the Reagan administration adopted a new approach designed to explore some degree of engagement with North Korea to make progress on various issues, an approach that was continued by the Bush Sr. administration; informal contacts between North Korean and American officials were now permitted. Sanctions were eased to permit humanitarian trade. More substantial improvements in relations between the DPRK and the United States would be possible if there was progress on a range of issues, including relations between Seoul and Pyongyang, human rights, the recovery of American soldiers missing in action from the Korean War, and North Korea's renunciation of terrorism.

THE ORIGINS OF THE NUCLEAR PROGRAM

North Korea's involvement in the development of nuclear technology (which the United States had closely observed since its inception) dates back to the 1950s when the DPRK was an ally of the Soviet Union, which was then prepared to cooperate with other communist states in various aspects of industrial development, including civil nuclear technology. In 1956 North Korea and the Soviet Union signed two agreements on increased cooperation and North Korean scientists began to receive training on nuclear physics at the Joint Institute for Nuclear Research in Dubna in the Soviet Union. In 1959 Soviets helped set up a research center on the bank of the Kuryon river, close to the town of Yongbyon. It was referred to as the furniture factory, presumably to keep its real purpose secret.[3] Programs in nuclear technology were set up at the Kim Il-sung University and the Kim Chaek College of Technology. North Korea also began collaborating in the field of nuclear energy with China.

In September 1961, at the fourth conference of the KWP, Kim Il-sung told scientists to work on the peaceful uses of nuclear energy. The core of North Korea's nuclear program in the early stages was a small research reactor known as the IRT-2000 research reactor. This reactor was procured from the Soviet Union in January 1962 and construction began in 1963 under Soviet supervision. In August 1965 the Soviet Union provided a research reactor called IRT 2000 and rated at 2 MWt (the output of a nuclear reactor is measured either in terms of MWt [megawatts of heat produced] or MWe [megawatts of electricity generated]). The pool-type reactor uses a mixture of uranium fuel elements of different levels of enrichment, designed to produce small quantities of isotopes for medical and industrial purposes. North Korea's reactor became operational in 1967. (The power rating increased to 4 MWt in 1974 and 8 MWt in 1987.)

It is not known exactly when the leaders of the DPRK decided to pursue a nuclear weapons program, although this may well have been on Kim Il-sung's mind from very early on after the Korean War, an intention that firmed up after the Cuban Missile Crisis of 1962 (when Kim Il-sung declared a new self-reliant military policy) and the deployment of U.S. nuclear weapons in the Republic of Korea. According to North Korean defectors interviewed by Daniel Pinkston from the International Crisis Group, Kim Il-sung gave a directive to develop nuclear warheads for missiles in 1966 or 1967.[4]

Anxieties generated by the Cuban Missile Crisis were exacerbated by the considerable reluctance of the Soviet Union to share nuclear technology with the DPRK. North Korea had been provided with a research reactor but not a full-scale nuclear reactor for generating electricity, in contrast with some East European countries (where such reactors were under construction by the mid-sixties), and Soviet assistance remained limited.[5] In 1964 Kim Il-sung suggested in a letter to Mao Zedong that China and the DPRK should share nuclear weapons technology, given their partnership in the Korean War, but China refused, stating that such a small country did not need nuclear weapons. A similar request made in 1974 was likewise rejected, but only after various hints were made by the Chinese that they might be prepared to provide tactical nuclear weapons to the DPRK sometime in the future.[6] Unlike other Soviet allies, the DPRK refused to ratify the NPT, which provoked concerns in Moscow about Pyongyang's intentions, in particular as the stance taken by the North Koreans was quite similar to that adopted by the Chinese government.

North Korea's interest in nuclear technology was not directed purely at the acquisition of nuclear weapons, but also involved civilian applications; there was a clear interest in acquiring nuclear power stations as the DPRK had difficulty generating sufficient electricity. The 1973–1974 oil crisis prompted the Soviet Union to raise the price of oil it sold to its allies. Although the price was still well below the world rate, it resulted in considerable resentment in Pyongyang at the Soviet Union for continuing to refuse to supply the DPRK with a nuclear power plant. For the North Koreans, this was not only a matter of economic necessity, but also of prestige. The DPRK wanted to be at the forefront of new technological developments, especially as the Republic of Korea, although prevented by Washington from pursuing nuclear weapons, began constructing nuclear power plants.[7] It is clear that Soviet leaders were alarmed by Pyongyang nuclear ambitions. The view had formed in Moscow that Kim Il-sung was harboring aggressive ambitions toward South Korea (rather than the other way around) and cooperation with North Korea on conventional weapons production was also tightly constrained. Various threatening statements from Kim Il-sung about the coming "liberation" of South Korea were accompanied by official hints about nuclear weapons (possibly being provided by China).[8]

NORTH KOREA AND THE NPT

North Korea joined the IAEA in 1974, although it did not at that point accede to the NPT. In 1978 it signed an INFCIRC/66 trilateral safeguards agreement with the IAEA to allow for the monitoring of the IRT-2000 reactor and a critical assembly that the Soviet Union had provided in addition to the reactor. Choi Hak-gun was assigned as counselor to the DPRK's office at the IAEA in Vienna, and reportedly spent his four years there using IAEA library facilities to acquire as much information as possible about nuclear reactors design and other aspects of nuclear technology. He became North Korea's atomic energy and industry minister in 1986.

In the late 1970s the DPRK embarked on a substantial expansion of its nuclear capabilities. This manifested itself in the development of the nuclear infrastructure at Yongbyon as the first step in the establishment of a nuclear weapons program. North Korean defectors reported that at that time a complex of nuclear facilities was constructed underground in the Pakchon area (about fourteen miles southeast of Yongbyon), where research to develop indigenous nuclear fuel enrichment technology and other aspects of nuclear weapons technology (including the design of a nuclear device) was undertaken. Other facilities constructed at Yongbyon during this period included a factory to refine yellow cake (U_3O_8) produced at the uranium milling factories at Pakchon and Pyongsan and facilities to produce uranium metal fuel elements. (North Korea has uranium ore deposits that could potentially yield 4 million tons of natural uranium.)

In 1980 construction of an indigenous 5 MWe (20 MWt) gas-cooled, graphite-moderated reactor based on the British 1940s gas-graphite design (known as Calder-Hall) began. In 1984 construction of a second, larger reactor with an output of 50 MWe (200 MWt) commenced (this reactor was detected by U.S. observation satellites in 1989). The 5 MWe reactor went critical in August 1985 and began regular operations in 1986. Plans for the nuclear program also included a full-scale 200 MWe (800 MWt) power plant whose construction began in Taejon in 1989. However, of these three projected plutonium reactors, only the original Yongbyon reactor has become operational, while the others remain unfinished projects. In addition, construction of the so-called Radiochemistry Laboratory began around that time, a full-scale reprocessing plant to extract plutonium from the fuel rods. The infrastructure developed at Yongbyon also included facilities to treat and store nuclear waste.

The graphite-moderated Magnox reactor is quite different from the so-called VVER (pressurized water) light water reactors (LWRs) which the Soviet Union had provided to Eastern European countries. Generating nuclear materials for use in weapons is more complicated if you're dealing with LWRs, whereas the North Korean reactor produces very pure plutonium. Moreover, East European countries were dependent on the Soviet Union for the provision of nuclear fuel, whereas the North Korean nuclear program was effectively out of Soviet control and the North Koreans even refused to supply data about the operation of its research reactor to the Soviet Union.

In 1985, in response to pressure from the Soviet Union, the DPRK decided to join the NPT. The Soviet Union consequently agreed to sell North Korea four LWRs to be used for the production of electricity; however, the LWRs were never delivered because after the Soviet Union put trade relations on a hard currency basis using world prices, North Korea lacked the resources to pay for them. North Korea acceded to the NPT on December 12, 1985.

Washington made a concerted effort to ensure that North Korean nuclear facilities would be subject to IAEA safeguards. Because the prospect of a North Korean nuclear weapon was of such serious concern to the United States, the nuclear issue thus became central to efforts to improve U.S.-DPRK relations. Consequently, nuclear weapons assumed the role of the most significant asset that North Korea had in any negotiations. During his visit to Pyongyang in January 1991, Soviet foreign minister Eduard Shevardnadze explained the new basis of relations with the DPRK, which would include the diplomatic recognition of South Korea.[9] In response the then North Korean foreign minister Kim Yong-nam openly declared that North Korea would no longer consider itself bound to forego the development of nuclear weapons and would open direct negotiations with the United States. However, the notion that the nuclear program might become a bargaining counter in the game of ensuring the survival of the state was probably not yet clearly developed as Pyongyang did not yet realize the kind of crisis that its program was about to provoke.

In 1989 the administration of President Bush Sr. was confronted with intelligence that North Korea had a reprocessing plant close to its 5 MWe reactor, which meant it could separate plutonium from the fuel. There was also information that North Korea was working on a warhead design and testing explosives for an implosion-based device. The Bush administration decided that isolating North Korea would not prevent it from going nuclear and instead decided on a policy of engagement, building on the initiatives introduced by Reagan. The *National Security Review 28* (an interagency review of U.S. policy on North Korea chaired by Assistant Secretary of State Solomon in the spring of 1991) developed the concept of a "comprehensive engagement" of North Korea while at the same time adopting a strong deterrent posture and promoting dialogue between the two Koreas. At the core was the idea that the DPRK should accept its nuclear nonproliferation obligations under the NPT. In addition, the sale of missiles should be curtailed, and North Korea should renounce terrorism. Eventually this process would lead to normalization of relations between the United States and DPRK. The Bush administration also put legislation in place permitting the export of $1.2 billion worth of U.S. goods to the DPRK, such as food or humanitarian supplies, prior to any progress on the nuclear issue.[10]

The presence of U.S. nuclear weapons in South Korea was identified as an obstacle to engagement in National Security Review 28. But President George H.W. Bush decided to withdraw all nuclear weapons from overseas bases (except for free-fall aircraft-based weapons), including bases on the Korean Peninsula, as part of a mutual worldwide reduction in nuclear deployments between the Soviet Union and the United States. In response to a secret order authorized by the president, aircraft-based weapons were removed from Korea as well. Soon after, South Korean president Roh Tae-woo publicly declared the Republic of Korea to be free of nuclear weapons and suggested talks to make the Korean Peninsula a nuclear-free zone. Negotiations between the prime ministers of the two Koreas resulted in a nonaggression pact and an agreement not to interfere in each other's internal affairs. President Roh Tae-woo declared that the Republic of Korea would not produce plutonium or manufacture and store nuclear weapons, and that the Korean Peninsula was now free of nuclear weapons. President Bush stated he would not argue with President Roh, even though normally the United States does not confirm or deny the deployment or storage of nuclear weapons in any given location. By the end of 1991 intensive diplomacy produced the North-South Denuclearization Declaration (NSDD). At the urging of the United States, the declaration included a prohibition on the production of plutonium and uranium enrichment, thus cutting off all avenues to nuclear weapons production as long as the declaration was adhered to. The declaration had potentially far-reaching implications because although the Yongbyon reactor could continue to operate under IAEA safeguards, the reprocessing of fuel rods in order to extract plutonium was now banned.

The declaration was followed by significant progress on the issue of IAEA safeguards. In December 1991 Pyongyang declared its intention to sign a safeguards agreement with respect to all of its nuclear facilities, provided the United States declared that there were no nuclear weapons on the Korean Peninsula. In support of the improvement in relations, the United States and South Korea agreed to cancel the annual Team Spirit joint military exercise for 1992 if the DPRK made good on its declaration. Conducted since 1976, Team Spirit was a large-scale military exercise involving hundreds of thousands of troops to demonstrate the capacity of the United States and South Korea to repel an attack from the North. In Pyongyang it was seen as a possible prelude to an invasion, and each year the North Korean military leaders felt obliged to mount a major mobilization of their own forces in response, which incurred substantial costs.

At a meeting between U.S. undersecretary of state Arnold Kanter and his North Korean equivalent, Kim Yong-sun, the United States further offered to improve relations between the two countries if North Korea fulfilled its obligations with respect to nonproliferation. However, Kanter was unable to offer "full normalization" of relations and the North Korean response was noncommittal. Nevertheless, the DPRK initialed the safeguards agreement by the end of January and ratified it in April of the same year.

The nuclear facilities that would be subject to inspection were visited by IAEA director general Hans Blix. In May 1992 Pyongyang submitted a declaration to the IAEA that confirmed the existence of a reprocessing facility at Yongbyon and the separation of ninety grams of plutonium in 1990 from damaged fuel rods that had been removed from the 5 MWe reactor. But inspections conducted in July and September indicated that there were discrepancies in the declaration. The inspectors concluded that more plutonium had been recovered than had been declared, and that reprocessing took place over a longer time period than indicated by the North Koreans. Indeed, laboratory analysis showed that three different batches of plutonium had been produced over a time period of three years, as opposed to the one batch declared by North Korea. U.S. intelligence also suspected that North Korea was concealing two underground sites from the inspectors that perhaps contained waste from additional reprocessing. U.S. specialists estimated that enough additional spent fuel might have been reprocessed to yield sufficient plutonium for one or two nuclear weapons.

The seemingly substantial diplomatic achievements of 1991 were lost very quickly. Tension mounted between North and South Korea over the implementation of the NSDD, namely the frequency and scope of mutual inspections. The IAEA sought access to the suspect sites, using the previously uninvoked right to "special inspections," demands that were rejected by Pyongyang. The United States and the ROK announced that preparations for the 1993 Team Spirit exercise would continue, given the lack of progress in the bilateral inspection regime (for which the two Koreas blamed each other). The South Korean intelligence services announced the discovery of a Northern spy ring involving some four hundred agents whose purpose it was to subvert the South. Moreover, the United States rebuffed North Korean requests for another high-level meeting with Kim Yong-sun.

In 1992 there were presidential elections in the United States and the Republic of Korea. In Seoul, the first democratically elected president of the Republic of Korea who was not a military officer, Kim Young-sam, took office. The election was a momentous event, completing the Republic of Korea's path to full democracy. Kim and the newly elected U.S. president Bill Clinton took office as relations with North Korea were moving toward a serious crisis. Paradoxically, the incoming South Korean administration was considering radical changes to policy vis-à-vis the North, whereas the new U.S. administration's policy exhibited great continuity with its predecessor. Three key officials dealing with North Korea, Daniel P. Poneman, William Clark, and Robert Gallucci, were holdovers from the Bush administration.

The Clinton administration came into office with a strong commitment to nuclear nonproliferation and this induced a determination to deal with all nuclear proliferation threats, including North Korea, and supporting the IAEA to the hilt.

In South Korea, meanwhile, the newly appointed unification minister Han Wan-sang supported the idea of a grand gesture toward the North. Consequently, various statements about a summit between Kim Young-sam and Kim Il-sung were made by South Korean officials. The government indicated that such a summit could take place once the nuclear issue was resolved. However, as we have seen, the IAEA was convinced that North Korea's declaration had been fraudulent and Hans Blix issued the first ever request for special inspections, resulting in a rise of tensions with the North. At a meeting in Vienna on February 13, 1993, between Blix and the North Korean atomic energy minister Choi Hak-gun, the IAEA director general attempted to persuade Choi to address the discrepancies in the declaration. The U.S. government had provided intelligence information about North Korea's nuclear activities to the IAEA, including satellite imagery of the suspect sites and activities, which Blix threatened to use, but to no avail.

Although the North Koreans tried to limit the escalation in the tension with the United States and the ROK, they rejected the request for special inspections, and consequently a special meeting of the IAEA Board of Governors was convened in late February, at which IAEA officials displayed satellite photographs of the suspect sites. The most dramatic element of the presentation was a demonstration of how the North Koreans had apparently buried a waste site and built a decoy building on top.[11]

China and Russia were clearly reluctant to confront North Korea. Nevertheless, the board adopted a unanimous resolution on February 25, 1993, giving the DPRK one month to comply with its safeguard obligations. In order to ensure Russian and Chinese support, the resolution did not insist on special inspections, but merely that the IAEA be granted access to the suspect sites. The North Koreans were confronted with the evidence but conceded nothing.

ON THE BRINK OF A NUCLEAR CRISIS

The atmosphere of an impending crisis was heightened further by the Team Spirit exercise, which began in February. By special order of Kim Jong-il, North Korean forces were put on a semi-war footing. On March 12, 1993, came the bombshell: Pyongyang announced that the DPRK would withdraw from the NPT, invoking a clause that permits a country to withdraw if its "supreme interests" are threatened by giving ninety days' notice. North Korea cited U.S. military threats (it considered Team Spirit a preparation for nuclear war against the DPRK) and the manipulation of the IAEA to get access to secret military sites in North Korea. Pyongyang stated it might reconsider its withdrawal if "the United States stops its nuclear threats against our country."[12] This statement caused the Republic of Korea to place its forces on high alert, but both Koreas quickly stepped back from the brink once the Team Spirit exercise ended.

With the general atmosphere of relations with North Korea deteriorating fast, the intentions of the Pyongyang government were unclear. For example, it is still unknown whether the North Koreans were determined to hold on to some amount of plutonium outside IAEA safeguards in order to preserve the option to develop a nuclear weapon, or whether they were simply ratcheting up the pressure in the face of the perceived hostility from the United States and South Korea (a very common North Korean diplomatic practice). One factor that became clear in the course of later discussions was that the North Koreans would never accept an IAEA finding that would essentially convict the DPRK of submitting a false declaration. This was a matter of saving face. At the same time, however, it had become clear that the policy of continuing a nuclear weapons program while at the same time being a signatory to the NPT as a non-nuclear state had become difficult to maintain. The crisis came at an inopportune time, as Kim Jong-il was named chairman of the National Defense Commission to replace his father. The regime was in the process of a leadership transition and Kim Jong-il was facing a foreign policy crisis at a point when the political elite and especially the military leadership had to be convinced that he was capable of leading the country. The then-recent confrontation between Iraq and the United States was a salutary example for North Korea. Although the Hussein regime survived the 1990–1991 Gulf War, it ended up in a situation where it was defeated and essentially under perpetual siege. This was a fate that the North Korean leadership wanted to avoid at all costs.

The Clinton administration rejected the idea of isolating North Korea by focusing solely on sanctions. Instead it opted for securing multilateral support for a policy of gradually escalating diplomatic pressure on the DPRK in order to persuade Pyongyang to reverse its decision to withdraw from the NPT, while at the same time engaging in direct talks with Pyongyang. The dual-track strategy was intended to put the maximum pressure on North Korea while gathering as much international support as possible and, most important, keeping China and Russia on board. The situation with regard to China was problematic insofar as it became clear that China was unwilling to adopt a stance of coercion against the DPRK. The IAEA was concerned about the continuity of safeguards as Hans Blix insisted that previous agreements still applied even if the DPRK withdrew from the NPT and the safeguards agreement. The North Koreans were planning to temporarily shut down the 5 MWe reactor to unload the fuel rods. The problem was the possibility of diversion of plutonium if there was no independent verification; moreover, the fuel rods contained the history of the reactor that could be destroyed if they were reprocessed without observation by IAEA safeguards inspectors.

In April Pyongyang agreed that IAEA inspectors could come to North Korea. During the four-day inspection the IAEA staff made sure that the monitoring equipment was in working order and installed some additional equipment. The anticipated unloading of the reactor was postponed, so the issue of IAEA presence during the refueling remained on the agenda. The inspectors were not given access to the suspect sites. On May 11 the United Nations Security Council adopted Resolution 825, which called on North Korea to retract its withdrawal from the NPT and implement the safeguards agreement, and called on "interested states" to assist with a solution. In the context of impending dialogue between the United States and North Korea, China abstained and indicated that it did not oppose the will of the international community.

The North Koreans responded eagerly to American signals about the prospects of direct talks, which began at the end of May. The North Korean delegation was led by Vice Foreign Minister Kang Sok-ju (relations with the United States had become the purview of the ministry of foreign affairs after Party Secretary Kim Yong-sun, who previously had the role of conveying North Korean policy to the United States, lost his place in the Politburo). Ambassador Robert Gallucci—a nonproliferation expert who had served at the Arms Control and Disarmament Agency (ACDA) for a long time and had been involved in inspecting the Iraqi nuclear program after the Gulf War—headed the American team that was made up of representatives from the departments of state and defense, the National Security Council, the Joint Chiefs of Staff, and the ACDA.

The first round of talks held in New York in June 1993 proved extremely difficult. Nevertheless, it became apparent that North Korea was interested in progress.

The Americans tried to browbeat North Korea with threats of sanctions and references to official North Korean statements that contradicted Kang's stance. Initially, Kang insisted that a reversal of North Korea's withdrawal from the NPT was impossible. In the course of the negotiations it became clear, however, that the North Koreans were trying to find a solution and wanted to know what the United States would offer. Although Gallucci failed to persuade the DPRK delegation to consider remaining in the NPT on a permanent basis, the talks ended with an agreement to "suspend" the withdrawal.[13] The joint document issued at the end listed a number of agreed principles, such as an assurance not to use force or the threat of force (including nuclear weapons), mutual respect for national sovereignty, and noninterference in the internal affairs of other countries. The most important statement was that North Korea "decided unilaterally to suspend for as long as it considers necessary the effectuation of its withdrawal" from the NPT.[14] This meant that the IAEA inspectors would be able to resume inspections, although the details still had to be ironed out. The statement did not reveal the fact that Kang had discussed at least the possibility of a more far-reaching arrangement to end the production of plutonium in North Korea.

At the second round held in Geneva in July 1993 the North Korean delegation made a proposal based on "bold new instructions" to resolve the nuclear crisis. The DPRK offered to abandon its graphite-moderated reactors that produced plutonium if it were to be given LWRs to provide for North Korea's energy needs. From the U.S. point of view, this proposal was promising. If the North Koreans continued to produce plutonium they could accumulate a stockpile of the fissile material, which could then be used to make nuclear weapons. Although in principle fissile materials could be extracted from LWRs, nevertheless there was confidence that this could be prevented by safeguards and measures to remove the spent fuel from North Korea on a continuous basis.

Although this meeting seemed to indicate that there was a deal to be had, it also clarified the fundamental disagreements between the two sides. Gallucci was adamant that North Korea had to enter into consultations with the IAEA. The United States remained exercised about the incongruities in the North Korean declaration and about any diversions of plutonium prior to 1992 (by U.S. estimates possibly enough for two nuclear devices). Kang, on the other hand, expressed the North Korean concern that further inspections would reveal discrepancies and this would lead to an unacceptable loss of face. At the same time he insisted that there could be no agreement unless the United States guaranteed the provision of LWRs. Special inspections could only take place after the DPRK had received the nuclear reactors. From the U.S. perspective, this was a non-starter; U.S. law would prohibit the provision of such items as long as there were proliferation concerns.

This argument about the sequence of various steps would recur again and again in U.S.-DPRK negotiations. The United States wanted the concerns about nuclear weapons to be resolved *before* it was willing to meet other demands by the DPRK; the North Koreans insisted that it had to be the other way around, and they would not be willing to give up their one card before having received what they needed.

The meeting ended without any formal agreement as the U.S. delegation was unwilling to provide any assurances regarding the provision of LWRs until the non-proliferation concerns were dealt with, beyond "considering" such a proposal. The North Korean delegation agreed that Pyongyang would talk to the IAEA about safeguards and to South Korea about the implementation of the NSDD.

Relations between the IAEA and Pyongyang proved to be difficult. North Korea considered the extent of inspections a political issue to be settled by negotiations. It perceived the IAEA to be a tool of American foreign policy, rather than an independent international agency. The IAEA considered inspections a technical matter. The acceptance of inspections was required for North Korea to fulfill its obligations under the NPT. The NSDD was subject to the same problems as the safeguards. In this case, too, North Korea considered verification and inspections to be a political issue, to be settled by political negotiations, and not a technical matter that required all possible sites of concern to be inspected in order to give confidence that the declaration was being adhered to. Inter-Korean relations were also under stress because President Kim Young-sam—in his reluctance to be seen making too many concessions and as an attempt to placate the more conservative elements—made some statements that incensed Pyongyang, such as that "he would never make an agreement with someone who had nuclear weapons."[15] Seoul was also concerned that the United States might move to make a deal with Pyongyang without proper consultation. The North Koreans did not really consider either the IAEA or the Seoul government to be appropriate partners for negotiations about their nuclear program. For them it was an issue to be settled between the DPRK and the United States through a bilateral deal.

Of course, the IAEA is not an agency of the U.S. government. Both the U.S. administration and the IAEA saw the issue of inspections as a matter of treaty compliance and nothing else, but the U.S. government had wider concerns. The IAEA was focused on the continuity of safeguards and believed that further inspections were necessary to achieve that. The Geneva talks in July 1993 had enabled the inspections to take place in August, but the North Koreans restricted the planned activities and the IAEA inspectors worked under difficult conditions. On September 1–3 there were talks in Pyongyang between the DPRK and the IAEA. The IAEA representatives were pushing for more extensive inspections by September 28, 1993, when the cameras the IAEA had installed at the Yongbyon nuclear facilities were running out of film (the IAEA had run the cameras at their maximum speed in order to put pressure on the North Koreans). They also wanted to discuss special inspections with North Korea. The North Koreans, on the other hand, wanted the IAEA to apologize for having sparked the nuclear crisis and to discuss the provision of new reactors. The IAEA was not about to apologize and the question of the provision of LWRs was clearly beyond its purview. At this stage the dialogue between the IAEA and the DPRK broke down. As the observation cameras at the nuclear sites shut off, the point was coming when the continuity of safeguards could no longer be preserved.

The third round of bilateral talks, scheduled for September 1993, was postponed, which meant that the agreements of the Geneva meeting were not being met. The Clinton administration sought to make its engagement with the DPRK dependent on North Korea's engagement with the South, but the inter-Korean dialogue was running into trouble.

By December 29, 1993, months of diplomatic wrangling between United States and North Korea produced a proposal for a package of four steps to be taken simultaneously on March 1, 1994, dubbed Super Tuesday. The IAEA would begin inspections at seven sites that had been specified by the agency; the DPRK promised it would allow these inspections to be completed. Working-level meetings between Pyongyang and Seoul would begin to arrange the exchange of special envoys. The Republic of Korea would announce the cancellation of the Team Spirit exercise in agreement with the United States. North Korea and the United States would announce the date of the next round of bilateral talks.

Despite the December agreement, in early 1994 there was a significant increase in tension, which could be explained by several causes. The first was North Korea's winter military exercises. U.S. military analysts had identified these exercises as a possible starting point for another invasion of the South. In conjunction with bellicose rhetoric emanating from the North, what alarmed the Americans was the fact that North Korean troops were being deployed increasingly closer to the DMZ. The second cause was the U.S. plan to begin the deployment of Patriot missiles, which would provide some reassurance against a ballistic missile attack from the North. From the U.S. perspective this was considered a necessary step to protect its forces based on the Korean Peninsula, and was not intended as a political signal. But it proved to be controversial in South Korea and provoked hostile rhetoric from the North. Third, discussions between the DPRK and the IAEA reached an impasse, with the prospect of dramatic escalation of the nuclear crisis if the IAEA board were to conclude that the continuity of safeguards had been broken. The combination of these events led a spiral of escalation in tension to the point that the national intelligence officer (NIO) for warning (a member of the CIA's National Intelligence Council whose job it was to watch where the United States faced hostile forces) came close to issuing a "warning of war" on the Korean Peninsula.[16] Although a warning of war does not indicate that military action is imminent, it means that in the estimation of the NIO the country in question is completing the preparations that would make it ready for war. Such a warning would have provoked actions from the U.S. commander in Korea that would most likely have produced an escalating cycle of steps and countersteps toward a military confrontation.

Gallucci became increasingly worried that the United States was drifting toward war with North Korea and that something had to be done. The opportunity to take a step toward reducing tension came with an initiative by the evangelist Billy Graham to visit Pyongyang. Graham carried a message from President Clinton for Kim Il-sung to the effect that the United States wanted to resolve the nuclear crisis peacefully. Kim told Billy Graham that North Korea would never build nuclear weapons and expressed his wish for a summit meeting with President Clinton. In the aftermath of Graham's visit the dialogue between the IAEA and the DPRK seemed to make progress to the point where it appeared that the main outstanding issues were being resolved.

The day of March 1, 1994, was the so-called Super Tuesday (based on an analogy to the Super Tuesday when a number of primaries in presidential elections are held on one day). The U.S. government released the following statement about the outcome:

Pursuant to the consultations, both sides have agreed to take four simultaneous steps on March 1, 1994 as follows: 1. The U.S.A. announces its decision to agree with the Republic of Korea's suspension of Team Spirit '94 joint military exercise. 2. The inspections necessary for the continuity of safeguards as agreed between the I.A.E.A. and the D.P.R.K. on February 15, 1994, begin and will be completed within the period agreed by the I.A.E.A. and the D.P.R.K. 3. The working level contacts resume in Panmunjom for the exchange of North-South special envoys. 4. The U.S.A. and the D.P.R.K. announce that the third round of U.S.-D.P.R.K. talks will begin on March 21, 1994, in Geneva. Each of these simultaneous steps is required for the implementation of these agreed conclusions.[17]

The Super Tuesday deal, however, soon fell apart. Two issues were decisive. The first was that although the IAEA inspectors were permitted to visit the seven sites they had specified, they were prohibited from undertaking the sampling that they required. In other words, the North Koreans were still refusing to allow the IAEA to undertake the work necessary to ensure that there had been no diversion of plutonium in the past. During the inspections in March 1994, the inspectors discovered that the North Koreans had made substantial progress in developing a second reprocessing line that was not subject to safeguards. It was disturbing evidence that North Korea was planning to accelerate reprocessing and increasing its plutonium stockpile.[18] On March 15 the inspectors left without having completed their activities.

The second issue was related to the exchange of envoys with South Korea. The South Koreans insisted that the timing should be closely linked to the resumption of the Geneva talks (virtually simultaneously). The North Koreans threatened to boycott the talks if the exchange of envoys was a precondition for their resumption and the cancellation of the Team Spirit exercises.[19] On March 16 the United States cancelled the third round of meetings in Geneva and announced the resumption of planning for Team Spirit.

At the North-South working-level meeting in Pamunjom on March 19, the Super Tuesday deal was finally buried, when the North Korean representative Pak Yong-su said to his South Korean counterpart: "Mr. Song, your side has to deeply consider the dear price of war. Seoul is not far from here. If war breaks out, it will be a sea of fire."[20] (This remark was later disavowed by North Korean leader Kim Il-sung.)

The key dispute between the IAEA and Pyongyang centered on inspections designed to ascertain the history of the plutonium, to ensure there had been no diversions and to reconcile the facts with the declaration submitted by the DPRK. This dispute divided the U.S. government: the nonproliferation experts at the Department of State stressed the importance of ensuring that the history of the plutonium was preserved, whereas at Defense the more pragmatic view of preventing the accumulation of plutonium for weapons in the future was advocated by nonproliferation hawks such as Ashton Carter. The problem was that the insistence on the former could render the latter objective unachievable.

At the IAEA board meeting on March 21, Blix stated that the agency could not determine whether any nuclear material had been diverted from the Yongbyon reactor because the continuity of safeguards had been broken at the reprocessing plant. The resolution of the board referred North Korea to the UN Security Council, despite North Korean threats that the DPRK would permanently withdraw from the NPT if this were to occur and the Team Spirit exercise was to take place.[21] To the surprise of the Americans, China abstained when the resolution came to a vote, sending a strong signal to Pyongyang. The same day, the United States submitted a draft resolution to the UN Security Council, calling on North Korea to permit additional inspections by the IAEA. In order to ensure China's abstention, the draft did not seek to impose economic sanctions but gave the DPRK one month to comply.[22] (In the end, the United States would settle for a declaration by the UN Security Council president, which was essentially identical to the draft of the resolution—except for the one-month deadline, which was omitted—and was supported and proposed by China.[23])

Tension continued to escalate as the South Korean president Kim Young-sam placed his armed forces on high alert in response to the North Korean threat issued at Pamunjom and the United States began to deploy Patriot air defense missiles in South Korea.

On April 19, 1994, Robert Gallucci received a message from Kang Sok-ju that contained a bombshell: North Korea had decided to unload the approximately eight thousand spent fuel rods from the 5 MWe reactor at Yongbyon for "safety reasons." Gallucci warned Kang that any such unloading would have to be monitored by IAEA inspectors. In the meantime, in an effort to resurrect the Super Tuesday deal, the United States and South Korea agreed to decouple the third round of the Geneva talks from the exchange of envoys between North and South, and on April 28, 1994, at a working-level meeting, the U.S. State Department officials once again offered to resume talks and suspend Team Spirit if North Korea allowed additional IAEA inspections. All of this was overtaken by the events unfolding in Yongbyon. North Korea informed the IAEA the inspectors could observe the unloading of the reactor but not take any samples from individual fuel rods.[24] On May 12 the DPRK informed the IAEA that it had started removing fuel rods from the 5 MWe reactor. The IAEA assembled a team of inspectors to go to Pyongyang, while the United States began to talk about sanctions. Refusing to allow the IAEA to record the location of individual fuel roads, the North Koreans began to destroy the operational history of the reactor that the IAEA had fought so hard to preserve.

With the fuel rods out of the reactor, North Korea was moving one step closer to reprocessing to extract plutonium for weapons production. The IAEA estimated that the eight thousand fuel rods would yield approximately 25–30 kg (55–60 lb) of plutonium, enough for perhaps up to six nuclear warheads.

The crisis was escalating dangerously. By unloading the reactor North Korea had crossed a "red line." To quote from *Going Critical*, cowritten by Gallucci, "Whether North Korea's defueling was the product of delusion or desperation, in crossing that line it essentially dared the United States to cut off dialogue and to refer the nuclear issue to the Security Council for punitive action."[25]

In the United States, the storm was gathering. Defense Secretary Bill Perry pushed for military reinforcements to be sent to Korea. Perry wanted the reinforcements to be in place before sanctions were imposed by the UN Security Council. Preparing the United States for military action in the region was seriously discussed, as the Clinton administration came under fire in the press and in Congress for its seemingly weak and inconsistent response to North Korea's provocations. The possibility of a strike on North Korea's nuclear facilities was also considered.

Efforts to build an international consensus to impose sanctions began to bear fruit. Japan was considering measures to cut off the remittances of North Korean residents in Japan to the DPRK, which amounted to about $600 million per annum. China was indicating its impatience with Pyongyang's behavior and hinted to the North Koreans that unless they came into line, it would not oppose sanctions. South

Korea was in favor of a firm stance and was prepared to participate in sanctions against the North. Russia's president Boris Yeltsin told North Korea that it could not count on support from Russia against economic sanctions over its nuclear program or in the event of war.[26]

After briefings on the likely casualties of a war on the Korean Peninsula Clinton actively discouraged any war talk. The analysis presented to the U.S. president confirmed that the United States and South Korea would win a war, but with 30,000 U.S. casualties and 450,000 South Korean casualties. These projections did not include figures produced by the Department of Defense that estimated that there would be 1 million civilian casualties, the conflict would cost $60 billion, and the damage to the South Korean economy would amount to $1 trillion (figures presented to Clinton at another briefing).[27] Still, as North Korea announced its intention to withdraw from the IAEA and a draft resolution for sanctions against the DPRK was circulated, the drift toward confrontation seemed inexorable.

As tension was rising former president Jimmy Carter proposed that he should go to North Korea for a personal visit with Kim Il-sung. Carter followed the suggestion of the U.S. ambassador to the Republic of Korea, Jim Laney, who had become increasingly disturbed about the mounting confrontation. Carter's involvement was a reflection of the seriousness of the risk of escalation to armed conflict in this crisis. The idea was that Carter might be able to reach the one person in North Korea who would be able to pull back from the brink and take the decisions necessary to avoid war. The administration was divided on the proposed trip (it was opposed by Secretary of State Warren Christopher), but it was approved by President Clinton after Vice President Gore persuaded National Security Advisor Tony Lake to support it. The South Korean government privately opposed the Carter trip. President Kim thought that support for sanctions was growing and Carter would have a different agenda.

On June 13, 1994, Jimmy Carter arrived in Seoul. The plan was to travel to North Korea by car through the DMZ. There was an extraordinary sense of crisis. Private citizens were stockpiling supplies and the South Korean government reviewed the mobilization status of over 6 million reservists. Two days later a previously planned nationwide civil defense exercise was held, which added to the sense of crisis. According to the South Korean National Ministry of Defense, the armed forces of the DPRK were in their highest state of readiness since 1990. Later it was reported by a defector that Kim Jong-il spent most of the period of the nuclear crisis in a bunker. Embassies in Seoul reviewed evacuation plans and some foreign companies had ordered dependents of their employees to leave the country. U.S. Ambassador Laney himself told his daughter and grandchildren to leave Korea.

The South Korean government feared that the United States was preparing to evacuate its citizens and take steps toward a conflict in North Korea without prior consultation with Seoul. This impression was mistaken, but discussions about increasing U.S. forces and a possible strike at the nuclear facilities were getting underway in Washington as Carter began his visit. On the day President Carter arrived in North Korea, the United States presented the other four permanent members of the UN Security Council with a draft resolution calling for sanctions on North Korea. The resolution called for five phases of increasingly severe sanctions if North Korea continued not to cooperate with the IAEA. In the first phase there would be an immediate cessation of all UN technical and scientific projects in North Korea as well as a total embargo on arms sales.[28]

At the initial meeting with Foreign Minister Kim Yong-nam, Carter was confronted with a hard line. The basic message was that IAEA inspectors would be asked to leave until an agreement was reached. However, a meeting with Kim Il-sung produced a breakthrough. The Great Leader stressed that his country could not and need not develop nuclear weapons. He also emphasized the need to be able to generate sufficient electricity.

Kim Il-sung also made it clear that North Korea would give up its graphite-moderated reactors if it were to receive LWRs. When Jimmy Carter sought a commitment that the IAEA inspectors should be able to complete their work without hindrance, it transpired that Kim Il-sung was not fully aware of the current state of the confrontation. The chief negotiator, Kang Sok-ju, advised the North Korean leader that he could make the commitment to full transparency, including remaining in the NPT, and said that a decision had already been made to permit the inspectors to stay. It transpired later that the opposite had been the case, but now with the commitment from Kim Il-sung the immediate crisis was resolved. Kim Il-sung also supported a proposal by Carter to hold the first ever North-South inter-Korean summit. Controversially, Carter suggested to Kang that reprocessing of the fuel rods from the reactor might be permissible, provided it occurred under IAEA safeguards. Although Carter was correct in terms of his interpretation of the NPT, reprocessing had been anathema to the Clinton administration, given that it would give North Korea sufficient plutonium for perhaps five nuclear weapons. Moreover, reprocessing was expressly prohibited by the North-South Declaration on Denuclearization.

Despite the unofficial nature of Carter's visit, the ex-president made a statement on CNN that criticized the move toward sanctions and made it difficult for the U.S. government to back away from the kind of "deal" that seemed to be on offer. In a videotaped message Carter informed Kim Il-sung that the process leading to sanctions had been halted. President Clinton decided to put the best face on it and interpret it in a way that satisfied U.S. requirements, putting the burden on North Korea to challenge the "interpretation." Thus the United States understood the commitment to mean that the 5 MWe reactor would not be loaded with fresh fuel and that there would be no reprocessing of spent fuel rods. This became the basis of the negotiations from thereon.

On July 8, 1994, three weeks after the meeting with Carter, Kim Il-sung died of a heart attack. These events interrupted the talks briefly but negotiations resumed, resulting in what came to be known as the Agreed Framework on October 21, 1994.

THE AGREED FRAMEWORK

The core of the Agreed Framework was that North Korea would abandon its nuclear program in stages, in accordance with the progress of the LWR project: the Korean Peninsula Energy Development Organization (KEDO) was formed in order to manage this project that involved the construction of two 1,000 MWe reactors to be completed by the target date of 2003. Among the other commitments in the Agreed Framework was the provision of heavy fuel oil that would be managed by KEDO as well. The South Korean government was to provide and pay for the nuclear reactors (with some contribution from Japan and smaller contributions from other countries), while the U.S. government was committed to provide the heavy fuel oil. The first step would be the freezing of additional plutonium production, but full compliance with safeguards (which would include whatever plutonium North Korea had produced prior to 1992) would not be required until a "significant portion" of the LWR project was completed in four or five years' time. U.S. and IAEA officials were to supervise the freezing of the Yongbyon 5 MWe reactor and the storage of the fuel rods. The second phase of implementation involved the supply of 500,000 tons of heavy fuel oil annually (funded by the United States). Other elements included the reduction of barriers to trade and investment, and improvements in political relations ultimately leading to full diplomatic relations.

Before the key nuclear components of the LWR would be delivered and the first reactor could come on line, the IAEA safeguards agreement would have to be implemented, "including all steps deemed necessary by the IAEA."[29]

In the third phase, after the first unit of the LWR project was completed, the eight thousand spent fuel rods would be removed from North Korea. The entire dismantlement of the graphite-moderated reactors and all elements of plutonium production in the DPRK would take place after completion of the LWR project. Once North Korea had complied with its IAEA safeguards agreement and was accepted as a non-nuclear weapons state in the NPT, the United States would provide formal assurances to the DPRK against the threat or the use of nuclear weapons.

The United Nations Security Council issued a statement on November 4, 1994, in support of the Agreed Framework, and North Korea agreed to cooperate with the freezing of the reactor at Yongbyon (by September 1999 the canning of the fuel rods had been completed). In March 1995 the Korean Peninsula Energy Development Organization (KEDO) was formed to implement the Agreed Framework. Its main task was to manage the construction of the light water reactors and provide 500,000 tons of heavy fuel oil to North Korea.

It is fair to say the Agreed Framework was controversial both in the United States and in South Korea, and political disagreements resulted in significant problems in its implementation (discussed in the next chapter). The signing of the Agreed Framework was not the end, but rather the continuation of complicated bargaining between the various parties. The Agreed Framework was a sole executive agreement, and unlike a treaty was based on presidential executive authority without any formal assent from Congress. Moreover, it was a "non-binding political agreement" that was not legally enforceable. While this meant that there were no obstacles to the adoption of the Agreed Framework, its status contributed to some of the problems of implementation.

These began before the ink was even dry. In Washington the agreement faced a barrage of criticism. The Agreed Framework was perceived to be a form of appeasement: most of the Republican leadership (including, for example, Senator John McCain, who attacked Robert Gallucci personally) believed that the North Korean leadership should have simply been faced down. William Safire quoted former U.S.

Defense Secretary James Schlesinger referring to the Agreed Framework as "nego-tiated surrender."[30] Bob Dole, the Senate majority leader, said about the Agreed Framework that it "shows it is always possible to get an agreement when you give enough away."[31]

Democrats were not exactly enthusiastic, either. The obvious criticism of the Agreed Framework was that it could be viewed as a form of extortion. From this perspective it could be argued that North Korea was being rewarded for breaking its international treaty commitments, and was using the threat to develop nuclear weap-ons to extort various political concessions and economic support on a large scale. The critics, however, ignored the realities of dealing with North Korea. They did not have any workable alternative options to deal with the plutonium program and failed to appreciate the extraordinary feat of diplomacy that was required to step away from the brink of nuclear crisis and obtain the Agreed Framework. Moreover, the Agreed Framework imposed requirements on the DPRK that exceeded those of the NPT, banning both the refueling of the 5 MWe reactor and the reprocessing of fuel rods.

The capacity of the Clinton administration to implement the Agreed Frame-work was constrained by congressional elections in November 1994, which resulted in a Republican majority in both houses. Although the Agreed Framework did not require congressional approval, the U.S. government needed congressional approval for meeting its financial obligations to fund KEDO and provide 500,000 tons of heavy fuel oil every year. Congress capped funding to implement the Agreed Frame-work at $30 million, assuming that heavy fuel oil shipments could be funded with foreign contributions and that the Department of Energy would submit a separate funding request for the storage of fuel rods from the North Korean reactor. Congres-sional funding was made conditional on certification that the DPRK was in compli-ance with its obligations under the Agreed Framework and that it was also imple-menting the 1992 Declaration on Denuclearization as well as engaging in dialogue with South Korea. Funding for the provision of heavy fuel oil was often inadequate and consequently the United States fell behind schedule in delivery, once again giv-ing the North Koreans grounds for complaining the United States was not holding up its end of the bargain.

Although the Agreed Framework was not an international treaty, it involved various powers who were not formally party to the agreement and had not been engaged in the negotiations, but whose acceptance and participation in the imple-mentation was nevertheless crucial. The Republic of Korea was one such power.

President Kim Young-sam formally endorsed the Agreed Framework, though the South Koreans were conflicted about it.[32] ROK conservatives, in particular, opposed it based on their opinion that the Agreed Framework gave another lifeline to the North Koreans, delaying Korean unification. In the government there was an informal opinion that the DPRK might collapse soon anyway.[33] The Republic of Korea was to provide about 70 percent of the Agreed Framework financing (estimated at $4.5 billion). The rest of the funding would come from Japan. The North Koreans were distinctly unenthusiastic about South Korean involvement in the provision of the nuclear reactors. They preferred a reactor of Russian design, though of course there was no way that the South Koreans would pay for that. By June 1995 American negotiators, in particular Gary Samore, convinced the North Koreans that they had to accept a South Korean model (although the origins of the design and active involvement of South Korea were not formally acknowledged).[34]

The construction of the reactors was a complex engineering task, but also posed financial and legal difficulties relating to the status of the land and the foreign workers. It is not surprising that the project continued to fall behind schedule, resulting in bitter complaints from the North Koreans. Three different countries, each with their own political agenda and domestic political issues, had to provide the funding. The North Koreans could be relied upon for creating trouble at the most inopportune moment.

There was considerable opposition to the Agreed Framework in U.S. Congress on grounds of principle. This was fueled by two issues in 1998. One had to do with reports by the Defense Intelligence Agency about an underground facility at Kumchang-ri that was suspected of being a secret nuclear site. In 1999 the North Koreans agreed to inspections of the site in return for the provision for grain, and nothing suspicious was found.

The other issue was North Korea's missile program, provoked by the launch of a Taepodong missile. It demonstrated that North Korea had the technical capability to add a third stage to their missiles, a key step in the development of an ICBM. Although the launch was a failure insofar as the third stage carrying a satellite failed to reach orbit, it was nevertheless cause for alarm. The trajectory of the missile brought it hurtling over Japan, exposing that country's vulnerability to missile attack from North Korea and eliciting a very strong political reaction, including a temporary suspension of Japanese funding for KEDO. It became evident later that North

Korea had not planned for the remains of the rocket to fall down where they did and the launch was not aimed to intimidate Japan as such.

Against odds, the Agreed Framework survived congressional obstinacy and North Korean provocations, and toward the end of the Clinton administration there was considerable improvement in U.S.-DPRK relations. Vice Marshal Jo Myong-nok, the first vice chairman of North Korea's National Defense Commission and one of Kim Jong-il's closest military advisors, came to Washington for talks with President Clinton, Secretary of State Madeleine Albright, and Defense Secretary William Cohen. Albright also attended a summit meeting with Kim Jong-il in Pyongyang. North Korea agreed to a moratorium on long-range missile tests with the prospect of an agreement to end the missile program in the future. By the end of the Clinton administration the engagement of North Korea seemed to have borne fruit.

UNDERSTANDING THE FIRST NUCLEAR CRISIS: THE LESSONS OF THE NEGOTIATIONS LEADING TO THE AGREED FRAMEWORK

What caused the so-called first North Korean nuclear crisis? On the surface the answer seems obvious—it was the diversion of plutonium from the Yongbyon reactor and the subsequent efforts by the United States and the IAEA to compel North Korea to comply with its safeguards obligations under the NPT. But this does not answer the deeper question as to what was at stake for North Korea, the United States, and the international community, and how to explain the manner in which this crisis unfolded and was (at least temporarily) resolved.

The effort to develop nuclear weapons had been ongoing in North Korea for quite some time before the crisis erupted. There is no evidence that there was a crash program to build a bomb, but rather that it was a program that was moving forward under its own momentum and reached the critical stage in the early 1990s, when reprocessing of fuel rods enabled North Korea to produce and stockpile plutonium. The fact that this program became the principal means whereby North Korea could engage the United States emerged only after the attempts to make North Korea comply with the safeguards agreement.

Nevertheless this was an industrial-scale nuclear program, which involved uranium mining, milling, processing, fuel fabrication, reprocessing, and three graphite-moderated nuclear reactors (of which only one became operational). The North Korean leadership clearly made a decision that the continuation of this program could take place even though the DPRK had joined the NPT. For North Korean nuclear materials to be under safeguards posed a threat to this strategy, but evidently the North Koreans underestimated both the breadth and the technical sophistication of IAEA inspections.

Similar problems were implicit in the North-South Denuclearization Declaration. As North Korea most probably did not have any nuclear devices at this time, the signing of the declaration itself had no impact on the nuclear program. But the difficulties emerged when the two Koreas started to have meetings in order to implement it. From the outset it was unclear whether the North Koreans were hell-bent on the acquisition of nuclear weapons or wanted to leverage their capability in order to get relief for the severe economic difficulties they were facing. The answer to this question turns on a number of different factors. The nuclear crisis began to develop well over a decade before North Korea finally conducted a nuclear test, and the North Koreans themselves did not indicate any level of certainty about their capabilities until about 2003. At the beginning of the 1990s the North Koreans may still have been uncertain about whether they could in fact manufacture a nuclear device or not. On the other hand, the shortfalls in the production of electricity were becoming very serious as the country's ability to import oil was severely constrained due to the changing international situation and North Korea's limited access to hard currency.

The essence of the deal governing the Agreed Framework, namely the provision of light water reactors, was put on the table by the North Koreans fairly early on. This would imply that Pyongyang was prepared to forego the security benefits of a nuclear deterrent (at least in terms of developing a full-blown nuclear weapons capability) in return for political and economic benefits. This raises the question of how the North Korean leaders assessed the threat from the United States. In official statements there was a persistent refrain of the "hostile policy of the United States" and allusion to the nuclear threat. The annual tantrums against the Team Spirit and other military exercises clearly reflect concerns about the use of such exercises to mobilize for a large-scale attack against the North. It is likely, however, that the North Koreans are aware that the only scenario seriously considered in Washington is that of a small-scale, targeted attack on nuclear facilities. The paradox here is that North Korea's nuclear program is generating precisely the kind of threat that it is presumably intended to deter.

During the Cold War North Korea was protected by security guarantees from the Soviet Union and China. Although its allies were not prepared to countenance another attempt to conquer South Korea, Pyongyang could rely on the security guarantees for deterrence against U.S.–South Korean aggression. The end of the Cold War completely changed the strategic balance and left the DPRK in a very weak position. Not only could its previous powerful allies no longer be counted on, but the military capabilities of the DPRK itself had degraded through the aging of equipment and the general lack of resources (in particular fuel for aircraft and vehicles), thus changing the conventional military balance on the peninsula. How precisely North Koreans assess the strategic situation in Korea is unknown, but there is a persistent belief that the morale and the fighting spirit of the North Korean army is such that it will prevail in any conflict. At the same time their military leadership must be aware of the weaknesses of their capabilities and the overwhelming power that the United States can bring to bear.

In light of this situation the DPRK adopted an asymmetric strategy. By signaling a willingness to take risks to the point of annihilation and threatening all-out war on the Korean Peninsula it sought to counter the superior military power of the United States. The history of U.S.–North Korean relations since the early 1990s has proven this strategy to be very successful. In particular, the North Korean capacity to launch large-scale artillery and missile attacks on the Seoul metropolitan area even without the use of nonconventional weapons means that any attack on North Korea risks a conflagration with a level of casualties that U.S. presidents so far have not been willing to contemplate.

But there is another element to North Korea's military strategy, namely the manipulation of threat to promote its political objectives. Here the record is more mixed. Although it could be argued that the Agreed Framework represents the crowning achievement of this approach to crisis manipulation, direct threats usually backfire. If North Korea had been more cooperative and less combative, it is likely that opposition in the United States to the Agreed Framework would have been reduced, and there are many other examples of how North Korea has had to forego tangible benefits due to its recalcitrant demeanor.

Just as there is no clear articulation of the external threat to the DPRK, there was no clear view presented by the U.S. government either internally or externally of the threat to international security posed by North Korea. There seems to have been a consensus that, with or without nuclear weapons, North Korea was essentially contained. Any estimates of North Korean nuclear weapons stockpiles (should they exist) were very low (less than twenty nuclear devices). The main threat appears to have been the prospect that an unchecked North Korea might eventually accumulate a substantial stockpile of nuclear weapons and acquire the capability to target ICBMs on the continental United States. Such a development would change the strategic environment in unpredictable ways, even if it were decades away, although even then the United States would still be able to deter a North Korean attack. The other threat posed by North Korea is that of the proliferation of nuclear and ballistic missile technology. In the 1990s North Korean ballistic missiles were sold to clients such as Iran and Pakistan, constituting the most successful line of exports for the DPRK. Finally, there is the threat of collapse, which (as discussed) could bring chaos to Korea and its neighbors.

The long-term threat of the nuclear program and the threat of collapse have been instrumentalized by North Korea to great effect. Not only did the regime manage to survive the famine in the mid-nineties, but it managed to extract enough economic support from the United States, South Korea, Japan, and China to marginally improve the economy in subsequent years. From this point of view, North Korea's strategy has been successful. The threat of proliferation, on the other hand, which has on occasion been articulated explicitly by the North Koreans, has always elicited a very negative response from the United States and has not proven useful to extract further concessions.

In the United States there was considerable opposition to negotiations with North Korea during the first nuclear crisis. This was based on the view that the United States should not be in the business of lending any support to a totalitarian regime, and that negotiations over the termination or the freezing of the nuclear program were rewarding North Korea for breaching its obligations under the NPT. Unfortunately, the United States lacked the instruments to force North Korea to abandon its nuclear program. The use of force was considered but rejected, because of the uncertainty of eliminating all elements of the program, the environmental consequences of an attack, and the threat of provoking a major war on the Korean Peninsula. The analysis that any attack on North Korea would involve unacceptable risks has been accepted by every U.S. president since Clinton. The alternative of isolating and containing North Korea until regime change occurs is not a plausible strategy as long as China and South Korea are not willing to go along. Such a policy has little chance of bringing about regime change or ending the nuclear program. Quite to the contrary, it could accelerate the nuclear program and bring the previously discussed undesirable developments closer. It could also provoke North Korea into other unpalatable attempts to generate military threats and confrontations. Nevertheless, U.S. critics of engagement with North Korea (such as Ambassador John Bolton, commentator Charles Krauthammer, and various members of Congress) persistently ignore the lack of availability of means to coerce North Korea.

The external strategic environment was not the sole or even the main determining factor in North Korean policy toward the United States. The nuclear crisis came to a head at a time when North Korea was undergoing a leadership succession. Kim Jong-il had been groomed for leadership for decades and was in charge of day-to-day affairs of state by the time Kim Il-sung died in 1994, but he still had to mount a great effort to consolidate his leadership, which was achieved by the introduction of the "military first" policy that reversed the power relationship between the Korean Workers' Party and the Korean People's Army. During the early phase of negotiations between the United States and the DPRK the diplomats conducted the talks but often seemed to come up against limitations imposed by the military.

The domestic power struggles in Pyongyang had several effects on relations with the United States. On the one hand the changed international environment and the dire economic straits that North Korea faced (as the public distribution system broke down in 1995 and there was a period in which the government was unable to contain mounting internal lawlessness) propelled the leadership into seeking a deal with the United States. On the other hand, the hostility of the United States and the threat of war were critical to the legitimation of the regime and the justification for the "military first" policy. The breakthrough occurred as a result of the intervention by former president Jimmy Carter, who met with Kim Il-sung. Once Kim Il-sung had laid down the direction of the policy, the North Koreans felt obliged to follow it. This does not mean that the North Korean leaders were willing to fully implement Kim Il-sung's expressed wish for the full denuclearization of the Korean Peninsula. But the provision of light water reactors, heavy fuel oil, and the prospect of reducing North Korea's international isolation made it seem prudent to accept the freezing of the production and reprocessing of plutonium. Still, given that the nuclear card was the only card that North Korea had to compel the international community to take it seriously, it was hard to see how it could give up this card entirely without being certain that the survival of the regime was assured. And it was unclear what the international community could provide to North Korea that would credibly give such an assurance.

The Clinton administration was of two minds about its objectives. The maximalist goal was to compel North Korea to reveal the full history of its nuclear program as well as curtailing future progress toward a weapons capability. But the priority of the nonproliferation absolutists led by Ashton Carter was to stop the program, even if it meant sacrificing the verification of past activities. This approach prevailed, and indeed there would not have been an agreement without it. But the Clinton administration was also constrained by domestic politics, and the implementation of the agreement was hampered by the failure of Congress to provide funds to fulfill its obligations.

Nevertheless, at the time the Agreed Framework appeared to be successful in dealing with the most critical problem posed by North Korea's nuclear program. Moreover, the willingness of the North Koreans to accept limitations on their missile programs in return for economic aid was also promising. However, the fundamental issues in relations between the United States and North Korea remained unresolved. While the economic benefits of the agreement could alleviate North Korea's plight, they did not settle the fundamental crisis of the regime. Even diplomatic relations with the United States and verbal security assurances would not change the fundamental threat that the Pyongyang regime was facing. From the U.S. perspective, although some kind of prolonged coexistence could be accepted because there was no realistic prospect of bringing about regime change, any acceptance of the North Korean regime would at least be superficial. Ultimately the United States would seek regime change through engagement, reform, and the opening of North Korea to the world. This is exactly what the Kim regime had to prevent in order to maintain its hold on power. These structural contradictions meant that any settlement of the strategic conflict between the United States and the DPRK could only be temporary.

6

The United States and
the Two Koreas
Confronting the Nuclear Issue

At the end of the twentieth century, it seemed that fundamental progress had been made toward transforming the crisis on the Korean Peninsula into a stable form of peaceful coexistence. The threat of the North Korean nuclear program had been contained by the Agreed Framework, while the historic summit between the two Korean leaders promised a new era of inter-Korean relations. The prospect of a meeting between President Clinton and Kim Jong-il was mooted as Vice Marshal Jo Myong-nok, number-two in the hierarchy of the DPRK, traveled to the United States and Secretary of State Madeleine Albright traveled to Pyongyang to meet with Kim Jong-il. There were signals from the North Korean leadership that other security issues, such as the North Korean missile program, might be susceptible to similar solutions.

Despite the evident success of the diplomatic process that had evolved during the Clinton administration, there remained substantial opposition in principle to the notion of making deals with North Korea. Republicans in Congress, opposed to "giving in to North Korean blackmail," demanded a more robust policy toward the Kim regime and attempted to sabotage the Agreed Framework by denying funds, thereby delaying its implementation. Although North Korean leaders were hopeful about improving relations with the United States, the delays in the provision of heavy fuel oil and the construction of the light water reactors raised doubts in their minds about the virtues of the Agreed Framework.

Toward the end of 2000 the Bush transition team signaled quite strongly that it had a very different view of North Korea. Nevertheless, President Clinton and National Security Advisor Samuel Berger concluded after a meeting with Bush that the new administration would continue to negotiate with Pyongyang. It seemed that the outgoing administration should not saddle its successor with any new commitments. The decision to cancel Clinton's trip to North Korea was confirmed on December 28, 2000, when it was clear that the frantic endeavor to reach a settlement between Israel and the Palestinians meant that there was no more time either to conclude an agreement on the North Korean missile program or prepare a summit adequately.[1]

When George W. Bush assumed the presidency of the United States in 2001, he initiated a fundamental review of U.S. national security policy. The Bush national security team took pride in its radical tactics, finally abandoning the Cold War approach to international security. But its worldview remained rooted in old-fashioned realism, according to which states are the main actors in the international system. The Bush administration was not ready to deal with, or even recognize the importance of, the "new wars" that were emerging as the main threat to international security and stability. Bush wanted to reduce U.S. responsibilities abroad and focus on the U.S. national interest rather than support efforts to build global collective security. He signaled that he was not going to get involved in further attempts to resolve the Israel-Palestine or the Northern Ireland conflict, or in any sort of nation building in crisis regions. The initial focus of the security policy of the Bush administration was on National Missile Defense, even though it was uncertain whether a strategically significant system would ever materialize.

The new strategic outlook and the general tendency to eschew international regimes and depend on unilateral or bilateral arrangements, relying on the overwhelming military power of the United States and neglecting soft power, were evident first of all in arms control and nuclear policy, but then extended to other areas of international security. While Bush himself was inclined to reduce U.S. global responsibilities, a different impulse came from the so-called neoconservatives and their supporters in the government, such as Paul Wolfowitz, Richard Perle, and Donald Rumsfeld. They advocated a form of hegemonist realism and the use of U.S. military power to constrain "rogue states" and bring about either regime change or at minimum a fundamental change in the behavior of these regimes, which were seen as posing a threat to international security and U.S. interests. Neoconservatives believed that rogue states that sponsored terrorists and sought to acquire WMD could either be coerced to move toward conformity with international norms or be replaced by democratic governments.[2]

The Bush administration took some time to review its policy on North Korea, which resulted in a policy vacuum in the final days of the ROK's Kim Dae-jung government. Secretary of State Colin Powell made statements in support of further diplomatic efforts, but the State Department was alone in its desire to continue engaging North Korea, and the locus of decision-making shifted away very swiftly. Two working groups were set up to deal with the issues surrounding policy toward North Korea: the Korea working group chaired by Thomas Hubbard from State, and a nonproliferation group chaired by Robert Joseph. Deputy National Security Advisor Stephen Hadley had to approve all documents.

In a difficult meeting with President Kim Dae-jung, President Bush openly voiced his doubts about attempting to engage North Korea, and little effort was made to disguise the fundamental disagreement between the two leaders. Bush made it clear how skeptical he was of Kim's Sunshine Policy and that he was not going to resume negotiations with North Korea over its missile program anytime soon. Bush's remarks caused deep offense, partly because they seemed to ignore Kim's stature as the leader of the democratic resistance during the struggle against South Korea's authoritarian government, as well as his achievements in dealing with North Korea that had been rewarded with a Nobel Peace Prize. This was especially jarring because in an earlier meeting with Secretary of State Powell, Kim had gotten the impression that the United States and the Republic of Korea were in basic agreement.

The disastrous U.S.–South Korean summit was a significant turning point in the development of the Bush administration's North Korea policy. The president himself had made his views clear. While the North Koreans were expecting to continue the dialogue begun under Clinton, the new administration began to move toward a policy of isolation. John Bolton was appointed undersecretary of state for arms control. The smart and knowledgeable hard-liner entered office determined to kill the Agreed Framework.[3]

On June 6, 2001, the results of the Bush administration's review on policy toward North Korea were announced. The statement indicated support for the Agreed Framework as long as North Korea fulfilled its conditions, despite the fact that conservative Republicans disapproved of the agreement. The Bush administration even secured increased funding for the heavy fuel oil deliveries to North Korea. It also promised to continue to provide humanitarian food assistance. At the same time it rejected a continuation of the previous talks on missiles and instead stated that future talks should follow a broad agenda, including "improved implementation of the Agreed Framework relating to North Korea's nuclear activities; verifiable constraints on North Korea's missile programs and a ban on its missile exports; and a less threatening conventional military posture."[4] In return the United States would ease sanctions and take other steps to help the North Korean people.

The review did not go as far as repudiating the Agreed Framework, despite the fact that various members of the administration strongly believed that this is what the U.S. government should do. Nevertheless, it embodied a radically changed attitude to North Korea. This manifested itself in the refusal to reaffirm the commitment to the "no hostile intent" principle that had been included in a communiqué when Jo Myong-nok was in Washington in 2000. Not only was Washington not open to trading the missile program for financial support, but instead of offering inducement the Bush administration expected North Korea to deliver on U.S. demands before any concessions would be made.

The outcome was not conducive to any further progress in relations with the DPRK. The military was the one strong card that the regime, with its collapsed economy, had to play. A demand to both eliminate its nuclear program and reduce its conventional forces deployed at the DMZ must have seemed absurd from the perspective of Pyongyang, unless economic and security guarantees were provided that would ensure the stability of the country and the regime. Those would have to be in place before North Korea could contemplate giving up its leverage. But there was nothing on offer (such as reductions in U.S. and ROK forces or ironclad security guarantees) that came even close to this.

POLICY CHANGE POST-9/11

The events of September 11, 2001, had a profound impact on U.S. national security policy in general and relations with North Korea in particular. The demonstration of the willingness of international terrorists to cause mass casualties raised the fear of the confluence on rogue states that pursue WMD and sponsor international terrorism. The review of U.S. nuclear strategy presented by Defense Secretary Rumsfeld stated that the United States was prepared to use force, including conventional and nuclear strategic weapons, against states or terrorists with WMD.[5]

The president's 2002 State of the Union address referred to rogue states as "the axis of evil." Bush stated that the United States had the right to take preemptive action against threats, rather than wait until it or its allies were attacked with WMD. North Korea and Iran were absent in the initial draft of the speech and were included at the insistence of National Security Advisor Condoleezza Rice in order to avoid an exclusive focus on Iraq.[6]

North Korea reacted strongly to its inclusion in the axis of evil, which it interpreted as a manifestation of Washington's desire to put pressure on North Korea in order to "stifle" the regime. The reference was seen as a rebuff to North Korea's attempts to reach out to the United States in the aftermath of 9/11 when Pyongyang condemned the attacks and pledged to ratify the International Convention for the Suppression of the Financing of Terrorism and the International Convention Against the Taking of Hostages. Ignoring such an overture from North Korea, public statements by President Bush continued to reflect his hostility to Kim Jong-il and his regime.

The "axis of evil" remarks had an explosive impact in South Korea. President Kim Dae-jung had lobbied for some gesture toward North Korea in order to resume dialogue. Soon after the speech President Bush visited South Korea, where he was told that the South Koreans gravely objected to the use of the term "axis of evil" insofar as it included North Korea. But Bush also made it clear to President Kim that unless North Korea abandoned WMD and changed its behavior, the United States would continue to oppose the regime. However, he refrained from repeating the phrase "axis of evil" in his public statements in Korea. On a more positive note, Bush stated publicly that the United States had "no intention of invading North Korea."[7]

The U.S. administration remained split between those who wanted to resume dialogue with North Korea and those who rejected any form of engagement with Pyongyang, resulting in mixed signals to a North Korean leadership that was already deeply skeptical about the intentions of the U.S. government. On the one hand the State Department reassured the North Koreans that the United States wanted to resume a dialogue. On the other hand the hard-liners, led by John Bolton, managed to persuade the administration to deny certification in 2002 that the DPRK was in compliance with the Agreed Framework. This occurred despite strenuous objection from the State Department and a rather skeptical Senate Foreign Relations Committee. Deputy Secretary of State Richard Armitage admitted to Senator Biden that the U.S. government did not have evidence that North Korea was cheating, but nevertheless did not have confidence that the DPRK would abide by the agreement.

The final irony was that in order to prevent a collapse of the Agreed Framework, President Bush used his power to waive certification in order to be able to use $95 million to fund continued heavy fuel oil shipments to North Korea.

During a visit to Pyongyang in April 2002 South Korea's national security advisor Lim Dong-won tried to persuade Kim Jong-il to receive a special envoy from the United States, and North Korea decided to resume the bilateral dialogue with the United States. In the meantime, there was a second review of North Korea policy in Washington after President Bush's Asia trip, this time directed by the president himself. If previously Bush was in the camp of those who favored no dialogue with Pyongyang, he now had shifted toward the idea of taking the initiative and making a comprehensive agreement with North Korea (rather than pursuing protracted step-by-step negotiations). This concept, which was an idea without many specifics, was called the Bold Approach. Secretary of State Colin Powell outlined some of its features in a speech at the Asia Society on June 10, 2002:

> Working with South Korea and Japan, the United States is prepared to take important steps to help North Korea move its relations with the US toward normalcy. We expect soon to have meetings with the North Koreans to explore these steps. However, progress between us will depend on Pyongyang's behavior on a number of key issues. First, the North must get out of the proliferation business and eliminate long-range missiles that threaten other countries. It must take itself off the preferred-supplier list of rogue states. Secondly, it must make a much more serious effort to provide for its suffering citizens. America continues to be the world's biggest donor of humanitarian assistance to North Korea. Just last week President Bush authorized a further donation of 102 thousand metric tons of food aid for North Korea. We will continue generously to support the World Food Program's operations there, but we want to see greatly improved monitoring and access so we can be sure the food actually gets into hungry mouths. Third, the North needs to move toward a less threatening conventional military posture. We are watching closely to see if Pyongyang will live up to its past pledges to implement basic confidence-building measures with the South. And finally, North Korea must come into full compliance with the International Atomic Energy Agency safeguards that it agreed to when it signed the Nuclear Non-

proliferation Treaty. The United States remains committed to the Agreed Framework which freezes and ultimately dismantles North Korea's dangerous old nuclear reactors in exchange for safer light water reactors.[8]

In essence, the Bold Approach was a recasting of the previously announced policy. The crucial difference was a commitment to normalization of relations and talks with North Korea. In order to move forward with the Bold Approach, assistant secretary of state for East Asian and Pacific affairs, James Kelly, was supposed to visit Pyongyang on July 10, but due to clashes between North and South Korean naval forces the visit was postponed until October.

Another factor in the delay of Kelly's trip to North Korea was a secret U.S. intelligence assessment according to which North Korea had started a clandestine program to produce highly enriched uranium (HEU). Indications that North Korea was developing a clandestine uranium enrichment program had begun to emerge back in 1998 and 1999, during the final years of the Clinton administration. In 2001 U.S. intelligence issued their assessment: that North Korea had started a clandestine program to produce HEU using centrifuge technology it had acquired from Pakistan in return for Rodong missiles.[9] The centrifuge method is based on the concept of separating the various isotopes of uranium according to their different weights using large numbers of high-performance centrifuges. For a full-scale uranium enrichment plant that could produce significant amounts of weapons-grade uranium North Korea would need to manufacture thousands of centrifuges and also be able to produce substantial quantities of UF_6. According to the CIA, North Korea began to seek centrifuge-related materials in large quantities in 2001.

The information on which this assessment was based had come from a variety of sources. In 1999 Seoul informed Washington that North Korean scientists had visited Pakistan, and in March 1999 the Republic of Korea and the United States jointly prevented the purchase by North Korea of components for gas centrifuges in Japan. In 2001 a North Korean defector said that North Korea had been pursuing centrifuge technology for uranium enrichment for some time. Moreover, there was evidence that North Korea was seeking components such as certain types of aluminum and equipment for uranium feed-and-withdrawal systems, for which no other purpose appeared plausible.

The Pakistan connection came to public attention in 2004 when A. Q. Khan, the head of Khan Research Laboratories and widely celebrated in Pakistan as the "father of the Pakistani atom bomb," was arrested for the large-scale illicit proliferation of nuclear technology to a range of countries, including Libya and Iran. There were official dealings between the Pakistani and North Korean authorities whereby Pakistan acquired Rodong missiles as nuclear delivery vehicles. Hwang Jang-yeop, the former chairman of the Supreme People's Assembly of the DPRK who defected to South Korea in 1997, has stated that an agreement was made in 1996 between North Korea and Pakistan to trade HEU technology in return for missile technology.[10]

However, it remains unclear whether the Pakistani government entered into an official agreement with North Korea to supply nuclear technology. Pakistani authorities insist that A.Q. Khan was not authorized to make a nuclear deal with North Korea and that any such activities were not sanctioned. Nevertheless, according to Pakistan's former president Pervez Musharraf, "A.Q. Khan transferred nearly two dozen P-1 and P-2- centrifuges to North Korea. He also provided North Korea with a flow meter, some special oils for centrifuges, and coaching on centrifuge technology, including visits to top-secret centrifuge plants."[11] This was the first time that a transfer of P-2 centrifuges was mentioned; previous accounts only mentioned P-1 centrifuges. In Khan's 121-page confession he admitted to supplying "old and discarded centrifuge and enrichment machines" to North Korea along with "sets of drawings, sketches, technical data and depleted hexafluoride (UF_6) gas."[12] On the basis of available evidence U.S. intelligence concluded that since 1997 A. Q. Khan had provided the DPRK with technical details of the process of enriching uranium together with some equipment and design information on the nuclear warheads tested in 1998 that were based on an earlier Chinese design using HEU.

Whether this involved an exchange of nuclear technology for missile technology remains unproven. Various Pakistani leaders, beginning with Benazir Bhutto, who visited Pyongyang herself, insisted that Pakistan acquired North Korean ballistic missile technology for cash to the amount of $210 million, despite its low financial reserves in the 1990s when the annual defense budget amounted to $3 billion. It is possible that Khan's unauthorized dealings further encouraged the North Koreans to supply missiles, or that Khan sold nuclear technology for his own profit. Both in Pakistan and among experts there remains doubt that Khan could have acted without the knowledge of the Pakistani government, but the available evidence does not show that the Pakistani government at any time authorized Khan to supply the DPRK with nuclear technology and cause North Korea to break its obligations under the NPT.[13]

The provisional assessment of the CIA when the investigations of a possible North Korean uranium-based nuclear program reached a conclusion in 2002 was that North Korea was constructing a uranium enrichment plant that would be able to produce HEU for two weapons annually once fully operational, possibly by 2005. The briefing given by CIA Deputy Director John McLaughlin to the principals (including President Bush, Vice President Cheney, Secretary of State Powell, National Security Advisor Rice, and Richard Myers, the chairman of the Joint Chiefs of Staff) stated that the intelligence community had high confidence that North Korea had acquired materials for a uranium enrichment program, but could not say where these materials were located or the extent for any progress in building an enrichment plant or developing a uranium bomb.[14] The Defense Intelligence Agency, generally hawkish about North Korea (although its assessments have sometimes been proven to be incorrect), reported that in all likelihood North Korea had already produced some HEU warheads.[15] The IRT 2000 research reactor used uranium enriched to 80 percent supplied by the Soviet Union, and North Korea could have diverted some of this material for weapons use (even though normally weapons-grade material is supposed to be enriched to over 90 percent).

The Republic of Korea and China were doubtful about the existence of an actual HEU program. The refusal of the United States to give the Republic of Korea access to its HEU program intelligence was a deep source of frustration for the South Koreans.[16] An analysis by experts from the International Institute of Strategic Studies in the United Kingdom in 2004, using the information that had come into the public domain, showed that, although no definite conclusions could be drawn, it was unlikely that North Korea had an operational enrichment plant at present and might not have one for more than ten years. This tentative assessment was based on indication that North Korea was still seeking components for an enrichment plant, the difficulties of building other elements of the infrastructure required (i.e. a UF_6 feeder plant) given what is known about North Korea's nuclear facilities, and the technical difficulties of successfully operating a uranium enrichment plant based on centrifuge technology. Internal South Korean assessments seemed to broadly concur with the judgment that North Korea was not yet very close to possessing the capacity for producing HEU. Thus Kim Tae-woo from the Korea Institute for Defense

Analyses suggests that the Khan Research Laboratory may have provided North Korea with a number of P-1 and P-2 type centrifuges, 50 kg (110 lb) of UF_6 for calibration, and technical information for the construction of enrichment stages and cascades. Kim concluded (as of the autumn of 2004) that North Korea most likely did not yet have any full-scale enrichment facilities or weapons-grade HEU, but that it might have laboratory-scale centrifuge facilities.[17]

The alleged uranium enrichment program was interpreted as a substantial breach of trust and seen as evidence for the strong belief of the opponents of any accommodation with North Korea that the DPRK simply could not be trusted. In an internal State Department meeting John Bolton used the uranium program to pronounce the Agreed Framework dead. Although technically not a breach of the agreement, which was concerned only with plutonium, it was nevertheless incompatible with commitments under the Agreed Framework as it reaffirmed the North-South Declaration on Denuclearization, which banned uranium enrichment. It also violated North Korea's obligations under the NPT.[18]

However, the status of the uranium enrichment program was unproven and the location of any enrichment facility unknown. Confidence in the CIA's intelligence assessment was declared to be high, but in a briefing to the principals (including President Bush) there was no "smoking gun"; it was a very complex, if compelling for those present, circumstantial case.

The attitude of John Bolton and others in the administration was that there was no point in raising the matter of the HEU program with Pyongyang and that the United States should not engage in dialogue, but rather put in place some punitive measures. For Bolton the Agreed Framework was dead and he wanted it to stay that way. The hard line was endorsed by the vice president's office. However, the situation was complicated by the summit meeting between Japanese prime minister Junichiro Koizumi and Kim Jong-il on September 17, 2002, which resulted in a substantial and unexpected breakthrough: Kim Jong-il acknowledging for the first time that some Japanese citizens had been abducted by North Korea in the past and agreed that those who were still alive could visit Japan. Koizumi was preparing a substantial aid package for North Korea (up to $10 billion) and was hopeful about normalization of relations. At the behest of the Japanese, National Security Advisor Rice and President Bush were persuaded that dialogue with North Korea should resume and Kelly's trip to Pyongyang should go ahead after all. But at the insistence of the hawks, it was decided that this meeting in Pyongyang, which took place on October 4–5, 2002, would have the principal purpose of confronting North Korea about the clandestine uranium enrichment program.[19]

The meeting got off to a bad start due to an argument about dinner arrangements, as Kelly had been instructed not to provide a "reciprocal dinner" after the welcoming dinner for the delegation. When Kelly met with Vice Foreign Minister Kim Gye-gwan and other North Korean officials, he outlined the broad proposals, but then brought up the question of the clandestine uranium enrichment program, stating that no progress could be made until the uranium program was dismantled. The North Koreans, who had prepared to present their positions with some flexibility on what they thought were the salient issues were stunned by the accusations in Kelly's presentation. Kim Gye-gwan denied the existence of an HEU program and seemed to be genuinely unaware of it.

The next afternoon First Vice Foreign Minister Kang Sok-ju started the meeting with a thirty-minute monologue in which he stated that the United States had destroyed the Agreed Framework by including North Korea in the "axis of evil," its policy of preemptive attack, and the inclusion of North Korea in a list of possible targets for nuclear attack. This was a reference to Article 3 of the Agreed Framework, according to which the United States was not to use nuclear weapons against the DPRK or threaten it with nuclear weapons. Consequently North Korea needed to reinforce its "military first" policy and modernize its armed forces to the maximum extent possible. Subsequently, as Kelly raised the issue of the HEU program again, Kang stated that he understood the United States had evidence relating to North Korean uranium enrichment activities and went on to say that for Pyongyang to be able to engage in dialogue with the United States, North Korea needed leverage either from uranium enrichment or nuclear weapons. In addition to uranium enrichment, North Korea could produce all kinds of other things, Kang claimed, and it was entitled to possess nuclear weapons. Kang also referred to a weapon more powerful than a nuclear weapon. The last statement puzzled the delegation, and later analysts suggested that this was a reference to North Korea's ideology of *juche*.

All members of the U.S. delegation had the impression that Kang had, at least implicitly, acknowledged the existence of a uranium enrichment program. Not having any authority to enter negotiations, the meeting was concluded and the U.S. delegation announced its departure. After the meeting the delegation's Korean speakers compiled a transcript of Kang's remarks from memory based on Kang's actual remarks and not the translation. The delegation used secure communication facilities in the British embassy in Pyongyang to convey the news to the Secretary of State.[20]

Preoccupied with the debates over Iraq, the Bush administration waited for nine days before making a public announcement. In light of what it presumed to be the North Korean acknowledgement of the HEU program, which it claimed violated the Agreed Framework, the State Department spokesman Richard Boucher announced on October 16, 2002, that the U.S. government was no longer able to pursue the Bold Approach.[21]

The issue of whether Kang did in fact acknowledge the HEU program or not was never satisfactorily resolved. The transcripts of the meeting remain classified. Much of Kang's speech was reported by Jack Pritchard, who was present, but it remains open to interpretation.[22] Former South Korean minister of unification Lee Jong-seok told me he read the notes of the meeting produced by one of the U.S. interpreters and he did not interpret Kang's statements as an admission of uranium enrichment.[23] One possible explanation is that Kang was deliberately ambiguous about uranium enrichment in an effort to pressure the United States into resuming negotiations by emphasizing the alternatives to diplomacy. If this was the case, then the North Koreans misread the Bush administration, which was not susceptible to such pressure. Quite the reverse, the Kelly visit finally tipped the balance in favor of those rejecting dialogue with North Korea. During unofficial meetings after the Kelly meeting, North Korean officials refused to confirm Kang's alleged "admission," but they also refused to deny the existence of an HEU program. They backtracked from Kang's statement that the Agreed Framework was dead and sought dialogue in order resolve the issues between the DPRK and the United States.

In November the DPRK ambassador to the United Nations stated that North Korea would be prepared to satisfy all security concerns the United States might have, including those relating to the uranium enrichment program, and the possibility of inspections of all North Korean nuclear facilities would be considered.[24] A month later, North Korea seemed to change policy again and denied it had acknowledged the existence of a uranium enrichment program, claiming that Kang had merely asserted North Korea's right to have such a program. The author was witness to a debate at a conference at Wilton Park in the U.K. on Northeast Asian Security in October 2004, when the North Korean delegation first stated that the

DPRK did not have a uranium enrichment program as such. When pressed, the North Korean ambassador to the U.K., Ri Yong-ho, categorically denied that North Korea had a uranium enrichment program.[25]

In the aftermath of the 2002 Kelly meeting in Pyongyang, the momentum toward further sanctions against North Korea was unstoppable. The obvious measure was to halt heavy fuel oil shipments that were being made under the terms of the Agreed Framework. U.S. allies in the region were deeply opposed to this step, but in the end bowed to American pressure. The final decision was that heavy fuel oil shipments would be suspended once the shipment that was already en route was delivered. Technically this was a matter to be resolved by KEDO and not the United States, but Washington essentially bullied the Japanese and Koreans to vote in favor. The calculation in Washington was that North Korea was so dependent on outside support that the suspension of shipments and further pressure from the international community would eventually bring North Korea in line. But the conclusion drawn in Pyongyang was that the Agreed Framework was no longer tenable. An announcement indicating the DPRK's withdrawal from the Agreed Framework was published in the official newspaper *Rodong Shinmun*: "The present grave situation is pushing the DPRK to the phase where it cannot respect the Agreed Framework any longer. The U.S. should be held fully responsible for the serious consequences to be entailed by its decision to stop the supply of heavy oil to the DPRK."[26]

On December 12, 2002, the DPRK announced that it was restarting the 5 MWe reactor and resuming construction of the 50 MWe and 200 MWe reactors (two projects that had been started but not completed prior to the Agreed Framework). Toward the end of December 2002, IAEA monitoring equipment at the Yongbyon Nuclear Science Research Center was removed, and seals were removed from the 5 MWe reactor and the pond containing eight thousand nuclear fuel rods. The IAEA inspectors left the country on December 31, 2002.

The Bush administration, preoccupied with the developing confrontation with Iraq, had a muted reaction to these developments. In late December North Korean officials from the UN delegation visited the governor of New Mexico, Democrat Bill Richardson. During wide-ranging talks the North Koreans confirmed their desire to negotiate with the U.S. government and explained the resumption of the plutonium program as a tactical step. Even uranium enrichment was on the table as a subject for negotiation. But the internecine warfare that was still raging in the administration precluded a coherent response to the North Korean initiative.

The hard-liners in the administration, such as John Bolton, continued to believe that Pyongyang was too weak to retaliate against the suspension of heavy oil shipments and that North Korea would cave in to pressure from the international community and the threat of sanctions. In other words, they assumed that North Korea could be coerced into dismantling their nuclear programs. The fact that the United States was confronting Iraq over its WMD with military force was thought to constitute a powerful example for North Korea, indicating what fate might await them if they did not modify their stance with regard to the nuclear program.[27] This was a major tactical misjudgment. First of all, it flew in the face of past experience with North Korean negotiating behavior that was characterized by extreme brinkmanship in apparent defiance of practical realities and what outsiders might have calculated to be in the best interest of North Korea's leaders. Scott Snyder, in his path-breaking analysis of North Korean negotiating behavior, showed that when North Korean leaders judge the external environment to be unfavorable, they adopt a position of *kojip* (stubbornness or unyielding attitude) until the external environment becomes more favorable.[28] Second, like many commentators who asked why the United States was going after Iraq (with no real evidence that it possessed nuclear weapons) and not after North Korea, the North Korean leaders were confirmed in the view that they needed a nuclear capability to resist U.S. pressure: "The Iraq war teaches a lesson that in order to prevent a war and defend the security of a country and the sovereignty of a nation, it is necessary to have a powerful physical deterrent."[29] North Korea may have also calculated that the United States would be preoccupied with the Iraq crisis and could not afford to mount a similar confrontation in the Far East at the same time.

These events occurred as Kim Dae-jung's term as president of the Republic of Korea came to an end. During the election campaign, the Millennium Democratic Party and its candidate Roh Moo-hyun were committed to continue the Sunshine Policy and increased engagement with North Korea, whereas the GNP and its candidate Lee Hoi-chang opposed the Sunshine Policy. However, bowing to public sentiment, Lee declared that he was prepared to meet Kim Jong-il without preconditions.

President Kim and candidate Roh clearly distanced themselves from the U.S. position on North Korea during the election campaign. The rhetoric took on an increasingly anti-American flavor as Roh called for the revision of the SOFA in order to put the bilateral relationship on an equal basis and warned ominously that in the event of war the United States and the Republic of Korea might not be on the same side. An incident near the DMZ involving two Korean schoolgirls killed in a traffic accident by an American armored vehicle sparked off a wave of anti-American sentiment. The Bush administration's overt support for candidate Lee did nothing to enhance his electoral chances. On December 19 Roh Moo-hyun was elected by a narrow margin.

The reaction by the United States to North Korea's actions to restart the 5 MWe reactor appeared to be surprisingly muted. Secretary of State Powell played the whole thing down by saying: "What are they going to do with another two or three nuclear weapons when they're starving, when they have no energy, when they have no economy that's functioning?"[30] He also affirmed that the United States had no intention to attack North Korea. Even more surprisingly, conservative pundits such as Charles Krauthammer and William Safire who derided negotiations with North Korea in 1994 and called for military action now advocated doing nothing. Ivo Daalder and James Lindsay from the Brookings Institution noted acerbically: "The Bush administration and its hawkish supporters have found their match in Kim Jong Il's North Korea."[31]

Although the rhetoric coming from Washington was low-key, the United States sent some military signals, which reflected the more bellicose sentiments in the administration. Two dozen long-range bombers (B-52 and B-1) were sent to Guam a month later to be within striking distance of North Korea. Four F-15E fighters and six F-117 stealth fighters were sent to South Korea to take part in military exercises, but remained there after the exercises were completed. The exercise called Foal Eagle involved a large-scale amphibious assault, which North Korea interpreted as a rehearsal of an attack

Whatever message Washington was trying to send seemed to have been received in Pyongyang. Ri Pyong-gap, a foreign ministry official, stated that the United States had made it clear that North Korea would be next after Iraq.[32] On March 2, 2003, four North Korean fighter aircraft intercepted an American reconnaissance aircraft (an RC-135) and shadowed it for twenty-two minutes until it broke off and returned to its base in Japan.

There is no doubt that the North Koreans were alarmed. After February 12, 2003, Kim Jong-il was not seen in public for nearly two months. But the hawks in the U.S. administration who believed the serious saber rattling and the demonstration of military might against Iraq would intimidate the North Koreans and cause them to quietly dismantle their nuclear program were mistaken. If there was one lesson the North Koreans learned from all of this, it was that a nuclear capability was of critical importance for their security.

On January 10, 2003, the DPRK announced that it was formally withdrawing from the NPT. Although withdrawal from the NPT, which is permissible in cases on grounds of a threat to national security, requires a ninety-day notice, Pyongyang declared that it was simply announcing the end of the suspension of withdrawal, which had previously been announced in March 1993. As the threat to national security North Korea cited the nullification of the Geneva Agreed Framework as a result of KEDO's cessation of heavy fuel oil supplies, and the hostile policy of the United States, including the threat of preemptive nuclear attacks.[33]

THE ORIGINS OF THE SIX-PARTY TALKS

By early 2003 the positions on both sides had hardened. The North Koreans insisted adamantly on bilateral talks with the United States and seemed to think that their actions placed them in a stronger position. In Washington the demise of the Agreed Framework, which had been eagerly anticipated by John Bolton and others, produced a total rejection of bilateral talks, a position insisted on by President Bush. The simple fact of the matter was, both sides completely misjudged each other. The North Koreans believed that by reviving the threat of a nuclear program they could put pressure on Washington to come to the table. On the American side the hawks believed that by not talking to North Korea and increasing diplomatic and military pressure on Pyongyang they would force North Koreans to cave in to American demands.

Contrary to the belief held by Bolton and Cheney, the advantage was, at least for the time being, on the North Korean side. There was no realistic military option against North Korea and therefore the United States did not have sufficient leverage to really stop the North Koreans from proceeding with the production of more plutonium and the development of nuclear devices. Isolation and containment were not going to do the trick, both because of North Korean resistance to such external pressure and the unwillingness of China and South Korea to push the DPRK to the brink of collapse. The only real option was to negotiate.

In order to find a way forward, Secretary of State Powell proposed to his Chinese counterpart Tang Jiaxuan that China should host a multilateral forum for talks involving both Korean states. Powell suggested a set of multilateral talks involving the five permanent members of the UN Security Council plus the EU and four regional states (the ROK, the DPRK, Japan, and Australia). North Korea rejected the idea out of hand, insisting on direct bilateral talks with the United States. China then proposed a three-way meeting involving itself, the United States, and North Korea. This was also rejected.

In February 2003 North Korea announced that it was putting its nuclear facilities for the production of electricity on a normal footing, which presumably meant it was restarting the 5 MWe reactor at Yongbyon, confirming a previous announcement to that effect. Satellite observation detected very heavy activity at the spent fuel facility, indicating that North Korea might be moving fuel rods for reprocessing. On February 12, 2003, the Board of Governors of the IAEA found North Korea in violation of its NPT safeguards obligations and referred the matter to the UN Security Council.

North Korea continued to escalate the tension. On March 31 there was a meeting between Charles ("Jack") Pritchard and David Straub from the State Department with North Korean diplomats from the DRPK UN mission in New York. This meeting had been requested by the North Koreans and authorized by Colin Powell. The North Koreans told Pritchard and Straub that they were reprocessing the spent fuel rods and for the first time acknowledged they were seeking to make nuclear weapons. The proceedings of this meeting were not reported to the rest of the administration, which received the information later through different channels, a fact that caused a very negative impact on Powell's standing in the administration.[34]

The Chinese government was concerned that tension between the DPRK and the United States was rising. On the one hand, China wanted to avoid a collapse of the DPRK under U.S. military and economic pressure (after all, China would have to deal with many of the social and economic consequences and did not want a military conflagration in its backyard). China was under strong American pressure to use its influence with Pyongyang, which in private discussions it always claimed was minimal.

Extensive shuttle diplomacy by China's vice premier Qian Qichen resulted in Kim Jong-il's agreement for North Korea to take part in three-party talks that would be held on April 24–25, 2003, in Beijing. The Chinese reassured the North Koreans that they would have bilateral talks with the Americans while at the same time telling the Americans this would be a genuine three-way meeting. China temporarily halted oil supplies to the DPRK for "technical reasons," to put pressure on Pyongyang. At the same time Russia and China prevented action by the UN Security Council against North Korea in response to the IAEA report on April 9.

Powell discussed the proposed talks with South Korean foreign minister Yoon Young-kwan, who presented him with a three-stage plan to deal with the nuclear issue. Yoon was supportive of the three-way summit, but urged Washington to talk with the North Koreans on a bilateral basis.[35] President Roh received approval from the National Assembly to send a contingent of South Korean troops to Iraq as a symbolic gesture of support for the United States. This politically costly gesture was implicitly designed to increase influence on the American stance toward North Korea and the nuclear issue.

The trilateral meeting opened on April 23, 2003, in Beijing. Fu Ying, the of the Chinese delegation, affirmed China's position that nuclear weapons in North Korea would bring chaos to the peninsula. The leader of the DPRK delegation, Li Gun, presented a proposal called a "bold initiative." It was based on the concept of four stages of simultaneous steps to be taken by the United States and North Korea, resulting in the dismantlement of North Korea's nuclear weapons program. In the first stage, North Korea would declare its intention to dismantle nuclear weapons, and heavy fuel oil shipments would be resumed. In the second stage, inspections of North Korea's nuclear facilities would take place, and the United States and the DPRK would sign a nonaggression pact. In the third stage, other issues would be resolved—there would be an agreement on missiles, and political relations between the DPRK, the United States, and Japan would be normalized. In the final stage, once the LWRs were completed, North Korea would finally dismantle its nuclear program. This proposal was clearly intended to be the opening gambit for negotiations in the anticipation of bilateral talks with the U.S. delegation.

The head of the U.S. delegation, James Kelly, stated the position of the Bush administration, which was that political and economic agreements could only be reached after complete, irreversible, and verifiable dismantlement of the nuclear program. This reflected the philosophy that North Korea should not be rewarded for breaching its international obligations, but should come into line before any further progress could be made. In essence the conduct of the U.S. delegation and the content of its statements were a complete repudiation of North Korea's initiative. Li

Gun informally told Kelly that the DPRK already had one or two nuclear weapons and had completed reprocessing the eight thousand spent fuel rods from the 5 MWe reactor. Any attempt to demonstrate solidarity between China and the DPRK disintegrated as Li made these statements, which not only repudiated Fu Ying's admonitions, but also admitted facts which North Korea had previously denied in private meetings with the Chinese. More ominously, there was also a hint that North Korea could make more weapons or transfer them to other parties. The style of diplomacy at this meeting that was forced upon the delegations by their political masters made anything more than a formal statement of the position of each side virtually impossible. The North Korean delegation had instructions not to engage with the members of the American delegation in informal exchanges, whereas the U.S. delegation had instructions not to engage with the North Koreans in bilateral formal exchanges. The Chinese were desperate to coax the U.S. diplomats to have bilateral discussions with the North Koreans because they had induced Pyongyang to attend with a promise of such discussions. The Chinese mysteriously absented themselves suddenly during lunch and dinner, which facilitated some informal conversations, but the U.S. delegations followed its instructions and the trilateral meeting ended one day early without result.[36]

On May 12, 2003, the DPRK declared that the North-South Declaration on Denuclearization was nullified, completing the retreat from all of its international obligations in relation to its nuclear program. In July 2003 North Korea notified the United States privately that it completed the reprocessing of the eight thousand fuel rods.

South Korean president Roh Moo-hyun came to Washington on May 13, 2003, for his first summit meeting with President Bush, accompanied by Foreign Affairs and Trade Minister Yoon. During Roh's meeting with Bush his entire statement was focused on dissuading the U.S. president from attacking North Korea. Bush finally told him that he had no intention of launching an attack against North Korea.[37] Roh explained his Peace and Prosperity Policy (akin to the Sunshine Policy) of engaging North Korea and resolving issues through diplomacy. During his visit an argument broke out in Washington over whether the Bush administration was prepared to enter a dialogue with North Korea, which ended with Bush himself firmly declaring that one-to-one dialogue with North Korea was not his policy, and he told Roh that without an end to the nuclear program his administration could not take any further steps.[38]

In June 2003 the Bush administration launched a Proliferation Security Initiative as an international effort to interdict shipments of items related to WMD. This initiative had been conceived by John Bolton and the other nonproliferation hawks in the administration in order to deal with the threat of the proliferation of nuclear materials and technology. It was primarily directed at North Korea, but South Korea and China refused to join and it remained unclear how it could operate effectively, given questions about the legality of intercepting ships on the high sea. Even if there was international agreement it was not likely to entirely mitigate the dangers of proliferation from a state like North Korea.[39]

China was eager to resume the tripartite talks, but the Americans wanted to include other regional powers. Powell told the Chinese that Japan and South Korea needed to be invited to participate. When Powell informed Russian foreign minister Igor Ivanov of the proposal, he demanded that Russia should be included.[40]

In early July Russia and China once again prevented action by the UN Security Council against the DPRK, while China was engaged in the resumption of diplomacy. Pyongyang was offered extra food and oil deliveries as an inducement to accept participation in the new talks that would involve six parties, namely the United States, Russia, China, Japan, North Korea, and South Korea. Thus the Six-Party Talks were born.

The very concept of these talks was flawed. The fundamental split in Washington was about whether or not to have a dialogue with North Korea. For example, John Bolton opposed the talks because he did not believe that they would induce North Korea to give up nuclear weapons. According to him, what was needed was increased political, economic, and if need be military pressure. Indeed the decision to enter the Six-Party Talks contradicted the policy that had recently been articulated by President Bush that he was not prepared to enter into dialogue with North Korea unless the nuclear program was dealt with first. The Six-Party Talks clearly undercut this stance. Whatever intentions the U.S. government might have had to maintain the talks on a multilateral basis, this was an untenable position given that the whole structure of the dispute with North Korea was really bilateral, because only the United States could deliver what North Korea was seeking, and so it was inevitable that the bilateral discussions would ultimately form the core of the talks. The other fundamental issue was the role of the other parties. The Bush administration wanted to enlist the support of the other regional states to put pressure on

North Korea. There was no reason to believe, however, that this would be more effective than direct talks. Quite the reverse, the viewpoints of the various parties and their interests were not congruent with that of the United States. China, Russia, and South Korea saw the Six-Party Talks as a means of establishing a bilateral dialogue between the United States and the DPRK. North Korea came to the talks in order to talk directly with the United States, while the United States attended in order not to have bilateral negotiations with North Korea.

The first of the Six-Party Talks was held in Beijing on August 27–29, 2003. As expected, North Korea proposed once again a series of simultaneous steps beginning with the exchange of a U.S. security assurance and a North Korean pledge to give up its nuclear weapons, eventually leading to disarmament. The DPRK delegation hinted that it might accept a freeze on its nuclear activities as a first step. However, the United States continued to stick to the principle of "dismantlement first." Although the U.S. delegation did not present a detailed counterproposal to the DPRK, it suggested that North Korean disarmament could take place in several phases, leaving the door open to some "rewards" before complete, irreversible, and verifiable disarmament had taken place. Nevertheless, security assurances and the resumption of heavy fuel oil deliveries could only be discussed after some disarmament had occurred. Moreover, the United States made it clear that full diplomatic normalization would require more than the dismantling of nuclear programs; other issues such as ballistic missiles, biological and chemical weapons, and conventional forces would need to be addressed.[41] At the margins of the talks Kelly had an informal conversation with North Korea's deputy foreign minister Kim Yong-il. Kim asked various direct questions about U.S. policy, but Kelly simply directed him to his statement. The conversation ended with Kim stating that the United States had not changed its hostile policy toward North Korea and that therefore they had no choice but to declare their possession of nuclear weapons and demonstrate their deterrent.[42]

The South Koreans proposed a three-stage process, which was to be a compromise between the North Korean and the U.S. approach. The first stage would consist of simultaneous declaration of security assurances and commitment to nuclear disarmament, followed by sequential actions that would involve the implementation of disarmament in different stages, reciprocated by inducement on the part of the United States and other parties to the talks. After a resolution of all of the issues—nuclear weapons, missiles, other WMD, and conventional forces—full normalization of relations among North Korea, the United States, and Japan could take place. However, due to the attitude of some of the other parties, this proposal did not gain any traction.

The paradoxical feature of the Six-Party Talks was that there was a great deal of common ground regarding the shape of any final agreement. The disagreement was primarily about the modality of the disarmament process. North Korea was not willing to relinquish its tangible assets without some down payment, while the United States had adopted the principle that it could not afford to be seen as blackmailed into negotiations and did not want to reward illicit behavior, thereby completely restricting its freedom to maneuver in the discussions. In addition, however, the issue of the HEU program remained an insurmountable obstacle as North Korea again denied the U.S. allegations about its existence. In private conversations North Koreans told the Americans that Kelly had misunderstood what Kang said in October 2002. Such a denial, however, meant that the program was not on the table for inclusion in any disarmament deal, and without it there could be no such deal. True to form, the North Koreans again issued threats; this time they said they would declare their nuclear status and conduct a weapons test if there was no solution. This behavior, which was quite consistent with the DPRK's previous negotiating tactics, did nothing to improve North Korea's bargaining position and only hardened the American stance.

There was no joint final communiqué, but the Chinese Ministry of Foreign Affairs issued a statement as chair of the talks that summarized some general principles that all parties seemed to agree to, including the need to resolve the North Korean nuclear issue through dialogue, the denuclearization of the Korean peninsula, and the need to continue the Six-Party Talks.

Despite the lack of progress the United States was content with outcome of the talks insofar as a clear message was sent to North Korea. The North Koreans reacted negatively. Prior to leaving, the delegation issued a statement at Beijing airport to the effect that North Korea had no interest in future talks.[43] The Ministry of Foreign Affairs in Pyongyang issued a statement on the talks that said: "The six-party talk was nothing but empty discussions. We came to realize that there are no other alternatives but self-defense capability and nuclear deterrence capability unless the U.S. changes its hostile policy."[44] Nevertheless, North Korea's chief delegate, Vice Foreign Minister Kim Yong-il, stated: "The denuclearization of the Korean peninsula is our ultimate goal, and possessing nuclear weapons is not our goal."[45]

As China and the Republic of Korea made efforts to achieve the resumption of the talks, North Korea indicated a lack of interest. On October 2, 2003, Pyongyang made a public announcement to the effect that it had completed the reprocessing of spent fuel rods from Yongbyon and that the plutonium would be used to enhance its nuclear deterrent force. However, these claims could not be independently confirmed.

Some progress was made at the Asia-Pacific Economic Cooperation (APEC) summit in Bangkok on October 20, 2003. In separate conversations with Hu Jintao and Roh Moo-hyun, President Bush expressed his willingness to join in a multilateral written security guarantee to North Korea if the DPRK agreed to dismantle its nuclear weapons program. This indicated some movement in the U.S. position.

On November 4, 2003, KEDO formally suspended the LWR project for one year, which was not unexpected, given that the entire Agreed Framework was in effect in suspension. China's efforts to convene another round of the Six-Party Talks in December ran into difficulties as various public statements reemphasized the differences between North Korea and the United States. China's initial draft was rejected and the United States proposed its own text, supported by Japan and the Republic of Korea. On December 6 the North Korean foreign ministry issued the following statement:

> A package solution based on the principle of simultaneous action is the core issue to be agreed upon between the DPRK and the U.S., being the key to solving the nuclear issue. This is our consistent claim. The DPRK advanced a productive proposal to put into practice measures of the first phase if the U.S. found it hard to accept the package solution all at once. These measures are for the U.S. to delist the DPRK as a sponsor of terrorism, lift political, economic and military sanctions and blockade on it and for the U.S. and neighboring countries of the DPRK to supply heavy oil, power and other energy resources to the DPRK in return for its freeze of nuclear activities.[46]

But President Bush had rejected the concept of simultaneous action. North Korea was to give up its assets before the United States would agree to anything.

In view of the lack of progress, there was some shift of policy in Washington. This may have been the consequence of more intense lobbying on the part of Seoul, coupled with the politically risky commitment to send some South Korean troops to Iraq. It may also have been helped by the forthcoming presidential election in the United States, which meant that some of the potentially controversial foreign policy areas were given to Powell in order to diffuse any attacks by Senator John Kerry. Whatever the reason for the shift, at the next round of the Six-Party Talks Undersecretary of State Kelly for the first time presented a detailed U.S. proposal for the resolution of the nuclear crisis. It involved some concession to the concept of simultaneous action, in that the United States was willing to resume fuel shipments and was open to making a provisional guarantee not to attack North Korea. It also offered talks on lifting U.S. sanctions. In return, the DPRK would have to freeze its nuclear activities within three months, to be followed by complete dismantlement. This was the concept of complete, verifiable, and irreversible disarmament (CVID). Kelly's proposal involved significant elements of a proposal that had been developed by the Ministry for Foreign Affairs and Trade in Seoul previously, thereby narrowing the differences between Seoul and Washington about how to handle talks with the DPRK.[47]

During the two-hour bilateral meeting between the United States and the DPRK, the North Korea delegation discussed the proposal, but insisted on "freeze for compensation" and, characteristically, threatened to test a nuclear weapon if the United States would not accept their proposal.

After the talks the North Korean foreign ministry issued a statement to the effect that some common ground had been reached at the talks in Beijing but stressed that there were still "big differences," in particular with regard to the issue of whether North Korea had a secret uranium enrichment program. Moreover, the time frame was characterized as unrealistic. On June 30 the North Korean ambassador to Russia stated that the DPRK wanted 2 million kilowatts in energy compensation before freezing its nuclear program.

In July, John Bolton visited Seoul and affirmed in a lecture at Yonsei University that the United States was not interested in a temporary freeze of North Korea's nuclear activities. Instead he invited North Korea to follow the example of Libya, which had given up its support for international terrorism and its WMD programs in exchange for lifting of sanctions and a return to the international community. It was clear that the United States still required CVID as the final outcome of the process, even though this had been rejected by the DPRK.

Although the participants of the Six-Party Talks agreed to hold a fourth round in September 2004, North Korea soon began to send signals that it was backing away from holding another round so soon, even though U.S. Secretary of State Powell and DPRK Foreign Minister Paek Nam-sun met in Jakarta at the Association of South East Asian Nations (ASEAN) regional forum, the highest-level encounter since the crisis began. On July 25, 2004, the foreign ministry called the U.S. offer a sham, and after the passage of the North Korea Human Rights Act in the U.S. Congress on July 27, 2004, the ministry questioned the usefulness of the Six-Party Talks. There was a widespread view that North Korea had decided to postpone the resumption of the talks until after the U.S. presidential election in November 2004, an interpretation that North Koreans vigorously denied.[48] Instead they said that they would not attend the talks unless the United States abandoned its hostile stance toward North Korea.

Pyongyang did not yield many clues as to the real reason for its decision to stall the Six-Party process. For more than a year there were conflicting messages, and the participating governments appointed new representatives to the talks without any clear signal as to if and when they would resume. One school of thought suggested that North Korea had decided that as economic relations with China and the Republic of Korea continued, whereas relations with the United States remained tense, it needed to at least partially remove the ambiguity over its nuclear program in order to deter the United States. However, in many respects Pyongyang's behavior was similar to that in the past—by continuously ratcheting up the threat, completing the reprocessing of the fuel rods from the reactor, threatening the resumption of missile tests, claiming to have a working nuclear deterrent, and stopping the 5 MWe reactor to extract fuel rods, it seemed to be trying to increase its leverage while at the same time demanding the resumption of dialogue with Washington on a bilateral basis.

Reports from the U.S. Defense Intelligence Agency (DIA) that North Korea might be preparing a nuclear test and could have missiles capable of delivering nuclear weapons to the United States contributed to the growing atmosphere of crisis. The DIA had been consistently hawkish on North Korea—it was responsible for the (false) reports of nuclear facilities at Kumchang-ri, and in 2005 the DIA director testified that North Korea had the capability to strike at the United States with nuclear weapons, a judgment disputed by most experts.

By June 2005 this game seemed to have come full circle. During the meeting in Pyongyang to celebrate the 2000 unification summit involving a sizable South

Korean delegation, Kim Jong-il arranged an impromptu meeting with the ROK unification minister Chung Dong-young, in which he indicated a willingness to return to the Six-Party Talks in July 2005 and even give up nuclear weapons and medium- and long-range missiles, provided that the United States ceased its hostile attitude and respected North Korea rather than despising it.[49] After the meeting it became clear that the government of the Republic of Korea had now been success- fully enlisted in North Korea's diplomatic campaign. For example, the ROK's for- eign minister Ban Ki-moon (now the secretary-general of the United Nations) said that statements by Secretary of State Rice and Undersecretary of State Paula Do- briansky that North Korea was an "outpost of tyranny" were "regrettable," as they might prevent Pyongyang from rejoining the Six-Party Talks, and he questioned the intention of U.S. diplomacy toward North Korea.[50]

TOWARD A STALEMATE

U.S. policy underwent a gradual but radical shift during the second Bush adminis- tration. This was partly due to the preoccupation by Rumsfeld and Cheney with the deteriorating situation in Iraq. The public disaffection with the war in Iraq eroded support for any other military actions. The responsibility for North Korea policy essentially passed to the State Department, where Condoleezza Rice, a close con- fidante of the president, was now in charge. John Bolton was nominated ambas- sador to the United Nations and was thus removed from day-to-day policymaking in Washington.

Rice appointed Christopher Hill to replace James Kelly as assistant secretary for East Asia and essentially as the chief negotiator with North Korea. Victor Cha, an outspoken advocate of "hawk engagement" to resolve the nuclear crisis diplo- matically, was appointed to the National Security Council as an expert on Asia. Hill demanded and received more latitude than his predecessor in directly talking to North Koreans and stretched his authority to the very limit (and often beyond) in order to coax the North Koreans back to the Six-Party Talks and begin a process of direct negotiations, despite the continuing efforts by some in the administration (such as Robert Joseph and Douglas Feith) to constrain him because they did not want any agreement with North Korea to be reached. Nevertheless, Hill began to pursue negotiations on a basis that increasingly conformed to North Korean expec- tations about reciprocity and the process, while continuing to insist that the final outcome had to be the complete elimination of all nuclear programs (including the HEU program, whose existence Pyongyang continued to deny) and a return to the NPT. One thorny issue that raised it head at this point was the question of civilian nuclear energy. President Bush had decided that in contrast to the Agreed Framework any new deal should not include the provision of light water reactors and that North Korea should not have access to any nuclear technology.[51] Now North Korea's chief negotiator, Kim Gye-gwan, insisted that the DPRK could not give up its right to civilian nuclear energy. (Eventually this particular issue was fudged.) The result of the negotiations was the first time the six parties agreed in writing to a set of principles in relation to North Korea's nuclear program. The so-called September 19 Declaration stated:

> The Six Parties unanimously reaffirmed that the goal of the Six Party Talks is the verifiable denuclearization of the Korean Peninsula in a peaceful manner. The DPRK committed to abandoning all nuclear weapons and existing nuclear programs and returning, at an early date, to the Treaty on the Non-Proliferation of Nuclear Weapons and to IAEA safeguards. The United States affirmed that it has no nuclear weapons on the Korean Peninsula and has no intention to attack or invade the DPRK with nuclear or conventional weapons."[52]

On the issue of civilian nuclear energy, the declaration included the following sentence: "The DPRK stated that it has the right to peaceful uses of nuclear energies. The other parties expressed their respect and agreed to discuss, at an appropriate time, the subject of the provision of a light-water reactor to the DPRK."[53]

The impact of the September 19 Declaration, however, was immediately blunted by a unilateral U.S. declaration, which had been drafted by John Bolton's successor at the State Department, Robert Joseph, jointly with Deputy National Security Advisor J. D. Crouch, National Security Council nonproliferation chief John Rood, and John Bolton, and which was read out by Hill. It reintroduced the demand for the complete, verifiable, and irreversible elimination of all nuclear programs and stated that the "appropriate time" for considering the issue of LWRs would only come after the DPRK had complied with all aspects of the declaration (including rejoining the NPT and compliance with IAEA safeguards) and "had demonstrated a sustained commitment to cooperation and transparency and ceased proliferating nuclear technology."[54] As Jack Pritchard commented, this meant that the DPRK had to demonstrate compliance with all demands, including an arbitrary goal over an unspecified time period before there could be any discussion about LWRs.[55] The immediate response by Kim Gye-gwan was to elevate the provision of LWRs to a fundamental condition of disarmament. Thus the U.S. unilateral statement managed to convert a successfully fudged issue into a stumbling block for the progress of negotiations, negating much of what had been achieved.

As the talks had effectively stalled again, the North Koreans and the Americans tried to get the other side to move. Pyongyang attempted to open up a direct dialogue with the United States, which Washington staunchly resisted. For example, Kim Gye-gwan suggested a meeting with Hill at the Northeast Asia Cooperation Dialogue held in Tokyo on April 10–11, 2006. The U.S. delegation refused and insisted that any discussions should take place in the forum of the Six-Party Talks. The U.S. State Department also launched the Illicit Activities Initiative aimed at curbing foreign currency earned through criminal activities such as counterfeiting currency and drug trafficking.[56] The freezing of North Korean assets in the Banco Delta Asia based in Macao and other banks deprived Pyongyang of access to funds in excess of $20 million. The U.S. government also imposed sanctions on North Korean companies for engaging in activities related to proliferation, such as the Korea Mining Development Corporation and the Korea Ryonbong General Corporation. Such actions had been demanded by conservatives in the United States for a long time. Targeting North Korea's illicit foreign exchanges earnings seemed one of the few possible points of leverage against a state that was otherwise impervious to military or political pressures, and moreover it highlighted the allegedly criminal nature of the state. But if it was designed to compel North Korea to return to the Six-Party Talks and accept the joint statement of principles, it failed entirely. Instead it created yet another seemingly insuperable obstacle in the way of progress as North Korea made return to the talks conditional on the lifting of these sanctions.[57]

In North Korea the sanctions were interpreted as part of a coordinated effort to topple the North Korean government. On July 5 North Korea broke its missile-testing moratorium and launched seven missiles, including a Taepodong-2. Once again Pyongyang resorted to increasing the military pressure in the hope of inducing a shift in the U.S. stance. Although the Taepodong-2 exploded soon after liftoff, the intention was clear: as a missile of almost intercontinental range, it was meant to demonstrate that North Korea was increasing the capacity to hold U.S. forces at risk. The launches were timed to take place shortly after the United States launched the space shuttle Discovery to celebrate Independence Day. The gesture, however, backfired on Pyongyang. It was interpreted universally as a hostile and provocative act. The United Nations Security Council voted unanimously on July 15, 2006, to impose sanctions on North Korea in response to the missile launches.

Pyongyang's actions created a state of shock in the South Korean government. It was a deep embarrassment for Unification Minister Lee Jong-seok, who had described North Korean leader Kim Jong-il as a man he could do business with. President Roh, faced with a provocation that undermined the whole premise of his policy toward the North, refused to make any comments. For the first time the South Korean government stopped the shipment of supplies to the North, and this had an immediate effect on the entire range of inter-Korean relations, with talks reaching a dead end as South Korean tours were halted.

By September 2006 there seemed little prospect of the resumption of negotiations on North Korea's nuclear program. Then North Korea decided to escalate even further. On October 9, 2006, the North Korean news agency KCNA announced that the DPRK had tested a nuclear device.[58] According to the South Korean National Intelligence Service, the explosion occurred at Sangpyong-ri, North Hamgyong Province, near the town of Kimchaek. The relatively modest size of the detonation (estimated at the equivalent of less than a thousand tons of TNT and thus less than a tenth of the size of the atomic explosion over Hiroshima) initially raised some doubts as to whether a nuclear detonation had in fact occurred. After a brief investigation, the U.S. Director of National Intelligence John Negroponte confirmed that radioactive debris had been detected and that a nuclear test had taken place. It is possible that the small size of the detonation means that the test was a partial failure and that nuclear fission did not quite take place according to plan. This raised speculation that North Korea would have to conduct further tests to ensure that its nuclear devices were working properly and that they could be fitted to delivery vehicles.[59]

It did not take long for UN Security Council Resolution 1718, which imposed an array of sanctions targeted on North Korea's elite. These included a ban on military exports to and from the DPRK, a ban on the sale or export of nuclear- or missile-related items, a ban on the sale of luxury goods to North Korea, a freeze on

North Korean financial assets, and a travel ban for all persons involved in the nuclear and missile programs and their families. For South Korea the most controversial element was the inclusion of inspections of North Korean ships, which had the potential for producing a serious confrontation at sea.

The nuclear tests demonstrated the complete failure of the policy of the Bush administration to counter Pyongyang's nuclear program. North Korea had acquired precisely the capability that years of sanctions and negotiations were supposed to stop. Soon after the nuclear test North Korea signaled that it was prepared to attend another session of the Six-Party Talks, without preconditions. While on the surface this appeared to be surprising, and some believed that this was due to Chinese pressure, it was consistent with North Korea's negotiating behavior. Now that it had demonstrated its nuclear status, the DPRK expected that it had greater bargaining power and that it needed to be treated with the respect due to a nuclear power. Consequently it could afford to rejoin the talks without preconditions.

Another session of the Six-Party Talks was held in Beijing in December 2006. The North Korean chief delegate Kim Gye-gwan made it clear that the DPRK would only discuss the nuclear program after financial sanctions were lifted. He characterized U.S. policy as one of carrots and sticks, i.e. dialogue and pressure, and contrasted this with Pyongyang's policy of dialogue and a shield. He also stated that North Korea would improve its nuclear deterrent. The North Koreans also repeated their demand that in return for giving up the plutonium program it needed to be compensated with light water reactors in order to provide for the energy needs of the country. After five days of talks in which no further progress was made, the meeting ended on December 22, 2006, with a statement by the Chinese delegate Wu Dawei, which simply restated the agreement of September 2005 that the DPRK would disarm in return for security guarantees and aid.[60] Following the December meeting the United States began to engage in bilateral negotiations with North Korea in Berlin. These talks revealed greater flexibility on the part of the United States and North Korea, both regarding style and substance, as they resembled the kind of bilateral bargaining that occurred in the run-up to the Agreed Framework. The U.S. chief negotiator, Christopher Hill, agreed that the issue of financial sanctions could be resolved and that the United States was willing to remove North Korea from the list of sponsors of terrorism as well as lift trade sanctions. At a meeting in Beijing on February 13, 2007, it was announced that an agreement had been reached. It required North Korea to shut down its nuclear facilities at Yongbyon within sixty days, with the purpose of eventual abandonment. North Korea was to receive fifty thousand tons of fuel oil for concluding the agreement. A package of economic, energy, and humanitarian assistance was agreed upon, to be gradually implemented as the dismantlement of nuclear facilities proceeded. The agreement did not mention nuclear weapons or devices, the disposal of nuclear materials, or the uranium enrichment program (the latter of which led to the collapse of the Agreed Framework and triggered the second nuclear crisis). There were signals from the U.S. administration that it may have exaggerated the significance of the uranium enrichment program.[61] It also did not address the missile program.

On September 6, 2007, the Israeli Air Force attacked and destroyed a building in Syria that was suspected to be a site for a nuclear reactor to be built with North Korean assistance. Although any intelligence about the nature of this building was not made public, the incident highlighted the risk that North Korea might proliferate its nuclear technology to other states seeking nuclear weapons.

At the second meeting of the sixth round of the Six-Party Talks on September 7–30, 2007, there was an understanding with respect to a list of actions to be implemented for the second phase of the agreement issued in a joint statement on October 3, 2007. North Korea agreed to disable the nuclear facilities in accordance with the previous agreements—namely the 5 MWe reactor, the reprocessing facility, and the fuel rod fabrication plant—by December 31, 2007. The DPRK also agreed to provide a full declaration of all of its nuclear facilities by that date. The United States promised to fulfill its agreements to establish mutual trust and remove the DPRK from the list of state sponsors of terrorism as well as terminate the application of the Trading with the Enemy Act to North Korea. The provision of economic, humanitarian, and energy assistance to the equivalent of 1 million tons of heavy fuel oil (including one hundred thousand tons of oil already delivered) was to be implemented.

In November 2007 the DPRK provided an inventory of its facilities, which it said fulfilled its obligations under the February 13 agreement. Although the United States considered the information provided wholly inadequate, it seemed that North Korea was prepared to go through with the dismantlement of its plutonium-production facilities and took significant steps toward that goal, leading up to the spectacular destruction of the cooling tower of the 5 MWe reactor in Yongbyon in June 2008. On May 8, 2008, North Korea submitted 18,822 pages of information about its nuclear program to the United States delegation. On June 26, 2008, North Korea submitted a declaration of its nuclear activities to China as the chair of the Six-Party Talks. This prompted President Bush to lift some of the sanctions against North Korea under the Trading with the Enemy Act and to announce the intention to remove North Korea from the list of countries sponsoring terrorism within forty-five days. However, when the Six-Party Talks resumed on July 10, 2008, there was renewed discord as the U.S. deemed the declaration of nuclear facilities provided by North Korea to be insufficient and described it as a "limited declaration." Consequently the removal of DPRK from the list of sponsors of terrorism was postponed. North Korea came under pressure in other ways—in September it became clear that the country was experiencing a very serious food crisis, and there were reports that Kim Jong-il was very ill and had suffered a stroke when he failed to appear at the celebrations of the sixtieth anniversary of the foundation of the DPRK. There was a test of the engine of a long-range missile at the Tongchang-ri test site. On September 19, 2008, the North Korean government declared that it was reversing its decision on nuclear disarmament and would start to reconstitute the facilities at the Yongbyon site because the United States had failed to follow the "action for action" principle on which the implementation of the February 13 agreement was supposed to be based. North Koreans removed seals and cameras from the site and barred IAEA inspectors from entering it.

This reversal once again raised questions about the sincerity of the North Korean commitment to nuclear dismantlement. Christopher Hill sought to calm nerves by saying that it would take North Korea a year to completely reverse the disablement that had taken place. While the atmosphere of crisis appeared to prevail, the U.S. delegation met with the North Koreans in Pyongyang at the beginning of October 2008 to hammer out an agreement of the verification of denuclearization. On October 11 the U.S. State Department announced that such an agreement had been reached and that the DPRK was removed from the list of countries that sponsor terrorism. In response, the disablement of nuclear facilities was resumed. However, the Six-Party Talks stalled as no further progress on declaration of nuclear facilities and verification was made. The upcoming U.S. presidential elections meant a hiatus in negotiations, while the incoming Obama administration appointed its own officials and formulated its policy toward North Korea. The new administration was determined to continue where the Bush administration left off. Obama appointed very experienced people to continue the Six-Party process, with Hillary Clinton as secretary of state, Stephen Bosworth as successor to Christopher Hill, and Gary Samore as nonproliferation czar. (Meanwhile relations between North and South Korea continued to deteriorate due to the tougher line pursued by Roh Moo-hyun's successor, Lee Myung-bak. After a South Korean tourist was killed by a North Korean soldier in the Mount Geumgang resort in July 2008 and the sinking of the *Cheonan* in 2010, practically all North-South dialogue has ceased.)

Soon it became clear that Pyongyang was not willing to pick up with the Obama administration where things were left off; there had been a fundamental shift in North Korean policy, with those in the military leadership who insisted on preserving a nuclear capability prevailing. On April 6 North Korea launched a Taepodong-2 missile, ostensibly to launch a satellite. Pyongyang issued a warning against any action by the UN Security Council and asserted that it was the DPRK's sovereign right to engage in space exploration. The launch was technically a failure insofar as the third stage, which contained the satellite, failed and the payload did not achieve orbit. But the missile performed properly and demonstrated North Korea's increasing capacity to produce long-range missiles. The United States and other members of the UN Security Council were not impressed by North Korea's explanations or warnings and imposed sanctions on the basis that the missile launch violated UN Security Council Resolution 1718. Subsequently North Korea attacked the UN Security Council's action and declared it would no longer attend the Six-Party Talks or engage in negotiations about its nuclear program, instead focusing on developing its deterrent.[62]

On May 25, 2009, North Korea once again acted in defiance of the international community by conducting another nuclear test. The device apparently had a yield of about four kT.[63] The test was accompanied by the firing of short-range missiles. The timing was ironic: it occurred just two days after the suicide of former South Korean president Roh Moo-hyun, a staunch supporter of engagement with North Korea, in the wake of a corruption investigation, an event that induced a profound sense of shock and grief in the Republic of Korea. International condemnation of North Korea was swift and predictable. President Obama accused Pyongyang of directly and recklessly challenging the international community.[64]

The second test supported the views expressed in the U.S. intelligence community that North Korea had the capability to produce nuclear devices that could be mounted on long-range missiles (although the publicly available evidence was not wholly conclusive). The space launch in April, although the satellite failed to reach orbit, also demonstrated, apparently quite convincingly, the progress North Korea had made in its missile technology. This was alarming because if it continued unchecked, the day on which North Korea could launch a nuclear weapon at the continental United States was drawing nearer. Pyongyang's behavior could be seen as an effort to influence the Obama administration and use its growing military capabilities to induce further concessions. North Koreans wanted to abandon the Six-Party process, which they found tedious and unproductive, in favor of direct bilateral talks with the United States. There was no doubt that despite, and in defiance of, its commitments to disarm, North Korea had spent 2007 and 2008 significantly developing its nuclear capabilities.

Nevertheless, some of the signals that Kim Jong-il sent despite all the hostile rhetoric seemed to indicate that Pyongyang still did want to ultimately improve relations with the United States. The nuclear tantrum was apparently aimed at forcing the United States into the recognition of the DPRK as a nuclear state with a small arsenal and to deliver economic aid in return for capping its nuclear and missiles programs. But the Obama administration was adamantly opposed to this kind of deal. Its policy was now to wait and see, to let North Korea take the diplomatic initiative, a policy that Secretary of State Clinton called "strategic patience." The United States was prepared to resume the Six-Party Talks only if North Korea was willing to return the commitments previously made to fully disarm.[65]

Relations between the United States and North Korea further deteriorated as a consequence of the sinking of the South Korean frigate *Cheonan* in March 2010. President Obama accepted the results of the international investigation, which concluded that a North Korea torpedo attack caused the sinking, and sided with South Korean president Lee Myung-bak in his condemnation of North Korea. The ROK and the United States conducted joint naval exercises as a response to the North Korean aggression on the seas (plans to conduct these exercises in the Yellow Sea were shelved after China voiced concerns, and they confined themselves to the East Sea). After a presidential statement from the United Nations Security Council, which deplored the attack but did not hold the DPRK responsible, the North Koreans indicated their willingness to return to nuclear talks. This was the price that China extracted from Pyongyang in return for refusing to join in the condemnation of

North Korea for the attack. The United States was unresponsive to North Korea's approaches as Washington and Seoul waited for some statement of regret over the *Cheonan* incident as well as an indication that Pyongyang was serious about nuclear disarmament. The United States and South Korea were looking for a signal that North Korea was willing to move toward genuine denuclearization. Signals from North Korea were not encouraging. In order to put more pressure on the United States, North Korea decided to finally lift the lid on the uranium enrichment program whose very existence it had strenuously denied. The North Korean ministry of foreign affairs invited three American arms control specialists—Siegfried Hecker (the former director of the Los Alamos nuclear laboratory), Robert L. Carlin, and John W. Lewis—to visit the Yongbyon nuclear facilities on November 12, 2010. They were shown a uranium enrichment facility, and saw rows of first-generation and advanced centrifuges. They were surprised by the scale and the sophistication of the facility. Hecker afterward stated that he believed the North Korean account that they were constructing an LWR using their own technical resources and that they were enriching uranium in order to fuel the reactor, but said that it was very likely that a parallel program to produce highly enriched uranium for weapons purposes existed somewhere else. This revelation was not only a strong vindication of the analysis previously presented by the CIA, but also a complete refutation of liberal critics such as Selig Harrison and skeptics in Beijing and Seoul. It demonstrated that North Korea had secretly embarked on a second nuclear program despite the agreement with the United States.[66] Subsequently the North Korea artillery attacks on Yeonpyeong in November 2010 increased tension further. The current impasse means that it may be some time before diplomacy on the nuclear issue will resume.[67]

THE END OF NUCLEAR TALKS WITH NORTH KOREA?

U.S. efforts to engage North Korea and eliminate the North Korean nuclear program have come full circle. Although the Agreed Framework negotiated during the Clinton administration and the February 13 agreement reached in the Six-Party Talks during the Bush period indicated a willingness of the North Korean government to trade its nuclear program for significant political and economic benefits, it remains unclear whether the development of North Korean nuclear capabilities can be permanently constrained. The strategy to guarantee North Korea's continued existence in return for the freezing of the nuclear program ignored the fundamental dilemma that generated the nuclear issue in the first place: the very existence of North Korea.

From the U.S. point of view, North Korea is not part of the community of civilized nations whose collective identity is defined by the adherence to certain norms, both in domestic governance and international relations. In other words, it is a rogue state. The George W. Bush administration included North Korea in the "axis of evil" and emphasized the unacceptability of the North Korean regime. During the first term Bush sided with those in the administration who were against any form of engagement with North Korea or any deal on the nuclear program. Apart from the skepticism that North Korea would really disarm, such a deal not only involved rewarding North Korea for adhering to commitments and fulfilling obligations it had already undertaken, but it also pledged the United States to support the continued existence of the rogue state and underwrite its economic survival. The Clinton administration was willing to pay the price, because it considered the prevention of proliferation an absolute priority and was skeptical about North Korea's chances of survival in any event. The folly of this reasoning is that a resolution of the nuclear issue does not solve the underlying problem.

The North Korean regime will continue to remain unacceptable to the United States and most of the international community. No matter what agreements are signed, the outside world will seek gradual regime change. On the other hand, the North Korean state is not viable politically, socially, or economically. Its rulers reject internal reform, refuse to open the country up to the world, and conduct its foreign policy on the basis of threats. Its projection of the external threat is a major element of its internal legitimation. This leaves the North Korean leadership with the dilemma that it needs to improve its relations with the outside world, especially the United States, in order to mitigate the external threat and obtain the economic support it needs, even while any such improvement undermines the regime and its raison d'être. For these reasons, an unending cycle of confrontation and accommodation is inevitable while this regime endures. This explains why North Korea has defected from any settlement or agreement it has made when the conditions were no longer deemed advantageous. In the aftermath of the missile and nuclear tests President Obama made it clear that he was not willing to continue the cycle of agreements accompanied by generous economic support only for North Korea to abandon the agreements and further develop its WMD.[68] But an alternative to previous policies is not yet in sight.

7

China and the Future of the
Korean Peninsula

Written jointly with Chunyao Yi*

North Korea's relations with the international community are primarily mediated through its relations with the United States, partly because the United States is the ultimate provider of security on the Korean Peninsula and it has therefore taken on the responsibility to challenge North Korea with regard to its nuclear program. But many observers also believe that China is playing a key role as a country that has more potential leverage over North Korea, as well as closer political relations, than anyone else. China has played a leading role in dealing with the North Korean nuclear crisis by initiating and convening successive rounds of the Six-Party Talks in Beijing. Any resolution of the nuclear issue will involve China as an indispensable contributor and guarantor in the negotiation and implementation process.

China's active role has emerged at a time when China is constructing a new image of "responsible great power" following its rise.[1] A guiding principle of new Chinese foreign policy stresses that "the relations with big countries are the key, the neighboring areas are the primacy, the developing countries are the foundations, and the multilateral diplomacy is the main arena."[2] The North Korean nuclear issue seems to cover every aspect. Effectively managing the crisis has become a test for China to achieve the goals of protecting its national interests and at the same time becoming a "responsible stakeholder."

Before North Korea conducted its nuclear test, China's willingness and the limits of its influence over North Korea were subject to debate.[3] Many analyses of

---

* This chapter was drafted in her personal capacity and associated with her research work at the University of Leeds, UK.

China's policy have been conducted from the perspective of the triangle of relations between the United States, China, and the DPRK.[4] However, although both the United States and North Korea view China as aiming to protect its own self-interest, it is not sufficient to simply reduce China's behavior to a passive reaction to U.S. policy and North Korean demands, ignoring China's own policy goals, in order to understand its foreign policy. China's role and policy can only be understood through a better assessment of its perceptions, priorities, and limitations, all of which are integrated into its international strategies.

This chapter examines China's policy toward the North Korean nuclear program. It first looks closely at China's concerns, policy context, policy instruments, and policy goals. Before the nuclear test, Western analysts generally argued that while the idea of a nuclear-free Korean Peninsula is important, for the Chinese leadership and most Chinese strategic experts the survival of the North Korean regime and reform of North Korea are both China's greatest challenges and prime objectives.[5] Has the nuclear test had any impact on China's policy priority? By reviewing China's policy, this chapter will show that the years 2003 and 2006 were critical in China's policy development toward the North Korean nuclear crisis. China has actively responded to the urgent situation on the basis of a short-term goal of preventing the escalation of the crisis and paving ways for a long-term goal of peace, denuclearization, and economic development. Twice, China used its quiet diplomacy to bring the confrontational parties—the DPRK and the United States—together and establishing common ground among the six parties involved in the Six-Party Talks.

CHINA'S PERCEPTION OF NORTH KOREA

Chinese conventional perceptions of its relations with North Korea are reflected in two descriptions—the comrade and brotherhood friendship fortified by blood, and the metaphor of the closeness of "lips and teeth." The first description refers to the historical connections, such as the battlefield cooperation between China and North Korea against Japanese colonization in the first half of the twentieth century, the cooperation during the 1950–1953 Korean War, a de facto military alliance formed in 1961,[6] as well as the shared socialist ideology during the Cold War.[7] The second, the metaphor of "lips and teeth," describes the geopolitical significance of the Korean Peninsula to China.

Japan invaded China through Korea in the early twentieth century, and U.S. forces approached the Chinese border in the 1950s; Chinese leaders tend to view the

Korean Peninsula as a key bulwark against external hostilities, a strategic backyard and its natural sphere of influence.[8] Some Chinese scholars have argued that because of its southward-shifting economic and strategic center of gravity as well as the changed nature of contemporary war, with the decisive role of marine and air forces, the eastern coastal line would be the primary target if any attack on China occurred. From this point of view, the strategic importance of North Korea has declined as the effectiveness of a buffer zone for China's northeast land and the possibility of a springboard used by a third country are both reduced.[9] Nevertheless, due to the geographic proximity of the two countries as "lips and teeth," North Korea is still strategically important to China's core national interests of stability, security, and prosperity. Therefore, this strategic view remains popular in the decision-making and academic circles in China today.

While the second view has been slightly adjusted, the first has been gradually replaced by a third view, which sees North Korea as a troublesome neighbor, an isolated and backward country stubbornly sticking to the ideology doctrines which China has discarded,[10] and worst of all, that it has created the long-standing nuclear crisis which could threaten China's most fundamental economic and security interests.[11]

Since the collapse of the Soviet Union in 1991, North Korea has relied heavily on China's economic support in a variety of forms, such as direct government-to-government aid, subsidized trade, and private barter transactions, to ensure the survival of the isolated regime.[12] As the largest source of foreign aid to North Korea, China has provided nearly half of the total food import and almost all of the crude oil, between 300,000 and 1 million tons annually.[13] China's trade with North Korea reached $1.7 billion in 2006, which accounts for roughly 40 percent of the DPRK's trade, double that of South Korea and more than six times that of Japan.[14]

Although bilateral relations have been sustained by crucial Chinese political and diplomatic support, essential economic assistance, and limited military co-operation,[15] the two countries are no longer as close due to the establishment of diplomatic relations between China and the Republic of Korea in 1992 and China's equal-distance diplomacy toward the two Koreas since.[16] North Korea not only denounced China's betrayal of its one-Korea (pro-Pyongyang) policy (as well as of socialism) for more than three decades, but also resented the fact that China recognized the South without requiring the United States to do the same for the North.[17] However, "this [China-ROK] relationship has become extremely important to Beijing as well as to Seoul, and the PRC [People's Republic of China] is not about to sacrifice it to placate Pyongyang in any way."[18]

Regarding the nuclear program, on the one hand China seems to understand North Korea's concerns, particularly of defending its security against the United States.[19] North Korea has long been vulnerable to the U.S. nuclear presence in East Asia and the Pacific, and this sense of vulnerability was heightened significantly after the collapse of the Soviet Union and the PRC-ROK reconciliation, which removed the nuclear umbrella over North Korea. Therefore, following these events, Pyongyang started to accelerate its nuclear program. Later, the Bush administration not only listed the DPRK as one of the "rogue states" and part of the "axis of evil," the targets of the U.S. global policing actions, but also mentioned North Korea as one of seven countries (a list that included China) the administration saw as potential "nuclear attack targets for preemptive strike,"[20] and even once deployed nuclear weapons in South Korea.[21] With a deep sense of isolation and insecurity, North Korea was bent on expanding its military strength, especially nuclear weapons and long-range ballistic missiles, in spite of the fact that the country suffered from severe economic difficulties.[22] On the other hand, many Chinese experts believe that North Korea's request for nuclear weapons has become China's gravest near-term security threat and that North Korea's provocative behavior, not the United States', has ignited the recent nuclear crisis.[23]

HOW DID CHINA GET INVOLVED?

In the first North Korean nuclear crisis in 1993–1994, China was involved little, if at all, in the whole diplomatic process. When the crisis was resolved and the United States and DPRK signed the Agreed Framework, China hoped it would result in improved economic conditions in North Korea, keeping the regime functioning and enhancing the prospects of political stability.[24] However, China refused to join KEDO, the international consortium for the implementation of the Agreed Framework.

China's reclusive stance toward the U.S.-DPRK standoff in the first crisis has been completely replaced by a proactive role in 2002–2003. In December 2002, then presidents of China and Russia, Jiang Zemin and Vladimir Putin, respectively, issued a joint declaration after their summit in Beijing calling on North Korea to abandon its nuclear programs and urging the United States to reduce the tension by resuming negotiations with North Korea.[25] The year 2003 saw a significant shift in China's policy on North Korean nuclear crisis. The Chinese met with North Korean officials and took on the role of relaying messages between Pyongyang and Washington.[26]

Jiang Zemin had several conversations with President Bush, and the former foreign minister Qian Qichen made a quiet visit to Pyongyang in March 2003 to meet with Kim Jong-il.[27] In the same month, Leading Group on the North Korean Crisis (LGNKC)—directed by China's new president, Hu Jintao—was established in order to improve the assessment of the situation, especially on the DPRK's intentions and capabilities, and to develop a cost-effective strategy.[28] Then, in April 2003, China made unprecedented diplomatic efforts to bring Washington and Pyongyang to the trilateral talks. Contrary to the speculation that China might simply withdraw from an active role once the trilateral talks failed, the Chinese government immediately sought to initiate another trilateral event.[29] China's efforts greatly facilitated the formation of the Six-Party Talks, the major multilateral forum for the exclusive purpose of the resolution of the North Korean nuclear crisis.

Several factors led to such a dramatic change in China's policy. First of all, compared with its problematic situation in the early 1990s, when China was affected by both internal and external political turbulence—namely the Tiananmen incident and the collapse of transnational communism—China found itself with enhanced economic and geopolitical power in the new millennium.[30] In the decade following the mid-1990s China has oriented its foreign policy from Deng Xiaoping's "hiding its light under a bushel" (*tao guan yang hui*) to "peaceful rise" and active self-image construction of a "responsible regional power."[31] Second, China's active role in mediating the North Korean nuclear crisis has also been in line with its new security framework developed for the twenty-first century, known as the "new security concept" and elaborated by Chinese vice foreign minister Wang Yi as a "comprehensive, common, and cooperative" security framework.[32] This framework stresses cooperative relations with neighboring countries as well as more accommodating policies on multilateral security arrangements in the region. Concepts such as "common security" and "preventative diplomacy" have also attracted Chinese decision makers' attention and interests in fitting them into real situations. China has not only actively participated in regional and global multilateral organizations and mechanisms, but also initiated multilateral organizations such as the Shanghai Cooperation Organization (SCO).[33] The Six-Party Talks have been another multilateral cooperative effort initiated by China. In other words, in 2003–2004 China was able and willing to mediate between the United States and DPRK.

The catalysts for China's swift actions were the so-called Bush Doctrine and the DPRK's reaction to it.[34] The new U.S. national security doctrine announced in June 2002 set such strategic priorities as missile defense; the creation of a high-tech, rapid-reaction military of overwhelming scope and power; and the revitalization of the U.S. nuclear weapons industry, in a quest for absolute security so that no other state or coalition of states would be able to confront the United States. The invasion of Iraq has been perceived as the prototype of the Bush Doctrine—"regime change" by military force to punish any adversary who dared to stand up to American power.[35] The Bush Doctrine has been perceived by Pyongyang as a dominating threat to its own security and therefore motivated North Korea to build up a nuclear deterrent against the U.S. attack, should North Korea find itself the next target of regime change.[36] China feared that the mutual provocation between the United States and the DPRK would escalate the crisis and eventually lead to U.S. intervention or direct attack, which would in turn precipitate regime change in North Korea and bring American military forces to China's border.[37]

POLICY INSTRUMENTS AND INFLUENCE

China's policy instruments to address the North Korean nuclear issues have been developed along both multilateral and bilateral fronts. China initially intended to act only as a mediator between the United States and the DPRK to alleviate the tensions and promote dialogue between them. In April 2003 China hosted the trilateral talks in Beijing. When the talks did not produce any positive results, Deputy Foreign Minister Dai Bingguo traveled to Moscow, Pyongyang, and Washington to seek ways of finding some common ground. The United States was not inclined to hold direct bilateral talks with the DPRK, while North Korea demanded to negotiate with the United States bilaterally, so China initiated a "multilateral" setting that would satisfy Washington's wish to shift the security burden to other East Asian countries as well as Pyongyang's condition of talking to the United States directly.

The first round of the Six-Party Talks was held in Beijing in August 2003. In this multilateral setting, China constantly mediated between the United States and the DPRK, persuading each side to make reasonable concessions: for example, in the first two rounds the United States was convinced to make a promise of nonaggression against the DPRK, and the latter in return agreed to give up the ongoing nuclear program. When Kim Jong-il visited Beijing in April 2004, he was told by the top Chinese leaders that the United States was unlikely to invade the DPRK and that therefore it would be in Kim's interest to alter North Korea's hard-line stance. By doing so, China pushed the direct dialogue between the United States and the DPRK inside the multilateral talks. In the meantime, China also tried to seek the common ground among the parties, especially between South Korea and Russia. In the preparation for each new round of the talks, China repeatedly contacted other parties to set timetables for both working-level meetings and the talks themselves.

Although there were ups and downs along the six rounds of the talks, Chinese diplomats made considerable efforts to keep this process going. As hosts, they often used various tactics such as stating that "no one will leave until a diplomatic draft is worked out" or announcing an "adjournment" when no common ground could be found among the parties, in order to avoid the withdrawal of any party or, worse, the collapse of the talks.[38]

The Chinese also blended the Asian-style "informal diplomacy" into the process, which helped to build up consensus in a flexible way: on September 18, 2005, one day before the scheduled closing for the fourth round of the Six-Party Talks, Dai Bingguo invited the parties' delegations to an autumn moon festival banquet, in celebration of a traditional Chinese holiday. The banquet lasted until midnight, providing opportunity for delegation leaders to conduct last-minute informal negotiations and facilitating the first joint statement of the Six-Party Talks, reached the next day.[39]

In the bilateral relations with North Korea, China has tried to retain its erratic neighbor in the dialogue process through a variety of means. Although Pyongyang has relied on China's economic support for its survival, China had to frequently employ economic incentives to bring North Korea to the negotiation table. On initiating the Six-Party Talks, China pledged to offer the DPRK greater economic aid than previous years. Later, in order to urge Pyongyang to take part in the first round of the Six-Party Talks, China provided ten thousand tons of diesel fuel to North Korea; to secure North Korean acquiescence to the second round of the talks in February 2004, China offered new and significant amounts of economic aid and energy assistance, totaling around $50 million.[40] A considerable amount of fuel, worth 300 million yuan (approximately $40 million), was delivered to North Korea, which guaranteed Pyongyang's participation in the fourth round.[41] President Hu Jintao's state visit to Pyongyang on October 28–30, 2005, before the fifth round, brought an offer of more monetary aid to the DPRK and the Economic and Technological Cooperation Agreement, which was reported to be worth $2 billion in trade credits and investment.[42]

However, economic inducements have not always been effective in ensuring Pyongyang's participation and halting the progress of its nuclear program. When a new round of the talks was expected in February 2005, for instance, Pyongyang announced that it had no intention of returning to the negotiating table and admitted for the first time it was manufacturing nuclear weapons. And after the fifth round in November 2005, North Korea once again announced that it would not join the next round of the talks unless the United States halted the financial sanctions upon Pyongyang. Even though Chinese leaders made a commitment of development assistance, enhanced trading, and investment during Kim Jong-il's trip to Beijing in January 2006, as well as when Chinese vice minister Wu Dawei visited Pyongyang in February 2006 to try to revive the Six-Party Talks, China was not able to bring its elusive neighbor back to the table.

In spite of the fact that China managed to keep the talks going, there seemed to be considerable limits to China's influence over this crisis. First, China's reins over North Korea's nuclear adventure by means of economic aid have been weakened by North Korea's ungrateful attitude. Moreover, according to Ming Liu (Shanghai Academy of Social Sciences):

Pyongyang is wary of Beijing's international influence, its ability to collaborate with the United States and South Korea, its willingness to foster traditional friendship, and its credibility in fulfilling its commitments to the DPRK in case of crisis. Therefore, both openly and privately, the DPRK will try to limit or downplay China's role and influence during the resolution of the current crisis.[43]

China tried to persuade its errant neighbor to cooperate with the international community, but its ability to force concessions from North Korea was limited. Neither did China have much influence over the American hard-line policy toward North Korea. From China's perspective, until the American foreign policy makers acknowledge that the nuclear issue is not the only issue that needs to be resolved and accepts an engagement approach with the DPRK, China will not be able to play a greater role in mediating the tension and leading to a resolution.

On the other hand, critics have pointed out that China is unwilling to get tough, to exert coercive pressures on North Korea in order to compel its compliance. While China made efforts to keep the Six-Party Talks from collapsing, talking for talking's sake only gives Pyongyang more time to develop its nuclear arsenal.[44] It is true that from 2003 to 2005 China adopted limited coercive measures on a couple of occasions. China briefly shut down the only remaining oil pipeline between China and North Korea in February 2003, which is generally viewed as a form of pressure bringing Pyongyang to the original trilateral meeting in late April 2003 (China denied such intention). But in general, China has avoided exercising its influence on North Korea in an overtly coercive manner. For a long time the international community, including the United States, has regarded China as having greater influence on North Korea than any other country, simply because China maintains political and economic relations with North Korea on many fronts. China's trade, investment, and aid have been viewed as the most visible leverage and seemingly the most tangible form of influence over Pyongyang to end the security crisis in Northeast Asia. It is believed that if China were to join in economic sanctions against North Korea, the country would face a serious economic crisis. However, "China is unwilling to use wholly the lever that it is believed to have toward North Korea."[45]

Another criticism is that although it is performing as a mediator, China has not taken a neutral position between the errant North Korea and the world's sole superpower, the United States. China's public stance has been supportive of Pyongyang and critical of Washington. China has not supported the U.S. goal of CVID and instead openly pressed the United States to care for "the legitimate security concern of the DPRK,"[46] and strongly supported North Korea's demands that the United States should guarantee the survival of the Kim Jong-il regime.[47] In order to understand how China perceives its own influence in the first place and the way China has chosen to exercise it, as well as China's different approaches from the United States, we need to closely examine China's policy goals toward North Korea.

POLICY GOALS

China seems to have several foreign policy priorities. The first is the threat to China's domestic economic development and stability. In the past quarter century the Chinese government has gained domestic legitimacy and international confidence through sustained rapid economic growth. The fourth-generation leadership has officially proclaimed the maintenance of a "well-off society" (*xiaokang shehui*) and a "harmonized society" (*hexie shehui*) as the single greatest challenge in the years ahead. The primary concern regarding the North Korean situation is over the immediate impact of the political change and the prospect of economic collapse in North Korea on China's own domestic development. The three provinces that border North Korea—Jilin, Liaoning, and Heilongjiang—have been suffering from very high rates of unemployment, stagnating traditional heavy industries, and low economic growth. The refugees streaming from North Korea in a time of regime collapse would exaggerate the economic difficulties in northern China.

Second, North Korea's nuclear program threatens regional stability in Northeast Asia. Not only does China want to prevent DPRK's nuclear blackmail, but it also wants to avoid providing a justification for other regional states, such as Japan, South Korea, and Taiwan, to start a nuclear arms race, since China is already surrounded by three nuclear powers: Russia, India, and Pakistan. China sees the North Korean nuclear program as a serious destabilizing factor, wrecking the regional security balance in Northeast Asia and complicating China's security environment. The worst scenario for China is that North Korea's nuclear program might trigger a military conflict on the Korean Peninsula that may in turn bring the American military presence to the region, a threat to China's security interests. Therefore, China has highlighted its commitment to a nuclear-free Korean Peninsula.

China has made great efforts to create a favorable international environment that promotes domestic development. Such a conflict at the doorstep would have profound economic consequences and curb economic growth by interrupting international trade and financial investment. Since China has resolved or cooled down the border disputes with Central and Southeast Asian countries (although there are still frictions between China and Japan), it seems that North Korea stands out as a dangerous and, most important, an imminent regional threat to China's economic and security interests.[48]

Third, a China-friendly Korean Peninsula serves China's core interests. The two-Korea status quo policy is popular with the Chinese, as long as China is able to maintain both Pyongyang and Seoul within its circle of influence.[49] Although China officially supports Korean unification through a gradual approach, China does not want to see a unified Korea emerge under U.S. domination. A long-term view might be that the North Korean nuclear issue offers an opportunity of fundamentally addressing this country's structural problems and reoccurring crises. A solution to the current nuclear stalemate will be expected to involve a comprehensive arrangement, a great bargain plan, which is able to impact upon other sectors of North Korea.[50] In other words, the nuclear crisis offers a chance for China to increase its influence over North Korea and adjusts its traditional relations with and approach to the North.

The last, but not least, consideration is China's relationship with the United States, which remains the single superpower in the world. The Sino-U.S. relationship is one of the decisive factors influencing China's foreign and security policy.[51] China and the United States have disagreements over several issues: bilateral trade, currency revaluation, intellectual property, human rights, and Taiwan. The North Korean nuclear crisis has become a primary focal point for the Sino-U.S. relationship in the field of international security. It is instructive that the Special Office on the North Korean Nuclear Issue of the Ministry of Foreign Affairs, which is in charge of the Six-Party Talks, is entirely staffed with Chinese officials who are experts on America instead of on Korea,[52] and that the newly appointed Chinese ambassador to Pyongyang, Liu Xiaoming, is also an American expert.

On the one side, China's proactive role in the Six-Party Talks and its perceived influence on North Korea is one of the few checks on American anti-China sentiment and provides impetus for a closer Sino-U.S. strategic relationship. The ongoing process of the Six-Party Talks itself is evidence of strengthened cooperation between the United States and China. The crisis has created an opportunity to expand the basis for Chinese-U.S. security cooperation, which has loomed large after 9/11, and allowed the two countries to make efforts to achieve strategic cooperation. For this reason, Secretary of State Powell claimed in 2004 that the U.S.-PRC relationship was the "best ever."[53]

On the other side, the North Korean nuclear crisis may further complicate the Sino-U.S. relationship. It has been rather difficult to coordinate the two countries' stances on North Korea. As China prioritizes the stability of Korean Peninsula and the United States presses for denuclearization, North Korea itself could become a wedge issue further dividing the two countries. Fundamentally different from the Bush administration's unilateralist, preventative-war strategy and determination of shaping the world by force, or threat of force, China has adopted a multilateral approach to build cooperative institutions among different states in order to achieve solutions to a common security problem. The United States has pursued "counter-proliferation": a coercive-diplomacy strategy designed to use international pressure to force such countries as Iran and North Korea to give up their potential nuclear weapons capacity, while China rejects this approach in favor of a more conventional "arms control" or "nonproliferation" approach.[54] Meanwhile, the North Korea crisis may give Beijing leverage in Washington on the peaceful resolution of the Taiwan issue, which has been China's enduring core national interest as well as the most sensitive factor in Chinese-U.S. relations. China would have to consider the Korean situation from a geopolitical perspective if the United States was to strengthen military relations with Taiwan.

Before North Koreans conducted the nuclear test, there had been a debate about China's "top priority" of policy toward North Korea. A Chinese scholar, Shi Yinhong, argued that the worst scenarios for China were North Korean nuclear blackmail directed at China, Japan going nuclear, and a U.S.-DPRK war.[55] Many Western observers have also drawn the conclusion that China's top priority is to prevent North Korea from going nuclear. A different analysis has insisted that China's greatest priority has been peace and stability on the Korean Peninsula, because China views the threat from North Korea more as a potential failed state and humanitarian disaster than a rogue state with solid nuclear capability.[56] According to this line of reasoning, while a nuclear-free Korean Peninsula is important, the survival of the North Korean regime and reform of North Korea are China's greatest challenge and prime objective. From China's perspective, the North Korean nuclear issue is more than nuclear proliferation, and it involves many complex issues: national security, geopolitical interests, relations with United States, and potentially the leadership in Northeast Asia. China is trying to gradually normalize the North Korean economy, with the long-term goal of a reformed, China-friendly North Korea.

As a matter of fact, these priorities can never be separated from one another, nor pursued independently. It is unlikely that China will tolerate an unfriendly new regime with American or South Korean military presence along its border as one of the outcomes of denuclearizing the Korean Peninsula. Similarly, the long-running nuclear crisis will undoubtedly deepen the isolation of this regime, reduce the chance of it attracting more economic support, and increase the possibility of its collapse, which will then grow into greater threats to regional security and stability.

THE THIRD CRISIS: CHINA'S RESPONSE

North Korea ended its missile test moratorium in July 2006 and then tested a nuclear device in October 2006, which has not only removed any previous doubt that North Korea was capable of producing nuclear devices but also led the diplomatic endeavor to resolve the crisis to a new phase. The missile launches were made in the midst of a new, concerted effort by Beijing (started in May 2006) to get the Six-Party Talks, which had stalled since November of the previous year, back on track, and seek common ground among the parties. As part of this effort, the Chinese arranged meetings with the foreign ministers of Japan, the ROK, and Russia, as well as the U.S. assistant secretary of state. The key decision makers in Beijing—Foreign Minister Li Zhaoxing, State Councillor Tang Jiaxuan, and Premier Wen Jiabao—all received the DPRK foreign minister Paek Nam-sun in Beijing in late May and early June. On June 1, 2006, President Hu Jintao personally called President Bush to urge the United States to accept North Korea's invitation of Assistant Secretary Hill to Pyongyang to resume the fifth round of the talks. China was eager to show the world that it was a responsible power, and the missile and nuclear tests seemed to have brought all of the efforts to naught. Pyongyang's tests have been described as a "deliberate slap in China's face" because China had publicly warned North Korea not to conduct any nuclear tests.[57] The DPRK's actions have also directly impinged on Chinese security interests by bringing all the speculations into reality—a possible nuclear blackmail from Pyongyang and the military augmentation of countries such as Japan and South Korea.

The statement of the Chinese government responding to the test was prompt and harshly worded: the test has a "negative impact" (*fumiande yinxiang*) on relations across the Yalu River and was "stubbornly defiant" (*hanran*), a term which has only ever been used in a few extreme cases, such as the Japanese prime minister's visit to the Yasukumi Shrine and the U.S. bombing of the Chinese embassy in Belgrade.[58] The test also forced China to adjust its diplomacy in the United Nations. Instead of protecting North Korea from sanctions in the international community, China chose to distance itself from North Korea's violation of international norms. Whereas during the first and second crises China objected to economic sanctions against the DPRK, this time China voted on two UN Security Council resolutions (1695 and 1718).[59] On October 5, 2006, as the DPRK announced its nuclear test, Chinese Ambassador to the UN, Wang Guangya, told reporters, "on this issue, everybody is unanimous. . . . No one is going to protect them."[60]

In addition to working with the UN, China adopted a severe measure of cutting off the crude oil export to North Korea for the whole month of September 2006 when Pyongyang showed signs of preparing for its first nuclear test.[61] Inspections on the cargos from North Korea were carried out at the Chinese border. The Chinese government gave instructions to Chinese banks to stop financial transactions with North Korea, which meant cutting Pyongyang's vital supply of hard currency and restraining North Korea's ability to conduct foreign trade.[62] China stopped investment in North Korea over the three months following the test and closed three customs offices in northeastern China that handled trade with North Korea.[63] The Chinese government also issued an order to halt a tourist train service as well as suspend regular flight service to Pyongyang.[64]

On the military front, additional troops were sent to the PRC-DPRK border in mid-July 2006. This was officially reported as part of a "routine military exercise" to reinforce the border and carry out missile drills in the Changbai mountains.[65] Nevertheless, this movement has been interpreted as intensifying preparation for and enhancing China's ability to react to a contingency involving North Korea.[66]

When both Western and Chinese analysts saw the disappointment, embarrassment, and anger in China's new actions following the nuclear test, they predicted that "a once unthinkable harder line" has become more likely because China was "running out of choices," which might include halting the supply of oil and food to the DPRK and therefore bring China's policy closer to the United States.[67] However, China's policy has not followed this logic, and largely showed a rather restrained position. China has never believed that its sanctions will force Kim Jong-il to simply kowtow to China and stop working on the second nuclear test. Chinese officials "were clear that Beijing did not and will not stop fuel and food donations, because North Korea will only 'grow stronger' if pressured," not to mention the negative effects on the starving population in the DPRK.[68] From China's own experience of being sanctioned and of exerting pressures on Pyongyang, sanction would only push the regime to find another way out. "The more sanctions against North Korea, the more hostile North Korea would be toward China."[69] Moreover, comprehensive economic sanctions would either cut off the connections between Beijing and Pyongyang and cause China to completely lose its long-term influence on the DPRK, or induce a regime collapse. From this perspective, a hard-line and confrontational policy would very likely cost China's crucial geopolitical interests without solving the problem at all. As Liu Jianchao, the state spokesman, said, "we will com-ply with the Security Council resolution, but China's aim is not for sanctions."[70] China's aim was to get North Korea to back away from the nuclear brink and rejoin the talks. China had to swallow its anger and continue to play its role of mediator in a new scenario.

Therefore, after a period of isolation imposed by withholding economic as-sistance to and freezing financial transactions with the DPRK, China sought to re-establish top-level dialogue with Kim Jong-il and to restore its influence with North Korea. China's short-term goal was to lessen the tensions and prevent the crisis from further escalation. Within three weeks of the nuclear test, Chinese special envoy Tang Jiaxuan visited Washington, Moscow, and Pyongyang, and China brought North Korea and the United States back to the negotiation table after more than a year of stalemate. In particular, Tang's meeting with Kim Jong-il discouraged a second nuclear test, which was widely believed to be a possibility at the time.[71] Al-though the Chinese delegation did not receive an apology from Kim for the nuclear test, they did receive assurances that there were no plans for a second nuclear test and that Pyongyang was willing to return to international negotiations on the condition that "certain questions, including the matter of U.S. financial sanctions against it, [be] resolved first."[72] Most important, the Chinese delegation secured a visit to Bei-jing by the North Korean chief nuclear negotiator Kim Gye-gwan.[73] Having faced the comprehensive sanctions imposed by the international community, it seemed to be high time for Pyongyang to go back to negotiation and use its increased bargain-ing weight after gaining the nuclear capability to exchange for economic benefits, political recognition, and security assurance.

In the meantime, China appealed to the involved parties to "maintain cool-headness," not to take any steps that might "worsen tensions" in the region, and to adhere to a diplomatic solution.[74] The fact that the United States (and Japan) did not resort to the extreme measures of military intervention and actually retreated from their previous strong positions left China much room to mediate between the DPRK and the United States. China urged Washington to suspend the financial measures in order to restart the Six-Party Talks. During the last week of October 2006, Vice Foreign Minister Wu Dawei invited Christopher Hill, Kim Gye-gwan's U.S. counterpart, to Beijing. History was repeating as another trilateral meeting was held before the official Six-Party Talks. But this time, the resumption of the Six-Party

Talks was due to a breakthrough in the trilateral negotiations, not its failure. "The three parties had a candid and in-depth exchange of views on continuing efforts to advance the process of the Six Party Talks," reported Xinhua News Agency on October 31, 2006. A few weeks' intensive behind-the-scenes diplomatic efforts by Beijing brought results, and on November 1, 2006, three weeks after the nuclear test, North Korea announced its commitment to return to the Six-Party Talks.

China also explored the occasion of the annual APEC summit in mid-November 2006 to consult individually with the leaders of the four parties (but not the DPRK).[75] Contrary to the immediate anticipations of more severe confrontational policies, the Six-Party Talks reached an agreement on a Denuclearization Action Plan (also called the Beijing Agreement) on February 13, 2007, only four months after North Korea's nuclear test.[76] In the subsequent weeks, a further round of the Six-Party Talks was suspended as North Korea halted its participation until it had received $25 million held by the Macau-based Banco Delta Asia that the United States had promised to unfreeze. Upon the release of the funds in mid-June 2007, DPRK invited IAEA inspectors to visit the Yongbyon nuclear complex for the first time since being expelled from the country in 2002. In July, the shutdown of the Yongbyon reactor was verified by the IAEA inspectors.

Roughly one year after the nuclear test, in October 2007, the sixth round of the Six-Party Talks produced a joint document titled "Implementing the Second-Phase Actions of the Joint Statement," the second "road map" to carry out the Beijing Agreement, in which North Korea committed to disable three main nuclear facilities and declare all its nuclear programs by December 31, 2007. In this round of talks, the DPRK and the United States remained committed to improving their bilateral relations and moving toward a full diplomatic relationship. At this time, the leaders of North and South Korea also moved forward to a Korean Summit to seek talks to formally end the Korean War. As South Korean prime minister Han Duck-soo has commented, "the inter-Korean relations and the process of the Six Party Talks have formed a positive cycle."[77] One year after the nuclear test, with the shutdown of the reactor and a timetable on disabling some North Korean key nuclear facilities and examining its full nuclear capabilities, a weak but important and positive basis for mutual trust seemed to have been established. China will also continue to highlight the importance of the Six-Party Talks, which will serve as a means for closing gaps in the respective positions of participants and building common grounds on the issues related to the DPRK's denuclearization.

A POLICY CHANGE?

There are different views on the extent that the nuclear test has changed China's policy. One view is that the missile and nuclear tests have not fundamentally changed the relationship between Beijing and Pyongyang because the bottom line of China's policy toward North Korea is still regime survival. The policy goals discussed in this chapter, especially those regarding regime survival and economic stability, remain unchanged. For example, after Pyongyang agreed to return to the Six-Party Talks, China firmly stated that Beijing was not going to cut off oil or food aid to the DPRK. Nevertheless, the nuclear test and the February Agreement did have significant influences on China's policy development. First of all, the clarification effects of the test have not been limited to the fact of Pyongyang's nuclear ability. For a long time other countries' concerns about Pyongyang's nuclear ability, which China had seriously doubted, offered China the chance of maintaining the outside perception of its capability of keeping the DPRK under control. The nuclear test has made obvious China's limited influence on North Korea's behavior and weakened the expectation from other countries that China might be able to prevent North Korea from going nuclear.

Second, if before the nuclear tests China had perceived the crisis as largely an issue between the United States and North Korea, after the crisis China started to regard the nuclear issue as its own problem as well.[78] From imposing the coercive measures to rapidly reviving the Six-Party Talks, it seems that China no longer merely wanted North Korea to attend the talks, but was willing and trying to put an end to its nuclear program.

Third, there has been a subtle change in China's overall stance and its policy priority toward the crisis. Since 2002, China's official stance toward the DPRK nuclear program has been: (1) peace and stability in the Korean Peninsula; (2) resolving the crisis through diplomatic and political means; and (3) denuclearization of the Korean Peninsula.[79] If China had downplayed the aim of denuclearization under the previously ambiguous circumstances and stressed the priority of stability and regime survival, a nuclear North Korea forced China to adjust the sequence of its policy aims and to pursue the goal of denuclearization, because the nuclear presence has become the primary threat of instability and peace in Northeast Asia. Immediately after the nuclear tests, therefore, Foreign Ministry Spokesman Liu Jianchao said, the "number-one priority" is "denuclearizing the Korean Peninsula."[80]

Chinese officials claim that China has always had a genuine interest in preserving the global nonproliferation regime and is willing to make more efforts on North Korean nuclear disarmament.[81] It was reported that before the nuclear tests China had intercepted a shipment of chemicals that could have been used in the separation process of weapons-grade plutonium.[82] Some critics maintain that for China, nuclear proliferation is a general concern but has never been a top priority. Whether before the nuclear tests or after, what matters is not whether the nuclear issue is the number-one priority, but the fact that the nuclear tests have severely increased China's stakes on the issue, and therefore failure to resolve the North Korean nuclear issue raises it to a higher priority.

The *Cheonan* incident in 2010 was a serious test for China's North Korea policy. The South Korean government fully expected that China, confronted with the evidence of the international investigation, which concluded that the *Cheonan* was sunk by a North Korean torpedo, would acknowledge the outcome and join in the condemnation of the DPRK. President Obama likewise dropped clear hints that the United States expected China to come out against North Korea, which it conspicuously failed to do.

The South Koreans did little to hide their monumental anger against the Chinese, and the joint naval exercises conducted in response to the incident also sent a signal to China, although the United States and the ROK relented from their original plan to hold the exercises in the Yellow Sea. China held steadfast to its policy because it perceived Seoul's reaction to the *Cheonan* incident as a precursor to an excessive reaction that could result in a dangerous rise in tension. For Beijing, the *Cheonan* controversy was an embarrassment that it wanted to overcome as quickly as possible. Providing diplomatic cover for Pyongyang came with a price—Kim had to agree to return to the Six-Party Talks after all.

From China's perspective, the key to the resolution of this issue is not held by China, but by the United States and the DPRK, and is about building trust. The tense nature of the North Korea nuclear crisis was rooted in the fact that both the United States and the DPRK lost basic trust in each other, each believing the other was untrustworthy and capricious in their words. Any U.S. policy perceived as unfriendly by North Korea has always been followed by DPRK's retaliation in a pattern of mutual provocation. Therefore, it has been difficult to reach a consensus, and even harder to implement it, let alone to implement it thoroughly. Without the support of basic trust, all agreements and policies are nothing more than empty words.[83]

UNDERSTANDING CHINA'S KOREA STRATEGY

This chapter has reviewed China's role in the process of resolving the North Korean nuclear crisis. In its efforts to become a "responsible great power," China has taken on the great challenge to defuse tensions and to transition to peaceful dialogues. The Six-Party Talks have been the primary diplomatic forum to resolve the North Korean nuclear crisis, and China has been a dominant force in creating and sustaining this process. The process of the Six-Party Talks itself has been a credit to Chinese diplomacy. For China, the North Korean nuclear crisis has never been just an issue of nuclear proliferation and it cannot be solved by only pursuing one goal. Instead its solution will have to be a comprehensive one. From China's perspective, nuclear proliferation is only one part of the overall set of policies, and China's goal is to focus on supporting the ongoing reform process in North Korea and eventually integrating it into the region and reducing its xenophobic threat perceptions. China will not consider the extremity of a complete set of economic sanctions (which most Western observers believe would constitute the real influence of China on North Korea), because such sanctions would greatly increase the likelihood of political collapse, civil war, and a renewal of international hostility on the Korean Peninsula. This also explains why China has refused to publicly support the idea of using coercive measures such as shutting down the oil pipeline, which would have pleased the United States. China traded no oil with North Korea in September 2006, according to Chinese trade data, but China officially denied that it had imposed a temporary oil sanction on North Korea.[84] China does not want to use these measures in the first place and if it has to, it uses them quietly and does not want to capture the American attention, which may lead to anticipation that China will use them in the future. In the meantime, these measures were all used suddenly at sensitive timings so as to send clear signals to Kim Jong-il: we can but we really don't want to, so you had better not force us to. Therefore, China prefers economic incentives or small steps of coercion to bring North Korea to the talking process. Although there have been some policy adjustments in response to the North Korean nuclear tests, including using more coercive measures, China has kept the measure of sanctions at a minimal level and stressed dialogue and negotiation in which it plays an active role. In the meantime, although China still maintains multiple goals toward this issue, denuclearization has attracted China's greater attention than before.

The years of 2003 and 2006 were critical in China's policy development toward the North Korean nuclear crisis, when China underwent clear adjustment in its policies. Twice, China actively responded to the urgent situation with a short-term goal of preventing the escalation of the crisis and paving the way for a long-term goal of peace, denuclearization, and economic development. During the entire process, China has consistently kept a style of quiet diplomacy and of behind-the-scene actions, only giving low-key public accounts in the aftermath of events, which is the exact opposite of the diplomatic style of the United States and the DPRK, who attract public attention by making announcements, denouncements, nuclear tests, and sanctions, and both are tough and unyielding, keen to show "strength" and "having face." China has fulfilled its role as mediator to providing "face" to both sides by quietly and repeatedly giving hints to each side to save face for the other so as to create an atmosphere for a diplomatic solution.

Despite concerns over the DPRK's nuclear ability, compared with 2002–2003 when China first got involved in this issue, the Chinese government should be feeling relieved on several accounts. The United States has effectively eliminated the option of the use of force toward North Korea, Japan has assured China of its intention not to develop its own nuclear ability, and the United States has not only entrusted the key role in resolving this issue to China, but also started to regard China as an essential diplomatic partner and a "responsible stakeholder."[85] It is in China's interest to see North Korea's denuclearization in exchange for normalization of relations with the United States, economic benefits, and the peace and stability on the Korean Peninsula as outlined in the Joint Statement of Principles of the Six-Party Talks on September 19, 2005. It would be a true breakthrough and success of the Six-Party Talks if North Korea would become the first state to have tested a nuclear device and subsequently reversed its program, and China could take considerable credit for such an achievement. Therefore, China will continue to highlight the importance of the framework of the Six-Party Talks and of working together with the United States.

However, China is alert about North Korea's maneuvers and attempts to reduce its dependence on China and even to play one big power against another.[86] From the beginning of the second nuclear crisis, North Korea has asked for direct dialogue with the United States, and following the February Agreement the United States and North Korea have developed a direct line of serious communication, in which North Korea appears to assert itself as an independent player.[87] North Korea originally even opposed China's participation in the Korean Peninsula Peace Summit, which aims at declaring the end of the Korean War.[88] Some North Korean officials have recently suggested that the United States can serve as a counterweight to the growing influence of China in East Asia and North Korea, and that the United States should cooperate with the DPRK to prevent Chinese hegemony in the region. China watches these matters with vigilant attention, as they may undermine China's role in resolving the crisis and any future incidents in the peninsula.

Currently, a prominent challenge for China is the intention of the DPRK and the ultimate goal of its nuclear program. According to China, the DPRK's motivation behind the nuclear program is to pressure the United States to continue negotiations on a nonaggression agreement and political recognition, and as a means to bargain for economic support and regime survival. In the meantime, there is good reason to doubt that North Korea will ever give up nuclear weapons completely. China understands that once the nuclear ability is achieved, it is not easy to relinquish. This is why China was alarmed about statements from the North in 2009, that the DPRK will not return to the Six-Party Talks and will not give up nuclear weapons. China supported unusually harsh sanctions in response to the long-range missile launch and the second nuclear test. The end of Six-Party Talks would constitute a serious setback for Chinese diplomacy, because it would most likely diminish China's role in the diplomatic negotiations with the DPRK and curtail China's influence over the evolving situation on the Korean Peninsula, in its backyard.

8

Conclusion

The Continuing Crisis on the Korean Peninsula

There seems to be no end to the crisis on the Korean Peninsula. As the Obama administration took office, signaling its desire to engage with Iran and North Korea, all the diplomatic achievements of the previous fifteen years seemed to have come to naught.

How can we explain the fact that even though the United States at various times seemed prepared to give North Korea much of what it demanded, Pyongyang never held on to the gains it made? Indeed, North Korean foreign policy behavior has seemed confusing and Pyongyang's intentions have been subject to controversy and different interpretations. But contrary to the impression made by the situation they find themselves in, there is a clear logic in the policies they pursue. During the Cold War period, the confrontation on the Korean Peninsula was embedded in the East-West confrontation. Both Koreas were kept secure and at the same time restrained by their respective superpower allies. For North Korea the geopolitical situation was somewhat more complex than for the South, because Kim Il-sung did not accept Soviet dominance such as was exercised in parts of Eastern Europe. Consequently he pursued a policy of equidistance between China and the Soviet Union. At the same time he gradually built up North Korea's military capabilities with a view to achieving unification under his leadership when the time would be ripe. Since the end of the Cold War and the loss of economic support and reliable security guarantees from its erstwhile sponsors, the top priority for North Korea has been regime survival. The Kim regime feels threatened by the changed geopolitical environment and in particular what it calls the hostile policy of the United States, as well as its severe economic difficulties.

The U.S. concern with North Korea's nuclear program provided Pyongyang with the opportunity to engage the United States. This engagement came to be perceived in Pyongyang as the key for addressing the external security concerns and the economic predicament of the DPRK. Essentially North Korea wanted the United States to accept the legitimacy of the regime, normalize diplomatic relations, take concrete steps to end the military threat to North Korea (for instance, sign a nonaggression pact), and remove economic sanctions.

It is important to not only understand the motivations that drive North Korean foreign policy, but also the tactics. Just as the United States uses coercive measures (such as unilateral and multilateral sanctions and UN Security Council resolutions) as well as incentives (the provision of fuel, the lifting of sanctions, diplomatic visits), North Korea uses its own form of pressure tactics (developing and demonstrating military capabilities, refusing to attend talks, issuing verbal threats, abandoning previous agreements) alongside cooperative gestures (permitting inspections, implementing parts of previous agreements, attending talks, entering into new agreements). The principle is "action for action." There are two reasons for this kind of negotiating behavior. The first is that North Koreans want to negotiate each element of a package deal separately in order to extract the maximum concession at each stage. The second is that the nuclear and missiles programs are the only cards that North Korea has. The Bush concept of CVID is not workable from the North Korean point of view because once they give up this card they have no further bargaining leverage. Consequently North Korean concessions have amounted to very partial resolutions of the nuclear issue. Although prior to its first nuclear test North Korea at various times reaffirmed that it was prepared to denuclearize the Korean Peninsula, the best that has ever been on offer is a freezing and the termination of the production of plutonium.

North Korea experts generally emphasize the rationality and the effectiveness of North Korea's foreign policy and diplomacy.[1] It is true that North Korea, a very weak state, has managed to gain significant concessions from very powerful countries. The fact that the United States has decided not to use force against North Korea is an important achievement for North Korea's asymmetric strategy of deterrence. However, the overall results of fifteen years of diplomacy are mixed. Although Pyongyang has received enough external support to muddle through and even somewhat improve its economic situation, it has not achieved its major objectives. Despite all of the investment into the construction of two light water reactors, by the beginning of the Obama presidency North Korea was further away than ever from having LWRs. By mid-2009 all of the previous diplomatic gains had been lost, and North Korea was under the most severe sanctions since negotiations over its nuclear program began. As a result of the *Cheonan* incident in March 2010, the South Korean government cut off all political and almost all economic links with the North. Its relations with Japan, the Republic of Korea, and even China had reached their lowest point ever.

The flaw in North Korea's diplomacy is that its policymakers incorrectly assess what drives U.S. policy and therefore the manner in which they employ the instruments available to them is to some extent ineffective: they project their own worldview onto others and do not anticipate the reaction of the United States correctly. For example, North Korea could have tried to save the Agreed Framework by portraying the United States as being in breach of the agreement for ceasing to supply heavy fuel oil, given that the evidence in relation to the HEU program was very circumstantial at best. The North Koreans seemingly believed that by restarting the Yongbyon reactor and reprocessing the fuel rods they increased their bargaining power. Instead the DPRK proved the opponents of the Agreed Framework in the U.S. government correct and freed the United States from its obligation to provide LWRs. Six years later Pyongyang may have nuclear devices, but it is further away from other benefits that were previously within its grasp. The regime's constant refrain is that its main aim is to change the hostile policy of the United States toward it. But many of its actions do not promote this aim—quite to the contrary, they strengthen the hand of those in the United States who believe North Korea can never be trusted and that any negotiations or agreements with the DPRK are a waste of time.

The concepts of national autonomy and sovereignty play a key role in North Korean diplomacy. The application of international law, external inspections, or the verification of agreements are seen as being in fundamental contradiction to these principles. The launch of a Taepodong-2 rocket on April 5, 2009, to put a satellite into orbit, is a good example. It was clearly designed to demonstrate North Korea's missile capabilities and defiance of UN Security Council Resolution 1718: that North Korea was standing up for its sovereign rights and was not cowed by international reaction.[2] It is clear from the history of U.S.-DPRK negotiations that North Korean diplomats are often under pressure to prove that they are standing up to the demands of the United States. This can mean that they become too inflexible and lose sight of the larger objectives, thus failing to obtain the results that they are seeking.

In retrospect it seems clear that the decision to produce a nuclear device and conduct a nuclear test was taken in 2003 after the eleventh round of the Supreme People's Assembly in September. A decisive factor was the Iraq war, which seemed to demonstrate the need for a capacity to deter a U.S. attack.[3] The belief of the North Korean elite that the nuclear program enhances the status of the DPRK, provides deterrence against external aggression, and facilitates a security dialogue with the United States that enables North Korea to also obtain much-needed economic support is deeply engrained. North Korea has been willing to freeze and limit its nuclear program, but the leaders in Pyongyang have not yet reached the point of being ready to finally give it up, and it is difficult to conceive any circumstances under which this might happen. Even if the various demands were met and the United States established diplomatic relations with DPRK, signed a nonaggression pact, and followed through with other promises about "changing its hostile policy," this would not be enough to permanently guarantee North Korea's security.

On the other hand, the external threat to North Korea is primarily created by the nuclear program in the first place. There is a curious paradox that underlies North Korean foreign policy, which is that it's fundamentally predicated on making North Korea appear dangerous to the international community. This motivates the United States and other countries to engage with North Korea in order to mitigate the threat, but in order for the engagement to be sustained the threat has to be periodically revived, which creates the seemingly inescapable cycle of conflict and cooperation. It also accounts for North Korea's diplomacy, which to outsiders sometimes appears erratic and even irrational.

UNDERSTANDING U.S. POLICY TOWARD THE KOREAN PENINSULA

U.S. policy toward North Korea has been driven by the nuclear program since the early nineties, but it has been difficult to achieve consensus on how to deal with the problem. The conflict over what U.S. policy should be is associated with different interpretations of the nature of the problem. To conservatives, North Korea is a "rogue," totalitarian regime that brutalizes its own population; to them, its propensity for external aggression is a result of its "nature" in common with other totalitarian regimes. According to this viewpoint, the international community should use all coercive means at its disposal, from isolation to sanctions and military action, to contain and deal with the threat that North Korea poses.[4] President Bush included North Korea in the "axis of evil" of states that pose a threat to the international community by their support for terrorism and the development of WMD.

The term "evil," of course, is just a label that says nothing about how the national interests of North Korea are constituted or what the objectives of its national policies are. In fact, a blanket term like that discourages further analysis. Apart from the fact that this particular approach substitutes name-calling for a real effort to understand North Korea, it does not provide a coherent basis for policy. In fact it is precisely this way of thinking that precipitated the end of the Agreed Framework and resulted in North Korea completing the development of nuclear weapons. Moreover, this approach embodies significant risks, given the support for military actions against North Korea and the advocacy of total economic sanctions in order to bring about regime change. Although there is little chance that these objectives will be achievable, given the refusal of China to cut off support for North Korea, consequences would be catastrophic.

The liberal perspective on North Korea is grounded in a realist approach to international relations and interprets North Korean foreign policy behavior as a rational response to the geopolitical situation in which the DPRK finds itself in the aftermath of the Cold War. North Korea perceives the United States as constituting a real and present threat to its national security, threatening preemptive strikes and refusing to recognize the legitimacy of the North Korean state. Looking at North Korean actions in more detail, it is possible to explain many of them as countermoves to American political pressure and military threats. The corollary of this opinion is that if the external threat is mitigated, North Korea's behavior will change. The more extreme version of this perspective, which is espoused by policymakers in China and many on the left in South Korea, sees the United States as the real source of instability in the region.[5]

Those officials and politicians in the United States who became directly involved in negotiations with North Korea were not necessarily located in one or the other camp. Unlike those in the Bush administration, the Clinton officials never attempted to provide an explanation for North Korea's behavior. It came down to the pragmatic issue of how the nuclear program could be stopped. Once the military option was ruled out, diplomacy backed up by sanctions was the only course of action. Ironically the Bush administration adopted a similarly pragmatic approach in its second term, despite the ideological predispositions of the president who included North Korea in the "axis of evil."

There is no doubt that the deep divisions in Washington about the nature of the problem and the appropriate means to deal with it seriously hampered U.S. diplomatic efforts. The unwillingness of Congress to support the Clinton administration meant that there could be no treaty with the DPRK, only a so-called Agreed Framework. Moreover, Congress could not be relied upon to provide any funds, so the financial burden of implementing the Agreed Framework had to be assumed mostly by the South Koreans and the Japanese. The funds for heavy fuel oil promised by the United States had to be taken from discretionary funding, which caused supplies to be behind schedule and meant the United States was seen as an unreliable partner.[6]

The more fundamental issue is that the basic principles of whatever agreement is arrived at with the DPRK simply cannot be fully implemented. During fifteen years of negotiation neither side has come to the point where they were really willing to hold up their end of the bargain. Moreover, just as North Korea will never fully relinquish its nuclear card, the United States will never fully accept the legitimacy of the Kim regime, and American policymakers are deluding themselves if they think otherwise. Consequently the manner in which the objectives of negotiations with North Korea have been framed defines ideals, rather than achievable goals. The two sides will have to settle for something in between.

DEALING WITH NORTH KOREA: WHAT IS TO BE DONE?

Much of the discourse in relation to North Korea has emphasized the threat that North Korea represents to the international community. Consequently the main focus of diplomatic engagement has been on the nuclear program. While this was inevitable, given that North Korea sought to leverage its military capabilities in order for the international community and especially the United States to engage with it, this has prevented the emergence of a holistic approach to the crisis on the Korean Peninsula. Thus all of the diplomatic resources of the United States have been devoted to stopping North Korea from acquiring a nuclear weapon. Now that this has failed, the objective is to put the genie back in the bottle and persuade Pyongyang to eliminate its nuclear capabilities. However, there is little chance that this can be achieved. The United States has both tried to compel and persuade North Korea to give up its nuclear program. The results have been mixed. The temporary freezing of the nuclear program under the Agreed Framework did stop the production of plutonium for a time and could be seen as the vindication of patient step-by-step negotiation based on a judicious mix of pressure and incentives ("sticks and carrots"). How long the Agreed Framework could have lasted if the Bush administration had taken a different approach is a matter for speculation. The agreement reached at the Six-Party Talks has seemingly been abandoned without provocation. North Korea has defected from almost every treaty or framework it has ever been party to. This includes all of agreements between North and South as well as the NPT, the Joint Declaration on Denuclearization, agreements between the DPRK and Japan, and even many commercial agreements where goods were received but not paid for. The institutionalist concept does not work in the case of North Korea because the North Korean leaders never adopt and internalize the principles and values underlying any institution that the DPRK becomes a member of. Small violations in any agreement are used as an excuse to defect as soon as the North Koreans believe that the agreement no longer suits their purposes or that a better deal could be had. Attempts to link various dimensions of relations with North Korea have also proven unsuccessful, as the leaders in Pyongyang will honor those provisions that are important to them and ignore others that are too insignificant or intangible to bring about a collapse of the agreement as a whole.

How to we explain this kind of behavior? There are two different aspects to this. The first is that the North Koreans only respect power, and have absolutely no respect for norms or values. Moreover, they believe that others act in precisely the same way that they do. From this perspective, international law and institutions have no merit in and of themselves, but are merely used as instruments of power to achieve certain objectives. This is why the notion that North Korea should permit intrusive IAEA inspections merely because they acceded to the NPT is incomprehensible to North Korean leaders: they see the IAEA as an instrument of U.S. policy, nothing more. Efforts to negotiate and enforce agreements once they have been reached are just part of a continuous power play, in which North Korea seeks to extract the maximum advantage at every turn.

The second aspect is that the confrontation over the nuclear program is merely a symptom of a problem for the North Korean state that is fundamentally unsolvable.

The general concept of negotiations over the nuclear program was that the international community would underwrite North Korea economically and normalize relations in return for the abandonment of WMD. However, these efforts were based on faulty premises. The North Korean regime will continue to remain unacceptable to the United States and most of the international community. No matter what agreements are signed, the outside world will seek gradual regime change. On the other hand, the North Korean state is not viable politically, socially, or economically. Its rulers reject internal reform, refuse to open the country up to the world, and conduct its foreign policy on the basis of threats. Its projection of the external threat is a major element of its internal legitimation. This leaves the North Korean leadership with the dilemma that it needs to improve its relations with the outside world and especially the United States in order to mitigate the external threat and obtain the economic support it needs, while at the same time any such improvement undermines the regime and questions its very existence. Thus, as we have seen, an unending cycle of confrontation and accommodation is inevitable while this regime endures.

Efforts to compel North Korea to eliminate its nuclear devices and materials or its ballistic missiles are doomed to failure. Sanctions have a limited effect as long as China provides enough food and oil to maintain a basic lifeline for the regime. Diplomatic pressure and UN Security Council resolutions produce a reaction of defiance. The use of force is so risky that no U.S. president can contemplate it.[7]

Another possible strategy would be to simply ignore North Korea and not to engage with it at all. This form of containment might look attractive, but there are significant dangers associated with it. First of all there would no longer be any constraints on the nuclear program and the development of ballistic missiles. If North Korea restores the facilities at Yongbyon and completes the construction of the 50 MWe and the 200 MWe reactors, it will be able to produce significant stockpiles of plutonium. Moreover, it is likely that in due course it will develop a ballistic missile of true intercontinental range, capable of reaching the continental United States. From Washington's point of view, this would represent an unacceptable risk and shift in the balance of power, which would constrain U.S. options in dealing with North Korea. For these reasons, a form of engagement, which enables the international community to put some constraints on North Korean nuclear capabilities and reduces military provocations, seems to be the only viable option, however unsatisfactory it might be.

It is important to understand that there is essentially no solution to the North Korean problem. As long as the Kim regime has sufficient resources to maintain itself in power (which means supporting the life of the political and military elite on which it depends), there is no prospect for meaningful political or economic reform because reform is (correctly) perceived to threaten the regime. Any efforts by external actors to get the regime to open up and modernize its economy are resisted. Although North Korea's leaders are acutely aware of the fact that the country needs economic support from abroad in order to survive, they also realize that such support can undermine their power. Humanitarian aid, although it is tolerated (given the difficulties the regime has in providing for the basic needs of its population), is not of much interest to those in power. What they seek is hard currency for their own requirements, international recognition to legitimize their position, and noninterference in their domestic affairs.

A sudden collapse of the North Korean state has potentially catastrophic consequences. Millions of refugees may stream into China or South Korea, many of them heavily armed. There is also the prospect of severe fighting between various military factions in the event of the collapse of central control. It is in the interests of all countries in the region to prevent this from happening. The concept of economic engagement with North Korea is predicated on the notion that even if there are no specific concessions from the regime in response to economic aid, it will create an increasing dependency of the regime on neighboring countries. This dependency is a reality, but the regime has been trying to limit its impact, and it has been almost impossible for either China, Japan, South Korea, or the United States to translate the dependency into tangible political leverage. The Lee Myung-bak government in Seoul proposed a very substantial investment in North Korea, mainly in the development of infrastructure, to double North Korea's GDP and modernize its economy in the hope that this would inevitably produce social and political change. So far this proposal has not gone anywhere due to the conditionalities (such as abandoning the nuclear program) attached. But the grip of the regime is weakening very gradually. Government control in the northern provinces has weakened as the central government no longer has the resources to sustain the public distribution system consistently at a level that meets basic needs. The border has become porous, and North Korean border guards are easily bribed. Many North Koreans, especially in the northern provinces, have access to Chinese cell phones. While there is no political space for the emergence of an opposition or rebellion, the North Korean regime cannot be sustained indefinitely. Change will come sooner or later. The problem is that it is really hard to conceive how there can be a soft landing.

Although there are secret contingency plans in the event that the North Korean state collapses, neither the United States nor the Republic of Korea have a clear vision for the future of the Korean Peninsula. The Republic of Korea is, according to its constitution, the sole legitimate Korea and therefore legally its territory comprises the whole of Korea, so in theory unification is the primary goal of public policy. While as a general sentiment this resonates deeply in the psyche of most Koreans, in practice there is not much appetite for the enormous burdens and sacrifices that unification would entail. The North has become another foreign country that happens to share a common language and ancient history. Likewise, the United States supports the goal of Korean unification in principle but has not done much in practice to help bring it about. There is no agreed plan for an endgame, no preparation for the dramatic change that will come one day (such as creating an international fund that would make it possible to manage the transition).

In the light of these realities, it is important to map out the key objectives in diplomacy with North Korea. The first priority must be to prevent the outbreak of war on the Korean Peninsula. In principle strategic deterrence in Korea is stable. However, the North Korean state is *not* stable and its leaders indulge in military provocations in order to compel changes in U.S. policy or extort economic concessions. Such brinkmanship is associated with a risk of escalation that could get out of control. It is important not to provoke any military action, while at the same time refusing to be intimidated by threats of war.

Another critical policy goal must be to stop the proliferation of nuclear and missile technology by North Korea. PSI and recent UN Security Council resolutions are useful tools, especially since South Korea fully joined PSI in May 2010. But prevention cannot be completely effective, especially as both North Korean consultants and equipment can travel by air to client states such as Pakistan, Syria, and Iran. Financial inducements may be needed, at least in the short term, to reduce the incentives to proliferate, given that for North Korea, ballistic missiles have been its most successful exports.

Finally, although a sudden collapse of the Pyongyang regime is in nobody's interest, it must be a foreign policy goal to weaken the hold of the regime over its people in the long run and promote Korean unification. Focusing economic support for North Korea on the needs of the population rather than the regime (food aid in particular) and finding ways of allowing more information about the outside world to seep into North Korea will be elements of such a strategy.

ENDING THE CRISIS ON THE KOREAN PENINSULA

Presidents Obama and Lee Myung-bak at their summit in Washington in June 2009 emphasized the threat posed by North Korea's nuclear program, and Obama vowed to break the cycle of allowing North Korea to create a crisis to reap further rewards. But it is unclear what means are proposed to deal with North Korea from now on. Not only is there no clear concept of how North Korea's nuclear arsenal is to be eliminated, the focus remains on the nuclear question rather than the regime itself, thus perpetuating the contradictions of previous policies.

It seems that the approach of "engaging North Korea" and the Sunshine Policy is too limited. The United States and the Republic of Korea should consider setting a framework for a controlled regime transition—not a regime change along the lines of the Bush administration, but using the already existing commitments from North and South Korea to begin the path to unification—as the center of policy toward North Korea.

Such an ambitious policy faces numerous obstacles. The first is to achieve international consensus. Without active support by China and Russia it will be difficult to pursue. The Republic of Korea and Japan also need to be convinced that it is worth taking the risks inherent in such an approach. China will need a number of reassurances, such as measures to prevent a massive refugee crisis at its border and an agreement to withdraw U.S. forces from the Korean Peninsula after unification. The prospect of other undesirable consequences, such as higher military tension in the region, may alter China's strategic calculations.

The second obstacle is that the regime in North Korea will resist fiercely. North Korea's leaders must be convinced that there is no way out, and this may not happen for a number of decades, and only if China adopts a different policy toward the North. In other words, we cannot expect much progress toward Korean unification until a post-Kim regime reforms substantially or the gradual decay of the existing power structure reaches a critical level. The third—and this is a bitter pill to swallow—is that personal safety, immunity from prosecution, and a reasonable lifestyle for North Korea's leaders must be guaranteed in some way in order for them to relinquish power.

The transition to a unified Korea will take decades to accomplish. This means that, as envisaged in the 2000 North-South summit agreement, there needs to be a period when there is a confederation. Unlike what was envisaged in the summit agreement, however, the existing regime in North Korea would be replaced by an interim government that would provide for internal security and embark on a program of economic reform. Gradually the North would adopt the laws of the Republic of Korea and develop its economy along free-market lines. Free movement of people would be gradually introduced in order to avoid a refugee crisis.

The first step for the U.S. government on this dangerous and difficult road would be to make Korean unification the central goal of its policy. The second step would be to create an international fund to provide for the enormous costs of unification, which cannot be borne by the Republic of Korea alone. The third step is to convince the international community that this is the only way forward.

It is easy to conclude that this approach is utopian and unrealistic. But if Western countries and their regional partners were to adopt Korean unification as the central goal of all policy toward the Koreas, this would radically change the public discourse and constitute the first step on the road toward a resolution of the crisis on the Korean Peninsula.

Notes

Chapter 1. Conceptualizing the Security Crisis on the Korean Peninsula

1. Andrei Lankov, *From Stalin to Kim Il Sung: The Formation of North Korea 1945-1960*, (London: C. Hurst & Company, 2002).

2. The principle of *juche* is somewhat complex and is actually better described as "socialism Korean style." For more discussion see Ralph C. Hassig and Kongdan Oh, *North Korea Through the Looking Glass* (Washington, DC: Brookings Institution, 2000).

3. Bradley K. Martin, *Under the Loving Care of the Fatherly Leader: North Korea and the Kim Dynasty* (New York: St. Martin's Press, 2004); Samuel S. Kim, *The Two Koreas and the Great Powers* (New York: Cambridge University Press, 2006).

4. Young Whan Kihl, *Transforming Korean Politics* (Armonk, NY: M.E. Sharpe, 2005).

5. Don Oberdorfer, *The Two Koreas* (New York: Basic Books, 2001).

6. Marcus Noland, *Avoiding the Apocalypse: The Future of the Two Koreas* (Washington, DC: Institute for International Economics, 2000).

7. Daniel A. Pinkston, "North Korea's Foreign Policy Towards the United States," *Strategic Insights*, 5, 7 (September 2006).

8. Robert L. Gallucci, Daniel B. Poneman, and Joel S. Wit, *Going Critical: The First North Korean Nuclear Crisis* (Washington, DC: Brookings Institution, 2004); James G. Strohmaier, *Extorting Cooperation: A Case Study of the Negotiation and Implementation of the 1994 U.S.-DPRK Agreed Framework* (PhD diss., University of Kentucky, 2003).

9. Joseph S. Bermudez Jr., *A History of Ballistic Missile Development in the DPRK*, CNS occasional paper 2 (Monterey, CA: MIIS, 1999); East Asia Nonproliferation Program, *CNS Special Report on North Korean Ballistic Missile Capabilities* (Monterey, CA: MIIS, 2006), http://cns.miis.edu/pubs/week/pdf/060321.pdf.

10. International Institute for Strategic Studies, *North Korea's Weapons Programmes* (Basingstoke, U.K., Palgrave, 2004); Michael O'Hanlon and Mike M. Mochizuki, *Crisis on the Korean Peninsula* (Columbus, OH: McGraw-Hill, 2003).

11. Kim Tae-woo, *Living with North Korean Bomb? Current Debates in and Future Options for South Korea*, KIDA Paper 2, June (Seoul: KIDA Press, 2003).

12. International Institute for Strategic Studies, *Nuclear Black Markets: Pakistan, A. Q. Khan and the Rise of Proliferation Networks* (Basingstoke, U.K.: Palgrave, 2007).

13. K. S. Kim, ed., *North Korea's Weapons of Mass Destruction: Problems and Prospects* (Seoul: Hollym Corporation, 2004).

14. H. S. Paik, "What Is the Goal of the U.S. Policy Toward North Korea: Non-Proliferation or Regime Change?" *Nautilus Policy Form Online* (April 7, 2005), www.nautilus.org; Y. B Jung, "The U.S. Response to the North Korea Nuclear Issue," *The Korean Journal of Defense Analysis*, 17, 2 (2005): 63–86.

15. For more analysis and sources see Leon Sigal, *Disarming Strangers* (Princeton, NJ: Princeton University Press, 1998).

16. Selig S. Harrison, *Korean Endgame* (Princeton, NJ: Princeton University Press, 2002).

17. Hazel Smith, *Hungry for Peace: International Security, Humanitarian Assistance, and Social Change in North Korea* (Washington, DC: United States Institute of Peace, 2005).

18. Kenneth Waltz, *Theory of International Politics* (New York: McGraw-Hill, 1979).

19. John J. Mearsheimer, *The Tragedy of Great Power Politics* (New York: W. W. Norton, 2001).

20. E. H. Carr, *The Twenty Years' Crisis: An Introduction to the Study of International Relations* (New York: Palgrave, 2001).

21. Adrian Hyde-Price, "'Normative' Power Europe: A Realist Critique," *Journal of European Public Policy* 13, 2 (March 2006): 217–34.

22. John H. Herz, "Idealist Internationalism and the Security Dilemma," *World Politics* 2, 2 (January 1950): 157–80.

23. Josef Grieco, "Understanding the Problem of International Cooperation: The Limits of Neoliberal Institutionalism and the Future of Realist Theory," in *Neorealism and Neoliberalism*, David A. Baldwin, ed. (New York: Columbia University Press, 1993), 301–39.

24. John Mearsheimer, "The False Promise of International Institutions," in *The Perils of Anarchy: Contemporary Realism and International Security*, Michael Brown, Sean-Lynn Jones, and Steven Miller, eds. (Cambridge, MA: MIT Press, 1995), 332–76.

25. For an analysis of balancing versus buck-passing, see Mearsheimer, *The Tragedy of Great Power Politics*, chapter 8.

26. Samuel S. Kim, "In Search of a Theory of North Korean Policy," in Samuel S. Kim, ed., *North Korean Foreign Relations in the Post-Cold War Era* (Oxford, U.K.: Oxford University Press, 1998), 3–31.

27. Alexander Wendt, *Social Theory of International Politics* (Cambridge, U.K.: Cambridge University Press, 1999), 196.

28. Charles Krauthammer, "The Unipolar Moment," *Foreign Affairs* 70, 1 (1991).

29. Andrew J. Bacevich, *American Empire: The Realities and Consequences of U.S. Diplomacy* (Cambridge, MA: Harvard University Press, 2002).

30. Samuel Huntington, *The Clash of Civilizations and the Remaking of the World Order* (New York: Simon & Schuster, 1996).

31. Francis Fukuyama, *The End of History and the Last Man* (New York: Free Press, 1992).

32. Joseph S. Nye, *The Paradox of American Power: Why the World's Only Superpower Can't Go It Alone* (Oxford, U.K.: Oxford University Press, 2002).

33. Bruce Cumings, "Creating Korean Insecurity: The US Role," in *Reconstituting Korean Security*, Hazel Smith, ed. (New York: United Nations University Press, 2007); Bruce Cumings, *Korea's Place in the Sun* (New York: W. W. Norton, 2005).
34. Tim Beal, *North Korea: The Struggle Against American Power* (London: Pluto Press, 2005).
35. Ken Booth and Nicholas J. Wheeler, *The Security Dilemma* (Basingstoke, U.K.: Palgrave, 2008), 284.
36. North Korean defector, in interview with author, Leeds, United Kingdom, September 2009.
37. Experts on North Korea, in interviews with author, Seoul, from 2004 to 2011.
38. Graham T. Allison, *The Essence of Decision* (Boston: Little, Brown, 1971).
39. This concept was first introduced by John Steinbruner to explain Kennedy's decision to sell Britain's Prime Minister Macmillan the Polaris system, but has not been used much in the strategic studies literature since then. See John D. Steinbruner, *The Cybernetic Theory of Decision* (Princeton, NJ: Princeton University Press, 1974).
40. Robert Jervis, *Perception and Misperception in International Politics* (Princeton, NJ: Princeton University Press, 1976), chapter 11.
41. David H. Dunn, *The Politics of Threat: Minuteman Vulnerability in American National Security Policy* (Southampton, U.K.: Southampton Studies in International Policy, 1997).
42. Jean-François Revel, *How Democracies Perish* (London: Weidenfeld & Nicolson, 1985).
43. Jervis, *Perception and Misperception*; Robert Jervis, Richard Ned Lebow, and Janice Gross Stein, *Psychology and Deterrence* (Baltimore, MD: Johns Hopkins University Press, 1989).
44. Ken Booth and Nicholas Wheeler have introduced the concept of unresolvable uncertainty in relation to assessing the intentions and capabilities of other states that gives rise to dangerous misperceptions in *The Security Dilemma*, 5.

Chapter 2. Preparing for Confrontation: North Korea's Armed Forces and Military Strategy

1. International Institute for Strategic Studies, *The Military Balance 2009* (Abingdon, U.K.: Routledge, 2009).
2. International Institute for Strategic Studies, *Military Balance*, 394; "DPRK Economy," GlobalSecurity.org, http://www.globalsecurity.org/military/world/dprk/economy.htm (accessed August 1, 2009).
3. Kongdan Oh and Ralph C. Hassig, *North Korea Through the Looking Glass* (Washington, DC: Brookings Institution, 2000), 105.
4. Daniel A. Pinkston and Shin Sungtack, *North Korea Likely to Conduct Second Nuclear Test* (Monterey, CA: James Martin Center for Nonproliferation Studies, January 8, 2007), http://cns.miis.edu/stories/pdfs/070108.pdf.
5. Mark Hibbs, "DPRK Test Shot Highly Inefficient, Maybe Design Flaw, Experts Say," *Nucleonics Week* 47, 41 (October 12, 2006).
6. Siegfried S. Hecker, *Report on North Korean Nuclear Program* (Stanford, CA: Center for International Security and Cooperation, Stanford University, 2006 [revised 2007]), 5.

7. Jeffrey Park, "The North Korean Nuclear Test: What the Seismic Data Says," *The Bulletin of the Atomic Scientists*, May 26, 2009; Bill Gertz, "Inside the Ring: North Korean Test," *Washington Times*, May 28, 2009; Kim Su-jeong and Yoo Jee-ho, "Expert: North's test not a surprise, more to come," *The Joongang Ilbo*, June 1, 2009.

8. *North Korea's Nuclear and Missile Programs: Asia Report No. 168* (Seoul: International Crisis Group, June 18, 2009), 10.

9. Richard L. Garwin and Frank N. Von Hippel, "A Technical Analysis: Deconstructing North Korea's 9 October Nuclear Test," *Arms Control Today* (November 2006).

10. Song Seong-ho, "North Korean Supreme People's Assembly Member Defects to South Korea," *Weolgan Chosun* (August 2005); *North Korea's Nuclear and Missile Programs*, 11.

11. Mary Beth Nikitin, *North Korea's Nuclear Weapons: Technical Issues* (Washington, DC: Congressional Research Service, 2009), report no. RL34256, 6.

12. Korean Central News Agency, October 3, 2006.

13. Kim Chol U, *Army-Centred Politics of Kim Jong Il* (Pyongyang: Foreign Languages Pub. House, 2002).

14. *North Korea's Chemical and Biological Weapons Programs: Asia Report No. 167* (Seoul: International Crisis Group, June 18, 2009).

15. Chris Schneidmiller, "South Korea Completes Chemical Weapons Disposal," Global Security Newswire, October 17, 2008; *North Korea's Chemical and Biological Weapons Programs*, 4.

16. International Institute for Strategic Studies, *North Korea's Weapons Programmes: A Net Assessment* (Basingstoke, U.K.: Palgrave, 2004), 53.

17. Ibid., 54

18. *North Korea's Chemical and Biological Weapons Programs*, 11.

19. Ibid., 11.

20. Based on interviews carried out by ICG staff with South Korean officials: see *North Korea's Chemical and Biological Weapons Programs*, 11; Barton Gellman, "4 Nations Thought to Possess Smallpox," *Washington Post*, November 5, 2002.

21. Joseph S. Bermudez Jr., *A History of Ballistic Missile Development in the DPRK*, Occasional Paper No. 2 (Monterey, CA: James Martin Center for Nonproliferation Studies, 1999).

22. *North Korea's Weapons Programmes*; Daniel A. Pinkston, *The North Korean Ballistic Missile Program* (Carlisle, PA: Strategic Studies Institute, 2008).

23. Gordon Jacobs and Tim McCarthy, "China's Missile Sales: Few Changes for the Future," *Jane's Intelligence Review* (December 1992): 560.

24. John Wilson Lewis and Hua Di, "Beijing's Defense Establishment: Solving the Arms Export Enigma," *International Security* (fall 1992): 5–40; *North Korea's Weapons Programmes*.

25. There have been various reports that North Korea received some Scud-B missiles from the Soviet Union directly. Pinkston, *North Korean Ballistic Missile Program*, 15; *SIPRI Yearbook 1989* (Oxford, U.K.: Oxford University Press, 1989).

26. Evgeni Tkachenko, "Korea Tried to Employ Russians to Modernise Its Missiles," ITAR-TASS, February 10, 1993; "Russian Scientists Assisting DPRK in Nuclear

Program," JPRS-TND-94-011, May 16, 1994, 51–52; Warren Strobel, "N. Korea Shops for Nuke Technology in Russia," *Washington Times*, July 5, 1994.

27. Testimony of Bok Koo Lee (alias), former North Korean missile scientist, before the Subcommittee on Financial Management, the Budget; International Security Committee on Governmental Affairs, United States Senate, May 20, 2003. See also Pinkston, *North Korean Ballistic Missile Program*, 21.

28. Pinkston, *North Korean Ballistic Missile Program*, 22.

29. "Weapons of Mass Destruction (WMD)," GlobalSecurity.org, http://www.globalsecurity.org/wmd/world/dprk/missile.htm (accessed December 20, 2009).

30. "Weapons of Mass Destruction (WMD): No-dong-A," GlobalSecurity.org, http://www.globalsecurity.org/wmd/world/dprk/nd-1.htm (accessed December 20, 2009); Pinkston, *North Korean Ballistic Missile Program*, 22.

31. Robert H. Schmucker, "3rd World Missile Development: A New Assessment Based on USNCOM Filed Experience and Data Evaluation" (presentation at 12th Multinational Conference on Missile Defence, Edinburgh, Scotland, June 1–4, 1999); cited in Pinkston, *North Korean Ballistic Missile Program*, 22; Jim Mann, "N. Korean Missiles Have Russian Roots, Explosive Theory Suggests," *Los Angeles Times*, September 6, 2000.

32. Based on conversations with IISS specialists in November 2010.

33. Korean Central News Agency, September 1, 1998.

34. Antony H. Cordesman, *North Korea's Missile Tests: Saber Rattling or Rocket's Red Glare* (Washington, DC: Center for Strategic and International Studies, 2006).

35. Mark Fitzpatrick, ed., *Iran's Ballistic Missile Capabilities* (London: IISS, 2010), 107; there have also been suggestions that the first stage of the Taepodong-2 could be derived from the Chinese CSS-2 or CSS-3, although there are no known examples of Chinese rocket motors for long-range missiles being made available to North Korea. See Stephen A. Hildreth, *North Korean Ballistic Missile Threat to the United States* (Washington, DC: Congressional Research Service, 2009), RS21473, 2.

36. For more technical details, see "Weapons of Mass Destruction (WMD): Taep'o-dong 2 (TD-2), NKSL-X-2," GlobalSecurity.org, http://www.globalsecurity.org/wmd/world/dprk/td-2.htm (accessed August 30, 2010).

37. *Seoul Sinmun*, December 7, 1991; for a critical evaluation of these reports see Pinkston, *North Korean Ballistic Missile Program*, 72–73.

38. Fitzpatrick, *Iran's Ballistic Missile Capabilities*, 26.

39. "NK Has 2nd Long-Range Missile Site," *Korea Times*, September 11, 2008; "North Korea Builds Nuclear Missile Site," *Daily Telegraph*, September 12, 2008.

40. Choe Sang-Hun, "Worry of a North Korean Missile Test," *New York Times*, February 24, 2009.

41. Edith M. Lederer, "UN Imposes Tough New Sanctions on North Korea," Associated Press, June 12, 2009, http://www.lexis-nexis.com.

42. "Seoul Must Work Out Responses to N.Korean Provocations," *Chosun Ilbo*, May 28, 2009.

43. "N.Korea 'Earning $2 Billion a Year in Arms Deals with Iran,'" *Chosun Ilbo*, July 16, 2009.

44. Pauline Jelinek, "North Korean Ship Kang Nam Turns Around," *Huffington Post*, June 30, 2009.

45. Yu Yong-won, "North Deploys New 4,000 km-Range Missiles," *Chosun Ilbo*, May 4, 2004. The dimensions of the missile cited here differ from those reported by the IISS (*North Korea's Weapons Programmes*, 81): a diameter of 1.65 m and a length of just under 10 m.

46. David C. Isby, "North Korea Has Deployed Intermediate-Range Missiles," *Jane's Missiles and Rockets* (September 1, 2004); Pinkston, *North Korean Ballistic Missile Program*, 35.

47. "Weapons of Mass Destruction (WMD): KN-02 Short Range Ballistic Missile," GlobalSecurity.org, http://www.globalsecurity.org/wmd/world/dprk/kn-2.htm (accessed August 30, 2009).

48. Fitzpatrick, *Iran's Ballistic Missile Capabilities*, 71.

49. Ibid., 69.

50. This is very well illustrated by the problems encountered by Raytheon, a company with considerable expertise and experience in the development of advanced rocket engines, in producing a reliable kill vehicle for the national missile defense program. For details see Bradley Graham, *Hit to Kill* (New York: Public Affairs, 2001).

51. For a photo, see Norbert Brügge, *The North Korean Nodong-missile Family*, http://www.b14643.de/Spacerockets_1/Diverse/Nodong/Dong.htm (accessed February 13, 2011).

52. Based on conversations with IISS specialists in February 2011.

53. Fitzpatrick, *Iran's Ballistic Missile Capabilities*, 141.

54. Ibid., 140.

55. "Russia: Makeyev Design Bureau State Missile Center (Makeyev GRTs)," NTI, http://www.nti.org/db/nisprofs/russia/delivry/makeyev.htm (accessed on February 13, 2011).

56. Bylaw of the Korean Workers' Party, cited from *North Korea's Chemical and Biological Weapons Programs*, 5.

57. Homer T. Hodge, "North Korea's Military Strategy," *Parameters* 33, 1 (spring 2003): 68–81.

58. International Institute for Strategic Studies, *Military Balance 2009*, 396–98.

59. Michael O'Hanlon and Mike Mochizuki, *Crisis on the Korean Peninsula* (New York: McGraw-Hill, 2003), 70.

60. Jae-Jung Suh, "Assessing the Military Balance in Korea," *Asian Perspective* 28, 2 (2004): 63–88; Taik-Young Hamm, *Arming the Two Koreas: State, Capital and Military Power* (New York: Routledge, 1999); Michael O'Hanlon, "Stopping a North Korean Invasion: Why Defending South Korea Is Easier Than the Pentagon Thinks," *International Security* 22 (1998): 135–70.

61. "Korea-U.S. Joint Military Exercise Begins," *Chosun Ilbo*, March 3, 2008.

62. Based on author's discussions with military experts in Seoul, 2008.

63. Michael O'Hanlon, e-mail to author, July 28, 2005.

64. O'Hanlon and Mochizuki, *Crisis on the Korean Peninsula*, Appendix 1.

65. Ibid., 77.

66. G. H. Snyder, *Deterrence and Defense* (Princeton, NJ: Princeton University Press, 1961).

67. Mark Mazzetti and Helen Cooper, "U.S. Confirms Israeli Strikes Hit Syrian Target Last Week," *New York Times*, September 12, 2007; Richard Weitz, "Israeli Air

Strike in Syria: International Reactions" (Monterey, CA: James Martin Center for Nonproliferation Studies, November 1, 2007), http://www.cns.miis.edu/pubs/week/071101.htm.

Chapter 3. North Korea and the World: From Soviet Colony to Failed State

1. Han Woo-Keun, *The History of Korea* (Honolulu, HI: East-West Center Press, 1970); James B. Palais, *Politics and Policy in Traditional Korea* (Cambridge, MA: Harvard University Press, 1975).

2. C. Kenneth Quinones and Joseph Tragert, *The Complete Idiot's Guide to Understanding North Korea* (New York: Alpha Books, 2003), 113.

3. Andrei Lankov, *From Stalin to Kim Il Sung: The Formation of North Korea 1945-1960* (London: C. Hurst & Company, 2002), 2.

4. Lankov, *From Stalin to Kim Il Sung*, chapter 1; Kathryn Weathersby, *Soviet Aims in Korea and the Origins of the Korean War, 1945-1950: New Evidence from Russian Archives*, Cold War International History Project working paper (Washington, DC: Woodrow Wilson International Center for Scholars, 1993).

5. Lankov, *From Stalin to Kim Il Sung*, 14.

6. Bradley K. Martin, *Under the Loving Care of the Fatherly Leader: North Korea and the Kim Dynasty* (New York: St. Martin's Press, 2004), 56.

7. David Rees, *Korea: The Limited War* (New York: Penguin, 1964); David Dallin, *Soviet Foreign Policy After Stalin* (Baltimore, MD: Lippincott, 1961).

8. Bruce Cumings, *The Origins of the Korean War*, vol. 1: *Liberation and the Emergence of Separate Regimes, 1945–1947*, vol. 2: *The Roaring of the Cataract, 1947–11950* (Princeton, NJ: Princeton University Press, 1981, 1990); Bruce Cumings, *Korea's Place in the Sun: A Modern History* (New York: W. W. Norton, 1997).

9. Weathersby, *Soviet Aims in Korea*.

10. Weathersby, *Soviet Aims in Korea*.

11. Quinones and Tragert, *Understanding North Korea*, 131.

12. Adrian Buzo, *The Guerilla Dynasty* (London: I.B. Tauris, 1999).

13. Andrei Lankov, *Crisis in North Korea* (Honolulu, HI: University of Hawai'i Press, 2005), chapter 5.

14. Nam Koon-woo, *The North Korean Communist Leadership, 1945-65: A Study of Factionalism and Political Consolidation* (Tuscaloosa, AL: University of Alabama Press, 1974); Buzo, *Guerilla Dynasty*; Lankov, *From Stalin to Kim Il Sung*.

15. Cited from B. R. Meyers, *The Cleanest Race* (New York: Melville House, 2010), 46.

16. Meyers, *Cleanest Race*, 47.

17. Ralph C. Hassig and Kongdan Oh, *North Korea Through the Looking Glass* (Washington, DC: Brookings Institution, 2000).

18. Martin, *Under the Loving Care of the Fatherly Leader*, 507; also based on extensive interviews in Seoul in 2005.

19. Buzo, *Guerilla Dynasty*, 212.

20. Scott Snyder, "Assessing North Korea's Strategic Intentions and Motivations," in Tae-Hwan Kwak and Seung-Ho Joo, eds., *North Korea's Foreign Policy Under Kim Jong Il* (Aldershot, U.K.: Ashgate, 2009), 57–80, 43; Ralph Hassig and Kongdan Oh, *The Hidden People of North Korea* (Plymouth, U.K.: Rowman & Littlefield, 2009), 177–81.

21. Cited from Hassig and Oh, *North Korea Through the Looking Glass*, 91.

22. Etel Solingen, *Regional Orders at Century's Dawn: Global and Domestic Influences on Grand Strategy* (Princeton, NJ: Princeton University Press, 1998), 161; Etel Solingen, *Nuclear Logics* (Princeton, NJ: Princeton University Press, 2007), chapter 118; Snyder, "Assessing North Korea's Strategic Intentions and Motivations."

23. Philip H. Park, ed., *The Dynamics of Change in North Korea* (Changwon, Republic of Korea: Kyungnam University Press, 2009), 62–63.

24. Lee Jong-seok, in interview with author, Sejong Institute, Seongnam, South Korea, July 2008.

25. Marcus Noland, *Korea after Kim Jong-il* (Washington, DC: Institute for International Economics, 2004), 47.

26. Ihk-pyo Hong, "A Shift Towards Capitalism?," *East Asia Review* (Winter 2002): 95–106.

27. Dick K. Nanto and Emma Chanlett Avery, *North Korea: Economic Leverage and Policy Analysis* (Washington, DC: Congressional Research Service, 2010), RL 32493, 28–36.

28. Mark E. Manyin and Mary Beth Nikitin, *Foreign Assistance to North Korea* (Washington, DC: Congressional Research Service, 2010), R40095.

29. Stephan Haggard and Marcus Noland, *The Winter of Their Discontent: Pyongyang Attacks the Market*, policy brief PB10-1 (Washington, DC: Peterson Institute for International Economics, January 2010).

30. Member of the National Assembly, interview with author, Seoul, January 2005.

31. Such accidents are usually viewed with suspicion, given the paucity of automobile traffic in North Korea. See Kang Chol-hwan, "The Trouble with Kim Jong-il's Succession," *Chosun Ilbo*, August 20, 2010.

32. Editorial, *Chosun Ilbo*, August 18, 2010.

33. Editorial, *Chosun Ilbo*, September 29, 2010.

Chapter 4. The South Korean Security Dilemma: Between Confrontation and Unification

1. Woo-Keun Han, *The History of Korea* (Honolulu, HI: East-West Center Press, 1970); Bruce Cumings, *Korea's Place in the Sun: A Modern History* (New York: W.W. Norton, 1990).

2. Tim Shorrock, "The Struggle for Democracy in South Korea in the 1980s and the Rise of anti-Americanism," *Third World Quarterly* 8, 4 (October 1986): 1195–218.

3. Don Oberdorfer, *The Two Koreas* (New York: Basic Books, 2001), 124–27.

4. Donald Kirk, *Korea Betrayed: Kim Dae Jung and Sunshine* (New York: Palgrave Macmillan, 2005), 62–83.

5. See In-Taek Hyun, "Domestic Controversies and changing U.S.-Korea Relations," in In-Taek Hyun, Kyudok Hong, and Sung-han Kim, *Asia-Pacific Alliances in the 21st Century* (Seoul: Oruem Publishing House, 2007), 261–85. Hyun was appointed by President Lee Myung-bak as minister of unification after the presidential elections in 2007.

6. For a searing indictment of the behavior of U.S. officials during that time, see Kirk, *Korea Betrayed*, chapter 4.

7. Narushige Michishita, *North Korea's Military Diplomatic Campaigns, 1966–2008* (Abingdon, U.K.: Routledge, 2009), chapter 1.

8. Young Whan Kihl, *Transforming Korean Politics* (Armonk, NY: M.E. Sharpe, 2005), 84.

9. This is a German term meaning "Northern policy" and was used in reference to West Germany's *Ostpolitik* ("Eastern policy") toward East Germany and Communist Eastern Europe.

10. Uk Heo and Terence Roehrig, *South Korea since 1980* (New York: Cambridge University Press, 2010) 133.

11. Dr. Park Jin, then an official in Cheong Wa Dae, in interview with author, Seoul, June 1997.

12. Yong-sup Han and Norman D. Levin, *Sunshine in Korea* (Santa Monica, CA: Rand Corporation, 2002).

13. For a more detailed conceptual analysis of South Korean engagement policies, see Son Key-young, *South Korean Engagement Policies and North Korea* (Abingdon, U.K.: Routledge, 2006).

14. Kirk, *Korea Betrayed*, chapters 10–11.

15. William Perry, *Review of United States Policy Toward North Korea: Findings and Recommendations*, unclassified report (Washington, DC: Department of State, October 12, 1999), http://www.state.gov/www/regions/eap/991012_northkorea _rpt.html.

16. Key-young, *South Korean Engagement Policies*, 84.

17. Selig S. Harrison, *Korean Endgame* (Princeton, NJ: Princeton University Press, 2002), 86; Oberdorfer, *Two Koreas*, 416.

18. Former minister for foreign affairs and trade Yoon Young-kwan, in interview with author, Seoul National University, July 2004.

19. Kirk, *Korea Betrayed*, 165.

20. Oberdorfer, *Two Koreas*, 431.

21. Kirk, *Korea Betrayed*, 191–208; Key-young, *South Korean Engagement Policies*, 117.

22. Lee Jong-seok, in interview with author, Seoul, July 2010. Lee is generally considered to be the architect of the national security policy of the Roh administration. However, one member of the government (chief economist Cho Yoon-je) told me that the outlines of the policy were developed by President Roh himself.

23. Haesook Chae and Steven Kim, "Conservatives and Progressives in South Korea," *Washington Quarterly* 31, 4 (autumn 2008): 77–95.

24. Officials, in interviews with author, Seoul, 2005.

25. Yoon Young-kwan, in interview with author, Seoul National University, July 2004; Lee Jeong-seok, in interview with author, Sejong Institute, Seongnam, South Korea, July 2008; Suh Jeo-seok, in interview with author, Korea Institute for Defense Analyses, Seongnam, South Korea, July 2008.

26. Presidential speech on Liberation Day in 2003, at http://english.president.go.kr/ pre_activity/speeches/speeches_list.php (accessed June 14, 2004).

27. Bruce Bechtol Jr., *Red Rogue* (Washington, DC: Potomac Books, 2007), 163.

28. Christoph Bluth, *Britain, Germany and Western Nuclear Strategy* (Oxford, U.K.: Oxford University Press, 1995).

29. Lee Jeong-seok, in interview with author, Sejong Institute, Seongnam, South Korea, July 2008.

30. Yoichi Funabashi, *The Peninsula Question* (Washington, DC: Brookings Institution, 2007), 252.

31. Harrison, *Korean Endgame*, chapter 8; Marcus Noland, *Korea after Kim Jong-il* (Washington, DC: Institute for International Economics, 2004).

32. Samuel S. Kim, ed., *Inter-Korean Relations* (Basingstoke, U.K.: Palgrave, 2004).

33. Kim, *Inter-Korean Relations*.

34. Roh Moo-hyun committed suicide on May 23, 2009, after an investigation of corruption in his administration resulted in allegations that he had accepted large sums of money from Park Yeon-cha, a Korean businessman.

35. Based on interviews with various members of presidential candidate's Lee policy team in Seoul 1997.

36. "Joint Vision for the Alliance of the United States of America and the Republic of Korea," June 16, 2009, cited in Mark E. Manyin, *US-South Korean Relations* (Washington, DC: Congressional Research Service), RL41481, http://www.fas.org/sgp/crs/row/R41481.pdf.

37. Evan Feigenbaum, "Korea Inter Pares: South Korea on the Global Stage," Council on Foreign Relations, http://blogs.cfr.org/asia/2010/07/10/korea-inter-pares/#more-1242 (accessed September 9, 2010).

38. Song Sang-ho, "North Korea Fires Artillery into Sea near Western Border," *Korea Herald*, November 23, 2010.

39. Background discussion with Pentagon official, December 2010.

40. Kwon Hyuk-chul, "President Lee Has Changed His Position from Controlled Response to Manifold Retaliation," *Hankyoreh Sinmun*, November 24, 2010.

41. Scott Snyder, "Lee Myungbak's Foreign Policy: A 250-day Assessment," *Korean Journal of Defense Analysis* 21, 1 (March 2009): 85–102.

Chapter 5. The North Korean Security Dilemma: After the Cold War and the First Nuclear Crisis

1. Nicholas Eberstadt, *The North Korean Economy Between Crisis and Catastrophe* (New Brunswick, NJ: Transaction Publishers, 2007), 116.

2. The estimates of premature deaths are disputed. For a detailed analysis, see Stephen Haggard and Marcus Noland, *Famine in North Korea* (New York: Columbia University Press, 2007).

3. Joseph S. Bermudez, "North Korea's Nuclear Program," *Jane's Intelligence Review* (September 1991), 405.

4. "North Korea Profile," Nuclear Threat Initiative, http://www.nti.org/e_research/profiles/NK/index.html (accessed September 21, 2010).

5. Balazs Szalontai and Sergey Radchenko, *North Korea's Efforts to Acquire Nuclear Technology and Nuclear Weapons: Evidence from Russian and Hungarian Archives*, working paper no. 53 (Washington, DC: Cold War International History Project, 2006).

6. Don Oberdorfer, *The Two Koreas* (New York: Basic Books, 2001), 252–53; Szalontai and Radchenko, *North Korea's Efforts*, 8.

7. Michael J. Siler, "U.S. Nuclear Nonproliferation Policy in the Northeast Asian

Region During the Cold War: The South Korean Case," *East Asia: An International Quarterly* 16 (autumn 1998): 41–79. Kim Il-sung was well aware of South Korea's nuclear ambitions.

8. Szalontai and Radchenko, *North Korea's Efforts*, 13.

9. James Clay Moltz and Alezandre Y. Mantsourov, *The North Korean Nuclear Program* (London: Routledge, 2000), 97.

10. Joel S. Wit, Daniel B. Poneman, and Robert L. Gallucci, *Going Critical: The First North Korean Nuclear Crisis* (Washington, DC: Brookings Institution, 2004), 7.

11. David Albright and Kevin O'Neill, eds., *Solving the North Korean Nuclear Puzzle* (Washington, DC: Institute for Science and International Security, 2000).

12. IISS, *North Korea's Weapons Programs: A Net Assessment* (Basingstoke, U.K.: Palgrave, 2004), 8.

13. Wit, Poneman, and Gallucci, *Going Critical*, 59.

14. Ibid.: "Joint Statement of the Democratic People's Republic of Korea and the United States of America."

15. Editorial, *Yonhap*, June 3, 1993.

16. "NUB Delivers Report on Trends in North Korea," *Dong-A Ilbo*, March 20, 1994; Wit, Poneman, and Gallucci, *Going Critical*, 127.

17. Statement on the Resumption of U.S.-DPRK Negotiations on Nuclear and Other Issues (press release), Department of State, March 3, 1994 (no longer available online).

18. David E. Sanger, "Nuclear Agency Chief Warns of Need for Access to North Korea," *New York Times*, April 15, 1994.

19. "North Korea Asserts U.S. Endangers Pact on Atom Inspections," *New York Times*, March 5, 1994; Korean Central Broadcasting Agency (Pyongyang), March 15, 1994, in "Foreign Ministry Spokesman on Implementing North Korea-US Agreement," BBC Summary of World Broadcasts, March 17, 1994.

20. Editorial, *Hankyoreh Sinmun*, March 23, 1994.

21. "North Korea Threatens Withdrawal from Nuclear Treaty," United Press International, March 20, 1994; David A. Sanger, "North Korea Bars A-Plant Survey; Threatens to Quit Nuclear Treaty," *New York Times*, March 21, 1994.

22. South Korean News Agency, March 22, 1994, in "UN Security Council Discusses North Korean Nuclear Issues," BBC Summary of World Broadcasts, March 23, 1994.

23. Victoria Graham, "U.S., China at Odds over Security Council Statement on North Korea," Associated Press, March 28. 1994.

24. Korean Central Broadcasting Agency (Pyongyang), May 3, 1994, in "Foreign Ministry Spokesman on Inspections and IAEA's 'Unreasonable' Request," BBC Summary of World Broadcasts, May 5, 1994.

25. Wit, Poneman, and Gallucci, *Going Critical*, 193.

26. Mike Trickey, "Yeltsin Warns North Korea Not to Expect Russia's Help," *Vancouver Sun*, June 3, 1994.

27. Wit, Poneman, and Gallucci, *Going Critical*, 181.

28. Paul Lewis, "U.S. Offers a Plan for U.N. Sanctions on North Koreans," *New York Times*, June 16, 1994.

29. Agreed Framework cited from Wit, Poneman, and Gallucci, *Going Critical*, 423.

30. William Safire, "Clinton's Concessions," *New York Times*, October 24, 1994.
31. Elaine Sciolino, "Clinton Ups Atom Stakes," *New York Times*, October 20, 1994.
32. Editorial, *Chosun Ilbo*, October 20, 1994; editorial, *Joongang Ilbo*, October 21, 1994.
33. Official, in interview with author, Cheong Wa Dae, Seoul, June 15, 1997.
34. Wit, Poneman, and Gallucci, *Going Critical*, 368.

Chapter 6. The United States and the Two Koreas:
Confronting the Nuclear Issue

1. For a detailed account see Mike Chinoy, *Meltdown* (New York: St. Martin's Press, 2008).
2. Ivo H. Daalder and James M. Lindsay, *America Unbound: The Bush Revolution in Foreign Policy* (Washington, DC: Brookings Institution, 2003); Christoph Bluth, "The Eagle Resurgent: National Security Policy in the Second Bush Administration," *The World Today* 60, 12 (December 2004): 10–12; Anthony D. Lott, *Creating Insecurity* (Aldershot, U.K.: Ashgate, 2004).
3. Chinoy, *Meltdown*, 6.
4. US White House, Statements and Briefings, "North Korea," June 6, 2001, at www.whitehouse.gov (accessed June 6, 2004).
5. "Nuclear Posture Review [Excerpts]," GlobalSecurity.org, http://www.global security.org/wmd/library/policy/dod/npr.htm (accessed January 8, 2008).
6. Chinoy, *Meltdown*, 69.
7. White House, "Remarks by President Bush during Press Availability with ROK President Kim Dae-hung, Seoul, Korea, February 20, 2002," press release.
8. Colin L. Powell, "Remarks at Asia Society Annual Dinner," U.S. State Department, June 10, 2002, at http://2001-2009.state.gov/secretary/former/powell /remarks/2002/10983.htm (accessed June 6, 2004).
9. Often referred to as the Nodong. This is just a different transliteration of the same Korean word, using the North Korean spelling.
10. Kim Min-cheol, "Hwang Tells of Secret Nuke Program," *Chosun Ilbo*, July 5, 2003.
11. Pervez Musharraf, *In the Line of Fire* (New York: Free Press, 2006), 296.
12. "A. Q. Khan Confesses," *Dawn* (Pakistani newspaper), February 5, 2004; see also *Nuclear Black Markets: Pakistan, A.Q. Khan and the Rise of Proliferation Networks*, IISS strategic dossier (London: IISS, 2007), 72–86.
13. Gauraf Kampani, "Second Tier Proliferation: The Case of Pakistan and North Korea," *Nonproliferation Review* 9, 3 (autumn 2002): 107–16.
14. Chinoy, *Meltdown*, 99–102.
15. "Uranium Program," GlobalSecurity.org, http://www.globalsecurity.org/wmd/ world/dprk/nuke-uranium.htm (accessed June 12, 2009).
16. Former unification minister Lee Jong-seok, in interviews with author, Sejong Institute, Seongnam, South Korea, June 2008.
17. Kim Tae-woo, "North Korean Nuclear Politics at the Crossroads," *Korean Journal for Defense Analyses* 16, 2 (fall 2004), 27–47.
18. James G. Strohmaier, "Extorting Cooperation: A Case Study of the Negotiation and Implementation of the 1994 US-DPRK Agreed Framework" (PhD diss., University of Kentucky, 2003).

19. Yoichi Funabashi, *The Peninsula Question* (Washington, DC: Brookings Institution, 2007), 1–92.

20. Charles L. Pritchard, *Failed Diplomacy: The Tragic Story of How North Korea Got the Bomb* (Washington, DC: Brookings Institution, 2007), 32–44; Chinoy, *Meltdown*, 115–26.

21. U.S. State Department, press statement, October 16, 2002.

22. Pritchard, *Failed Diplomacy*, 32–44, contains the fullest publicly available version of the text of Kang's speech.

23. Lee Jong-seok, in interview with author, Sejong Institute, Seongnam, South Korea, June 2008.

24. Daniel A. Pinkston and Phillip C. Saunders, "Seeing North Korea clearly," *Survival* 45, 3 (autumn 2003): 79–102.

25. Selig S. Harrison presented a truncated account of this meeting in an article that did not fully reflect what the North Korean ambassador said (the author was present at this meeting). Selig S. Harrison, "Did North Korea Cheat?," *Foreign Affairs* 84, 1 (January/February 2005): 99–110; Robert L. Gallucci and Mitchell B. Reiss, "Dead to Rights," *Foreign Affairs* 84, 2 (March/April 2005): 142–45; Richard L. Garwin, "HEU Done It," *Foreign Affairs* 84, 2 (March/April 2005): 145–46.

26. Korean Central News Agency, November 25, 2004.

27. Wade L. Huntley, "Ostrich Engagement: The Bush Administration and the North Korea Nuclear Crisis," *Nonproliferation Review* 11, 2 (summer 2004): 81–115.

28. Scott Snyder, *Negotiating on the Edge: North Korean Negotiating Behavior* (Washington, DC: United States Institute of Peace, 2002).

29. Korean Central News Agency, April 18, 2003.

30. Ivo H. Daalder and James M. Lindsay, *America Unbound: The Bush Revolution in Foreign Policy* (Hoboken, NJ: Wiley, 2005).

31. Ivo H. Daalder and James M. Lindsay, "Where Are the Hawks on North Korea?," *American Prospect*, February 1, 2003.

32. Chinoy, *Meltdown*, 163.

33. Korean Central News Agency, January 10, 2003.

34. Chinoy, *Meltdown*, 166–67.

35. Professor Yoon Young-kwan, in interview with author, Seoul, South Korea, June 2004.

36. Charles L. Pritchard, "The Korean Peninsula and the Role of Multilateral Talks," UNIDIR Disarmament Forum (Washington, DC: Brookings Institution, 2005); Korean Central News Agency, April 25, 2003; Yoichi Funabashi, *The Peninsula Question* (Washington, DC: Brookings Institution, 2007), 332–36.

37. Funabashi, *Peninsula Question*, 228.

38. Chinoy, *Meltdown*, 177–78.

39. Thomas D. Lehrman, "Rethinking Interdiction: The Future of the Proliferation Security Initiative," *Non-Proliferation Review* 11, 2 (summer 2004): 1–45.

40. Pritchard, *Failed Diplomacy*, 85.

41. Joseph Kahn, "Korea Arms Talks Close with Plan for a New Round," *New York Times*, August 30, 2003.

42. Chinoy, *Meltdown*, 186.

43. Moon Chung-in, "The North Korean Nuclear Problem and Multilateral Cooperation: The Case of the Six Party Talk," *Whitebook on the Korean Economy* (Seoul: Korea Institute for International Economic Policy, 2004), 25.

44. Korean Central News Agency, August 30, 2003.
45. Moon, "North Korean Nuclear Problem," 26.
46. Korean Central News Agency, December 6, 2003.
47. South Korean officials, in interviews with author, Seoul, South Korea, 2004–2006.
48. Based on discussions with North Korean officials in October 2004.
49. Editorial, *Korea Herald*, June 21, 2005.
50. Editorial, *Chosun Ilbo*, June 21, 2005.
51. Yuri Kim, in interviews with author, at the U.S. embassy, Seoul, South Korea, July 2004, and at the U.S. Department of State, December 2007.
52. Cited from Chinoy, *Meltdown*, 249.
53. Ibid.
54. Ibid., 250.
55. Pritchard, *Failed Diplomacy*, 122.
56. Dick K. Nanto and Raphael L. Pearl, "North Korea Counterfeiting of US Currency," CRS Report for Congress, RL33324, March 22, 2006.
57. Korean Central News Agency, April 24, 2006.
58. Korean Central News Agency, October 10, 2006.
59. Daniel A. Pinkston and Shin Sungtack, *North Korea Likely to Conduct a Second Nuclear Test* (Monterey, CA: MIIS, 2007).
60. "North Korea Talks End in Deadlock," BBC News, December 22, 2006.
61. Glenn Kessler, "New Doubts on Nuclear Efforts by North Korea," *Washington Post*, March 1, 2007; Hearing of the Senate Armed Services Committee, "Current and Future Worldwide Threats to the National Security of the United States," February 27, 2007, transcript.
62. For more detail, see *North Korea's Missile Launch: The Risks of Overreaction: Asia Report No. 91* (Seoul: International Crisis Group, March 31, 2009).
63. Jeffrey Park, "The North Korean Nuclear Test: What the Seismic Data Says," *Bulletin of the Atomic Scientists*, May 26, 2009; Kim Su-jeong and Yoo Jee-ho, "Expert: North's Test not a Surprise, More to Come," *Joongang Ilbo*, June 1, 2009.
64. Alexander, David, "Obama Says Nuclear Test a 'Grave Concern,'" *Reuters*, May 25, 2009.
65. Emma Chanlett-Avery and Mi Ae Taylor, *North Korea: U.S. Relations, Nuclear Diplomacy, and Internal Situation* (Washington, DC: Congressional Research Service, 2010), R41259.
66. Siegfried S, Hecker, "What I Found in North Korea," *Foreign Affairs*, December 9, 2010, http://www.foreignaffairs.com/articles/67023/siegfried-s-hecker/what-i-found-in-north-korea?page=show.
67. *North Korea: Getting Back to the Talks: Asia Report No. 169* (Seoul: International Crisis Group, June 18, 2009).
68. "Barack Obama to End Carrot-and-Stick Dance with North Korea," *Australian*, June 18, 2009.

Chapter 7. China and the Future of the Korean Peninsula
1. Li Baojun and Xu Zhengyuan, "Lengzhanhou zhongguo fuzeren daguo shengfen de goujian" [China's identity construction as a responsible big power after the Cold War], *Jiaoxue yu Yanjiu* [Teaching and Research], no. 1.

2. "Daguo shi guanjian, zhoubian shi shuoyao, fanzhangzhong guojia shi jichu, duo-bian waijiao shi zhongyao wutai." See "Xinjieduan de zhongguo waijiao" [China's new diplomacy in the new phase], *Liaowang*, October 22, 2007.

3. Jaeho Hwang, "Measuring China's influence over North Korea," *Issues and Studies* 42, 2 (June 2006): 205–32; Andrew Scobell, *China and North Korea: From Comrades-In-Arms to Allies at Arm's Length* (Carlisle, PA: Strategic Studies Institute, U.S. Army War College, 2004).

4. Russell Ong, "China, US and the North Korean issue," *Asia-Pacific Review* 13, 1 (2006): 118–35; John Park, "Inside Multilateralism: The Six Party Talks," *Washington Quarterly* 28, 4 (2005): 75–91.

5. Samuel Kim, "China's New Role in the Nuclear Confrontation," *Asian Perspective* 28, 4 (2004): 147–84; Scott Snyder, "Can China Unstick the Korean Nuclear Standoff?" *Comparative Connections* 6, 1 (2004): 98.

6. The Treaty of Friendship, Cooperation, and Mutual Assistance, see "Treaty of Friendship, Cooperation and Mutual Assistance Between the People's Republic of China and the Democratic People's Republic of Korea," *Peking Review* 4, 28 (1961): 5.

7. Jian Chen, *Mao's China* (Chapel Hill, NC: Chapel Hill Press, 2001).

8. David Shambaugh, "China and the Korean Peninsula: Playing for the Long Term," *Washington Quarterly* 26, 2 (2003): 43–56; Liping Xia, "The Korean Factor in China's Policy toward East Asia and the United States," *American Foreign Policy Interests* 27 (2005): 241–58; Ong, "China, US and the North Korean issue."

9. Limin Lin, "Chaohe weiji guanli yu zhongguo de waijiao juece" [the management on the North Korean nuclear crisis and China's foreign policy choices], *Xiandai Guoji Guanxi* [*Contemporary International Relations*] 8 (2006).

10. China and North Korea have lost their ideological affinity. They are separate in their views on socialism. North Korea's socialism is what China gave up three decades ago. The Chinese Communist Party sees its political legitimacy no longer relying on the existence of other manifestations of socialism in the world. Its ruling status more and more depends on what they are able to deliver. In contrast, North Korea has moved from the orthodox Marxist Leninism backward toward "feudalism," becoming a "post-modern dictator[ship]." Bruce Cumings, *North Korea: Another Country* (New York: New Press, 2004). A diplomatic dilemma that North Korea has created for China has been the North Korean asylum seekers. See *Perilous Journeys: The Plight of North Koreans in China and Beyond: Asia Report No. 122* (Seoul: International Crisis Group, 2006).

11. Kosuke Takahashi, "China's Worsening North Korean Headache," *Policy Forum Online* 05-10A (2005), http://www.nautilus.org/fora/security/0510A_Takahashi. html (accessed October 15, 2007); Gregory Moore, "How North Korea Threatens China's Interests: Understanding Chinese "duplicity" on the North Korean Nuclear Issue," *International Relations of the Asia-Pacific* (October 2007).

12. Hwang, "Measuring China's Influence over North Korea."

13. *China and North Korea: Comrades Forever? Asia Report No. 112* (Seoul: International Crisis Group, 2006), 3.

14. Ibid.; "Trade Statistics of 2006," Ministry of Commerce, PRC.

15. Scobell, *China and North Korea.*
16. China and South Korea concluded their normalization talks in a short period of time. The final PRC-ROK communiqué does not address anything about the past. For more on China and South Korean normalization talks, see Samuel Kim, *The Two Koreas and the Great Powers* (Cambridge, UK: Cambridge University Press, 2006), 58–63.
17. Xizhen Zhang and Eugene Brown, "Policies toward North Korea: A Time for New Thinking," *Journal of Contemporary China* 9, 25 (2000): 535–45.
18. Shambaugh, "China and the Korean Peninsula," 49. PRC-ROK trade reached $134 billion in 2006. "Trade Statistics of 2006," Ministry of Commerce, PRC.
19. Yongtao Liu, "Xinsikao chaoxian hewenti: anquan yu shenfen" [rethinking the North Korean nuclear issue: security and identity], *Shijie Jingji yu Zhengzhi* [*World Economy and Politics*], 3 (2007).
20. In March 2003 when President Bush officially hinted at the possibility of the United States using force against the DPRK, North Korea had believed that Washington would be very likely to make a policy and to mount preemptive strikes at the DPRK. *Nodong Sinmun Party* daily commented: "They are a revelation of the U.S. scheme for a preemptive attack on the DPRK, and a dangerous war outburst that drives the situation on the Korean Peninsula to the brink of war." Korean Central News Agency, March 20, 2003.
21. Zhang and Brown, "Policies toward North Korea"; Lin, "Chaohe weiji guanli yu zhongguo de waijiao juece."
22. Zhang and Brown, "Policies toward North Korea."
23. Moore, "How North Korea Threatens China's Interests"; Xuetong Yan, "Dongya heping de jichu" [the foundations of the peace in East Asia], *Shijie Jingji yu Zhengzhi* [*World Economics and Politics*], 3 (2004).
24. Samuel Kim, "China's Conflict-Management Approach to the Nuclear Standoff on the Korean Peninsula," *Asian Perspective* 30, 1 (2006): 5–38.
25. Philip Pan, "Putin and Jiang Criticize N. Korea Arms Program," *Washington Post*, December 3, 2003.
26. It is said that in the first quarter of 2003, Chinese officials met with North Korean officials more than sixty times and passed more than fifty messages between DPRK and the United States. John Pomfret, "China Urges N. Korea Dialogue," *Washington Post*, April 4, 2003.
27. Scott Snyder, Ralph Cossa, and Brad Glosserman, "Six-Party Talks: Developing a Roadmap for Future Progress," *Issues & Insights* 9 (2005).
28. *Meeting the North Korean Nuclear Challenge: Report of an Independent Task Force Sponsored by the Council on Foreign Relations* (New York: CFR, 2003), 28.
29. Charles L. Pritchard, *Failed Diplomacy: The Tragic Story of How North Korea Got the Bomb* (Washington, DC: Brookings Institution, 2007).
30. The Tiananmen incident took place in the summer of 1989. Western countries imposed sanctions in response to China's repression measures.
31. Evan Medeiros and M. Taylor Fravel, "China's New Diplomacy," *Foreign Affairs* 82, 6 (2003).
32. Michael Vatikiotis and Murray Hiebert, "How China Is Building an Empire," *Far Eastern Economic Review* (November 20, 2003): 30–3.

33. The new emphasis in China's foreign policy has shown up in many areas. At the UN Security Council, China has supported resolutions against Iraq under Chapter VII. China has also been increasingly involved in East Asian regional cooperation mechanisms, such as APEC, ASEAN + 3, and the East Asian Summit.

34. For the Bush Doctrine, see Robert Jervis, "Understanding the Bush Doctrine," *Political Science Quarterly* 118, 3 (2003): 365–88.

35. Mel Gurtov and Peter Van Ness, eds., *Confronting the Bush Doctrine: Critical Views from the Asia-Pacific* (London: Routledge, 2005).

36. Kim, "China's New Role in the Nuclear Confrontation," 147–84; Paul Pasch, "The North Korean Nuclear Crisis: Last Exit Beijing," *FES Bonn*, http://fesportal.fes.de/pls/portal30/docs/FOLDER/WORLDWIDE/ASIEN/ENGLISCH/BERICHTE/NORTHKOREAPASCH0805.PDF (accessed May 7, 2008); Charles Armstrong, "North Korea Takes on the World," *Current History* 107, 701 (2007): 263–67.

37. Robert Marquand, "Watching Iraq, China Begins to Lean on North Korea," *Christian Science Monitor*, April 8, 2003, online ed.; Scobell, *China and North Korea*.

38. Chinese official, in phone interview with Chunyao Yi, the Information Department, Ministry of Foreign Affairs, October 9, 2007.

39. "The Inside Story of the Fourth Round of Six-Party Talks on the North Korea Nuclear Crisis," *Sino-American Times*, September 29–October 5, 2005.

40. Edward Cody and Anthony Faiola, "North Korea's Kim Reportedly in China for Talks," *Washington Post*, April 20, 2004.

41. Hwang, "Measuring China's Influence over North Korea."

42. Cho Joong-sik, "China Announces Its Plan of $2 Billion Aid to North Korea," *Chosun Ilbo*, October 31, 2005.

43. Ming Liu, "China's Role in the Course of North Korea's Transition," in Ahn Choong-yong, Nicholas Eberstadt, and Lee Young-sun, eds., *A New International Engagement Framework for North Korea?* (Washington, DC: Korea Economic Institute of America, 2004), 36.

44. John Tkacik Jr., *Getting China to Support a Denuclearized North Korea* (Washington, DC: Heritage Foundation, August 25, 2003), http://www.heritage.org/Research/AsiaandthePacific/bg1678.cfm; John Tkacik Jr., *Does Beijing Approve of North Korea's Nuclear Ambition?* (Washington, DC: Heritage Foundation, March 15, 2005), http://www.heritage.org/Research/AsiaandthePacific/bg1832.cfm.

45. Comments by Christopher Hill, the assistant secretary of state of the United States in charge of East Asian affairs. See "Hill Doubting North Korea's Abandonment of Nuclear Ambitions and Asks for Greater Chinese Role," PRESSian.com, June 14, 2005.

46. "Chinese Vice FM Expounds China's Stance on Korean Nuclear Issue," Xinhua News Agency, August 26, 2003, http://www.china.org.cn/english/international/74165.htm; "DPRK's Legitimate Concerns Should Be Addressed: China's Top Legislator," Xinhua News Agency, September 3, 2003, http://www.china.org.cn/english/international/74165.htm.

47. Sun Cheng, "Tough Moves Get Nuke Issue Nowhere," China Daily, July 12–13, 2003.

48. Since 2001, China has resolved border disputes with Russia, Kazakhstan, Kyrgyzstan, and Tajikistan. In the south a code of conduct for the South China Sea has developed. China has also signed an agreement with the Philippines and Vietnam for joint surveying.

49. Kim, "China's New Role in the Nuclear Confrontation."

50. Liu, "China's Role in the Course of North Korea's Transition."

51. Jisi Wang, "China's Search for Stability with America," *Foreign Affairs* (September/October 2005).

52. Anonymous Chinese official, in phone interview with Chunyao Yi, Information Department, Ministry of Foreign Affairs, October 9, 2007.

53. Snyder, Cossa, and Glosserman, "Six-Party Talks: Developing a Roadmap for Future Progress."

54. John R. Bolton, "An All-out War on Proliferation," *Financial Times*, September 7, 2004.

55. Shi Yinhong, "How to Understand and Deal with the DPRK Nuclear Crisis," *Hong Kong Da Gong Bao*, January 15, 2003.

56. John Park, "Inside Multilateralism: The Six-Party Talks," *Washington Quarterly* 28, 4 (2005): 75–91.

57. The most notable message was Chinese Premier Wen Jiabao's public statement at the end of June. "DPRK Nuclear Test 'Fifty-Fifty,'" *Kyodo News Agency*, June 1, 2005.

58. The statement of the Ministry of Foreign Affair, PRC, on the DPRK's nuclear test, October 9, 2006, in *People's Daily*, October 9, 2007; Joseph Kahn, "The North Korean challenge," *New York Times*, October 10, 2006.

59. These movements led to a UN Security Council resolution (1695) of imposing sanctions of missile-related materials to North Korea and a resolution (1718) of imposing weapons and financial sanctions on North Korea. Resolution 1718 demanded that North Korea eliminate all its nuclear weapons, weapons of mass destruction, and ballistic missiles. It allowed nations to inspect cargo moving in and out of North Korea to check for nonconventional weapons but was not backed by the threat of force.

60. See Anna Fifield, "New UN Leader to Tackle N. Korea," *Financial Times*, October 5, 2006.

61. Tim Johnson, "North Korea to Return to Nuclear Arms Talks," *Lexington Herald Leader*, November 1, 2006; "North Korea Talks: Does Pyongyang Want to Give Up Its Nukes or Merely Ease the International Pressure?" *Washington Post*, November 1, 2006.

62. "China Sending Tougher Signal to Pyongyang," *Houston Chronicle*, October 21, 2006.

63. Except in some low-budget mining development. See "China Reportedly Makes Little Investment in North Korea Since Nuclear Test," Yonhap News Agency (Seoul), February 2, 2007.

64. "China to Halt North Korea-bound Tourist Train Service," Yonhap News Agency (Seoul), October 20, 2006.

65. Qiu Yongzheng, "Who Is Fabricating Rumours about the PLA," Elite Reference, August 6, 2006.

66. Feng Zhu, "Shifting Tides: China and North Korea," *China Security* (autumn 2006): 35–51.

67. Audra Ang, "Experts Say China Is Weighing Stronger Measures Against North Korea," Associated Press Financial Wire, October 20, 2006.

68. "U.S. Visitors Say China Has Not, Will Not Cut Off Aid to North Korea as Pressure," Yonhap News Agency (Seoul), November 16, 2006.

69. Yan Xuetong, quoted by Ang, "Experts Say China Is Weighing Stronger Measures."

70. Chinese Foreign Ministry Press Conference, October 24, 2006, http://www.fmprc .gov.cn/chn/xwfw/fyrth/t277291.htm (accessed on November 1, 2007).

71. Alexa Olesen, "North Korea Not Planning Second Nuclear Test," Associated Press Worldstream, October 24, 2006.

72. Chinese Foreign Ministry Press Conference, October 24, 2006.

73. "Quietly China Drew North Korea Back to the Table," *Straits Times* (Singapore), November 2, 2006.

74. Chinese foreign minister Li Zhaoxing's meeting with the Secretary of State Rice (press release), Department of State, October 20, 2006 (no longer available online).

75. North Korea is not a member of the APEC. Regarding the meetings, for example, President Hu Jintao "agreed" with Russian president Vladimir Putin "to work on the North Korean nuclear issue in a firm and coordinated fashion for a speedy resumption of the six-nation talks." President Hu and President Roh Moo-hyun "had a dialogue on how important it was for both North Korea and the U.S. to have many contacts within the framework of the six-party talks and show flexibility to get to a resolution of the issue," and for China and South Korea, they need "to persuade the U.S. and North Korea to have more trust in each other and engage in dialogue." See "China, Russia Leaders Agree on 'firm' Action to Resume North Korea Talks," ITAR-TASS news agency (Moscow), November 18, 2006; Bo-mi Lim, "South Korea, China Call on US, North Korea to Show Flexibility in Resolving Nuclear Standoff," Associated Press Worldstream, November 17, 2006.

76. According to this plan, the DPRK would take steps toward closing its main nuclear facility and allow IAEA inspectors back under an agreed timeline, in return for supplies of heavy fuel oil and the return of $25 million from a bank in Macau. The plan also established working groups to discuss the normalization of relations between the DPRK, the United States, and Japan. Implementation was intended to begin with the September 2005 Joint Statement (under which North Korea committed to abandoning all its nuclear weapons and nuclear programs and returning to the treaty of NPT).

77. Quoted in "Inter-Korean Ties, Six-Party Talks in Positive Cycle: S. Korean PM," Xinhua General News Service, October 4, 2007.

78. Yongnian Zheng, "Chaoxian wenti: zhongguo zhanliu de zhuanbian?" [the North Korean issue: a change in China's strategy?], *Lianhe Zaobao* [United Morning Paper] (Singapore), August 1, 2006.

79. The three propositions of China's stance on the North Korean nuclear issues, stated by Tang Jiaxuanat the Foreign Ministers Meeting of the Security Council on Anti-terrorism, January 20, 2003.

80. "Liu Jianchao: Zhongguo conglai weitong Chaoxian jinxingguo renhe xingshide he hezuo" [China has never engaged in any nuclear cooperation in any form with

North Korea], *Beijing Renninwang*, October 10, 2006, http://world.people.com
.cn/GB/8212/9491/57325/4901987.html.

81. Anonymous Chinese official, in phone interview with Chunyao Yi, Information
Department, Ministry of Foreign Affairs, October 9, 2007.

82. Christopher Twomey, "China Policy Towards North Korea and Its Implications
for the United States: Balancing Competing Concerns," *Strategic Insights* 5, 7 (2006).

83. "China's Pundit Urges US, North Korea to Adjust Policies," *Wen Wei Po* (Hong
Kong), February 9, 2007.

84. Chinese Foreign Ministry Press Conference, October 26, 2006.

85. The then Japanese prime minister Shinzo Abe promised that Japan would not seek
to develop nuclear weapons of its own, although some leading members of Abe's
ruling party had raised that possibility. Abe firmly denied that Tokyo would consider the nuclear option. See Eric Talmadge, "Japan, China Agree to Keep Pressure on North Korea to Return to Nuclear Talks," Associated Press Worldstream,
November 18, 2006.

86. The predecessor of the DPRK's maneuver was between China and the former
Soviet Union. In the triangle relation between Pyongyang, Beijing, and Moscow
from the 1960s to the mid-1980s, North Korea was playing the "Beijing card"
against the "Moscow card," which also effectively prevented China from moving
closer to Seoul.

87. There were eight announced dialogues and meetings between the United States
and the DPRK between January and October 2007. The turning point was the
DPRK-U.S. consultation in Berlin in January 2007, in the reached intent (*yixiang*)
on issues such as denuclearization, normalization, and financial sanctions. Christopher Hill's visit to Pyongyang in June 2006 was another step to build up mutual
trust, and the Geneva meeting in September 2007 made breakthroughs on the
issues of denuclearization and declaration, as well as the economic support and
removal from the "rogue state" list.

88. Yoo Cheong-mo, "N. Korea Initially Opposed China's Participation in Korean
Peninsula Peace Summit," Yonhap News Agency (Seoul), October 31, 2007;
"Foreign Ministry: China Supports the Peace Resolution in Korean Peninsula,"
China Daily, October 11, 2007 (in Chinese).

Chapter 8. Conclusion: The Continuing Crisis on the Korean Peninsula

1. A view shared by some U.S. diplomats. State Department official Yuri Kim, in
interviews with author, Seoul, 2004, and Washington, DC, 2007. See also Scott
Snyder, *Negotiating on The Edge: North Korean Negotiating Behavior* (Washington,
DC: United States Institute of Peace, 2002).

2. Jae-soon Chang and Kelly Olsen, "Analysts: Rocket Gives North Korea New Bar-
gaining Chip," *Associated Press*, April 6, 2009; see *North Korea's Missile Launch:
The Risks of Overreaction: Asia Report No. 91* (Seoul: International Crisis Group,
March 31, 2009).

3. Based on author's conversations with Prof. Lim Eul-chul, Kyungnam University,
Seoul (2008 and 2009), about his various discussions with North Korean foreign
ministry officials; see also editorial, Chosun Central News Agency, October 16,
2003.

4. "Beyond the Axis of Evil: Additional Threats from Weapons of Mass Destruction," by the Honorable John R. Bolton, Heritage Lecture #743, May 6, 2002; John R. Bolton, "The Post-American Presidency," *Standpoint* (July/August 2009): 42–45.

5. Leon Sigal, *Disarming Strangers* (Princeton, NJ: Princeton University Press, 1998); Leon Sigal, "Building a Peace Regime in Korea: An American View," *International Journal of Korean Unification Studies* 15, 1 (2006): 30–52; Hazel Smith, *Hungry for Peace: International Security, Humanitarian Assistance, and Social Change in North Korea* (Washington, DC: United States Institute of Peace, 2005); Hazel Smith, ed., *Reconstituting Korean Security* (New York: United Nations University Press, 2007); Bruce Cumings, *Korea's Place in the Sun* (New York: W. W. Norton, 2005).

6. James G. Strohmaier, *Extorting Cooperation: A Case Study of the Negotiation and Implementation of the 1994 U.S.-DPRK Agreed Framework* (PhD diss., University of Kentucky, 2003).

7. Ted Galen Carpenter and Doug Bandow, *The Korean Conundrum* (Basingstoke, UK: Palgrave, 2004).

Selected Bibliography

Albright, David, and Paul Brannan. *The North Korean Plutonium Stock Mid-2006.* Washington, DC: Institute for Science and International Security, 2006.

Albright, David, and Kevin O'Neill, eds. *Solving the North Korean Nuclear Puzzle.* Washington, DC: Institute for Science and International Security, 2000.

Allison, Graham T., and Philip Zelikow. *The Essence of Decision.* New York: Longman, 1999.

Bae, Jong-Yuan, and Chung-in Moon. "The Bush Doctrine and the North Korean Nuclear Crisis." *Asian Perspective (Special Issue on the Bush Doctrine and Asia)* 27, 4 (2003): 9–45.

Beal, Tim. *North Korea: The Struggle Against American Power.* London: Pluto Press, 2005.

Becker, Jasper. *Rogue Regime.* Oxford, UK: Oxford University Press, 2005.

Bennett, Bruce. "Weapons of Mass Destruction: The North Korean Threat." *Korean Journal of Defense Analysis* 16, 2 (fall 2004): 179–98.

Bermudez, Joseph S. "North Korea's Nuclear Program." *Jane's Intelligence Review*, September 1991.

———. *The Armed Forces of North Korea.* London, UK: I. B. Tauris, 2001.

Bluth, Christoph, "The Eagle Resurgent: National Security in the Second Bush Administration." *The World Today*, December 2004.

———. "Face Reality: Why Six-Party Talks Must Fail." *Korea Herald*, May 9, 2005.

Booth, Ken, and Nicholas J. Wheeler. *The Security Dilemma.* Basingstoke, UK: Palgrave, 2008.

Buzo, Adrian. *The Guerilla Dynasty.* London, UK: I. B. Tauris, 1999.

Carlin, Robert L., and Joel S. Wit. *North Korean Reform.* Adelphi paper 382. Washington, DC: International Institute for Strategic Studies, 2006.

Carpenter, Ted Galen. "A Hedging Strategy Is Needed Toward North Korea. *Korea Journal of Defense Analysis* 16, 1 (spring 2004): 7–23.

——— and Doug Bandow. *The Korean Conundrum.* Basingstoke, UK: Palgrave, 2004.

Cha, Do-hyeon. "Challenges and Opportunities: The Participatory Government's Policy Toward North Korea." *East Asian Review* 16, 2 (summer 2004): 97–110.

———. *The Future of the ROK-U.S. Alliance: Toward the Evolution of a Strategic Cooperation Alliance.* KIDA Papers 7, December. Seoul: KIDA Press, 2004.

Cha, Victor D., and David C. Kang. *Nuclear North Korea: A Debate on Engagement Strategie.* New York: Columbia University Press, 2003.

Chinoy, Mike. *Meltdown*. New York: St. Martin's Press, 2008.

Cordesman, Anthony H. *North Korea's Missile Tests: Saber Rattling or Rocket's Red Glare*. Washington, DC: Center for Strategic and International Studies, 2006.

Cumings, Bruce. *The Origins of the Korean War, Volume I: Liberation and the Emergence of Separate Regimes, 1945-1947*. Princeton, NJ: Princeton University Press, 1981.

———. *The Origins of the Korean War, Volume II: The Roaring of the Cataract, 1947–1950*. Princeton, NJ: Princeton University Press, 1990.

———. *Korea's Place in the Sun: A Modern History*. New York: W. W. Norton, 1997.

Daalder, Ivo, and James Lindsay. *America Unbound: The Bush Revolution in Foreign Policy*. New York: Wiley, 2005.

———. "Where Are the Hawks on North Korea?" *American Prospect*, February 1, 2003.

Downs, Chuck. *Over the Line: North Korea's Negotiating Strategy*. Washington, DC: American Enterprise Institute, 1999.

Eberstadt, Nicholas. *The End of North Korea*. Washington, DC: American Enterprise Institute, 1999.

———. *The North Korean Economy*. New Brunswick, NJ: Transaction Publishers, 2007.

Gallucci, Robert L., Daniel B. Poneman, and Joel S. Wit. *Going Critical: The First North Korean Nuclear Crisis*. Washington, DC: Brookings Institution, 2004.

Gallucci, Robert L., and Mitchell B. Reiss. "Dead to Rights." *Foreign Affairs* 84, 2 (March/April 2005): 142–45.

Garwin, Richard L. "HEU Done It." *Foreign Affairs* 84, 2 (March/April 2005): 145–46.

Han, Woo-Keun. *The History of Korea*. Honolulu, HI: East-West Center Press, 1970.

Han, Yong-sup, and Norman D. Levin. *Sunshine in Korea*. Santa Monica, CA: Rand Corporation, 2002.

Harrison, Selig S. "Did North Korea Cheat?" *Foreign Affairs* 84, 1 (January/February 2005).

———. "Harrison Replies." *Foreign Affairs* 84, 2 (March/April 2005): 146–48.

———. *Korean Endgame*. Princeton, NJ: Princeton University Press, 2002.

Hassig, Ralph C., and Kongdan Oh. *The Hidden People of North Korea*. Lanham, MD: Rowman & Littlefield, 2009.

———. *North Korea Through the Looking Glass*. Washington, DC: Brookings Institution, 2000.

Hastings, Max. *The Korean War*. New York: Simon and Schuster, 1988.

Hecker, Siegfried S. *Visit to the Yongbyon Nuclear Research Center in North Korea*. Senate Committee on Foreign Relations hearing, 2004.

Hodge, Homer T. "North Korea's Military Strategy." *Parameters* 33, 1 (spring 2003): 68–81.

Huh, Moon-Young. "60th Anniversary of Korea Liberation: Current Status of Inter-Korean Relations and Future Direction." *International Journal of Korean Unification Studies* 15, 1 (2006): 66–105.

Huntley, Wade L. "Ostrich Engagement: The Bush Administration and the North Korea Nuclear Crisis." *Nonproliferation Review* 11, 2 (summer 2004): 81–115.

———. "Rebels Without a Cause: North Korea, Iran and the NPT." *International Affairs* 82, 4 (2006): 723–42.

Hwang, Jaeho. "Measuring China's Influence over North Korea." *Issues & Studies* 42, 2 (June 2006): 205–32.

Hwang, Jang-yop. *I Saw the Truth of History*. Seoul: Hanwul, 1999.

International Institute for Strategic Studies. *North Korea's Weapons Programmes*. Basing-stoke, UK: Palgrave, 2004.

Jan, Suk. *Study on General Kim Jong Il's National Unification*. Pyongyang: Pyongyang Publishing House, 2002.

Jervis, Robert. *Perception and Misperception in International Politics*. Princeton, NJ: Princeton University Press, 1976.

Jung, Yeon Bong. "The U.S. Response to the North Korea Nuclear Issue." *Korean Journal of Defense Analysis* 17, 2 (fall 2005): 63–86.

Kampani, Gauraf. "Second Tier Proliferation: The Case of Pakistan and North Korea." *Nonproliferation Review* 9, 3 (autumn 2002): 107–16.

Kang, Chol-Hwan, and Pierre Rigoulot. *The Aquariums of Pyongyang*. New York: Basic Books, 2001.

Kihl, Young Whan. *Transforming Korean Politics*. Armonk, NY: M. E. Sharpe, 2005.

Kim, Byungki. "The Role of State Institutions, Organizational Culture and Policy Percep-tion in South Korea's International Security Policymaking Process: 1998–Present." *International Journal of Korean Unification Studies* 15, 1 (2006): 106–31.

Kim, Chul Woo. *General Kim Jong Il's Military First Politics*. Pyongyang: Pyongyang Publishing House, 2000.

Kim, Do-tae. "U.S.-North Korea Nuclear Talks: Pyongyang's Changing Attitude and U.S. Choice." *East Asian Review* 16, 1 (2004): 3–20.

Kim, Jae Ho. *Kim Jong Il's Strategy to Build a Strong and Rich Nation*. Pyongyang: Pyongyang Publishing House, 2000.

Kim, Jina. "An Endless Game: North Korea's Psychological Warfare." *Korean Journal of Defense Analysis* 17, 2 (2005): 153–82.

Kim, Keun-sik. "The North Korean Nuclear Crisis and Inter-Korean Relations." *East Asian Review* 16, 1 (2004): 21–36.

Kim, Samuel S., ed. *Inter-Korean Relations*. Basingstoke, UK: Palgrave, 2004.

———. *North Korea Foreign Relations in the Post-Cold War Era*. Oxford, UK: Oxford University Press, 1998.

———. *The Two Koreas and the Great Powers*. Cambridge, UK: Cambridge University Press, 2006.

Kim, Sung-han. "Anti-American Sentiment and the ROK-US Alliance." *Korean Journal of Defense Analysis* 15, 2 (fall 2003): 105–30.

Kim, Tae-hyo, and Sang-woo Rhee, eds. *Korea-Japan Security Relations*. Seoul: Oruem Publishing House, 2000.

Kim, Tae-hyo, and Woosang Kim. "A Candle in the Wind: Korean Perceptions of ROK-U.S. Security Relations." *Korean Journal of Defense Analysis* 16, 1 (2004): 99–118.

Kim, Taewoo. *Living with North Korean Bomb? Current Debates in and Future Options For South Korea*. KIDA paper 2, June 2003.

———. "North Korean Nuclear Politics at the Crossroads." *Korean Journal of Defense Analysis* 16, 2 (fall 2004): 27–47.

Korean Institute for National Unification. *White Paper on Human Rights in Korea*. Seoul, 2006.

Kwak, Tae-Hwan, and Seung-hoo Joo, eds. *North Korea's Foreign Policy Under Kim Jong Il*. Farnham, UK: Ashgate, 2009.

Laney, James T., and Jason T. Shaplen. "How to Deal with North Korea." *Foreign Affairs* 82, 2 (March/April 2003): 27–45.

Lankov, Andrei. *Crisis in North Korea*. Honolulu, HI: Hawaii University Press, 2007.

———. *From Stalin to Kim Il Sung: The Formation of North Korea 1945-1960*. London: Hurst, 2002.

Lee, Chung-Hoon, and Chung-in Moon. "The North Korean Nuclear Crisis Revisited: The Case for a Negotiated Settlement." *Security Dialogue* 34, 2 (2003): 135–51.

Lee, Nae-young, and Jeong Han-wool. "Anti-Americanism and the U.S.-ROK Alliance." *East Asian Review* 15, 4 (winter 2003): 23–46.

Lehrman, Thomas D. "Rethinking Interdiction: The Future of the Proliferation Security Initiative." *Non-Proliferation Review* 11, 2 (summer 2004): 1–45.

Mansourov, Alexandre Y., and James C. Moltz. *The North Korean Nuclear Program*. London: Routledge, 2000.

Martin, Bradley K. *Under the Loving Care of the Fatherly Leader: North Korea and the Kim Dynasty*. New York: St. Martin's Press, 2004.

Mazarr, Michael J. *North Korea and the Bomb*. New York: St. Martin's Press, 1995.

Mearsheimer, John. *The Tragedy of Great Power Politics*. New York: W. W. Norton, 2003.

Ministry of National Defense. *Defense White Paper*. Seoul, 2000.

———. *Defense White Paper*. Seoul, 2004.

———. *Participatory Government Defense Policy 2003* Seoul.

Moltz, James Clay, and C. Kenneth Quinones. "Getting Serious about a Multilateral Approach to North Korea." *Nonproliferation Review* 11, 1 (spring 2004): 136–44.

Moon, Chung-in. "The North Korean Nuclear Problem and Multilateral Cooperation: The Case of the Six Party Talk." *Whitebook on the Korean Economy*. Seoul: Korea Institute for International Economic Policy, 2004.

Moon, Chung-in, and David Steinberg, eds. *Kim Dae-jung Government and Sunshine Policy: Promises and Challenges*. Seoul: Yonsei University Press, 1999.

Moore, Gregory. "How North Korea Threatens China's Interests: Understanding Chinese 'Duplicity' on the North Korean Nuclear Issue." *International Relations of the Asia-Pacific*, October 2007.

Musharraf, Pervez. *In the Line of Fire*. New York: Free Press, 2006.

Myers, B. R. *The Cleanest Race*. Brooklyn, NY: Melville House, 2010.

Nam, Koon Woo. *The North Korean Communist Leadership, 1945-65: A Study of Factionalism and Political Consolidation*. Tuscaloosa, AL: University of Alabama Press, 1974.

Nanto, Dick K., and Raphael F. Perl. "North Korean Counterfeiting of U.S. Currency." CRS Report for Congress, Order Code RL33324, March 22, 2006.

Natsios, Andrew. *The Great North Korean Famine*. Washington, DC: United States Institute of Peace Press, 2001.

Noland, Marcus. *Avoiding the Apocalypse: The Future of the Two Koreas*. Washington, DC: Institute for International Economics, 2000.

———. *Famine and Reform in North Korea*. Washington, DC: Institute for International Economics, 2003.

———. *Korea after Kim Jong-il*. Washington, DC: Institute for International Economics, 2004.

Nuclear Threat Initiative. "DPRK, Nuclear" country profile, nti.org/e_research/profiles/NK/index.html (accessed February 10, 2011).

Oberdorfer, Don. *The Two Koreas*. New York: Basic Books, 2001.

O'Hanlon, Michael, and Mike Mochizuki. *Crisis on the Korean Peninsula*. New York: McGraw-Hill, 2003.

Paik, Haksoon. "What Is the Goal of the U.S. Policy toward North Korea: Nonproliferation or Regime Change?" Nautilus Policy Form Online, April 7, 2005, http://www.nautilus.org.

Palais, James B. *Politics and Policy in Traditional Korea*. Cambridge, MA: Harvard University Press, 1975.

Park, Han S. *North Korea: The Politics of Unconventional Wisdom*. Boulder, CO: Lynne Rienner, 2002.

Park, Ihn-hwi. "Toward an Alliance of Moderates: The Nuclear Crisis and Trilateral Policy Coordination." *East Asian Review* 16, 2 (summer 2004): 23–42.

Park, Sun Song. "Reform or Military Buildup: North Korea's Economic Policy 1994–2004." *East Asian Review* 16, 2 (summer 2004): 3–22.

Perry, William. *Review of United States Policy Toward North Korea: Findings and Recommendations*. Washington, DC: Department of State, 1999, http://www.state.gov/www/regions/eap/991012_northkorea_rpt.html (accessed November 4, 2007).

Pinkston, Daniel A. *The North Korean Ballistic Missile Program*. Carlisle, PA: Strategic Studies Institute, 2008.

——— and Phillip C. Saunders. "Seeing North Korea clearly." *Survival* 45, 3 (autumn 2003): 79–102.

Quinones, C. Kenneth, and Joseph Trager. *Understanding North Korea*. New York: Alpha Books, 2003.

Rees, David. *Korea: The Limited War*. London: Penguin, 1964.

Sagan, Scott. "Why Do States Build Nuclear Weapons?" *International Security* 21, 3 (1996): 54–86.

Samore, Gary. "The Korean Nuclear Crisis." *Survival* 45, 1 (spring 2003): 7–24.

Saunders, Phillip C. *Military Options for Dealing with North Korea's Nuclear Program*. Monterey, CA: James Martin Center for Nonproliferation Studies, 2004, http://cns.miis.edu/research/korea/dprkmil.htm.

Scobell, Andrew. *China and North Korea: From Comrades-in-Arms to Allies at Arm's Length*. Carlisle, PA: Strategic Studies Institute, 2004.

Shambaugh, David. "China and the Korean Peninsula: Playing for the Long Term." *Washington Quarterly* 26, 2 (spring 2003): 43–56.

Sheen, Seongho. "Preempting Proliferation of WMD: Proliferation Security Initiative (PSI) and Its Challenges." *Korea Journal of Defense Analysis* 16, 2 (fall 2004): 109–30.

Shorrock, Tim. "The Struggle for Democracy in South Korea in the 1980s and the Rise of Anti-Americanism." *Third World Quarterly* 8, 4 (October 1986): 1195–1218.

Sigal, Leon. "Building a Peace Regime in Korea: An American View." *International Journal of Korean Unification Studies* 15, 1 (2006): 30–52.

———. *Disarming Strangers*. Princeton, NJ: Princeton University Press, 1998.

Smith, Hazel. *Hungry for Peace: International Security, Humanitarian Assistance, and Social Change in North Korea.* Washington, DC: United States Institute of Peace, 2005.

Snyder, Scott. *China's Rise and the Two Koreas.* Boulder, CO: Lynne Rienner, 2009.

———. *Negotiating on the Edge: North Korean Negotiating Behavior.* Washington, DC: United States Institute of Peace, 2002.

———. "Response to North Korea's Nuclear Test: Capitulation or Collective Action?" *Washington Quarterly* 30, 4 (2007): 33–43.

———. "South Korea's Squeeze Play." *Washington Quarterly* 28, 4 (2005): 93–106.

Strohmaier, James G. *Extorting Cooperation: A Case Study of the Negotiation and Implementation of the 1994 U.S.-DPRK Agreed Framework.* PhD diss., University of Kentucky, 2003.

Szalontai, Balazs, and Sergey Radchenko. *North Korea's Efforts to Acquire Nuclear Technology and Nuclear Weapons: Evidence from Russian and Hungarian Archives,* working paper 53. Washington, DC: Cold War International History Project, 2006.

Waltz, Kenneth. *Theory of International Politics.* New York: Random House, 1979.

Wampler, Robert A., ed. *North Korea and Nuclear Weapons: The Declassified Record.* National Security Archive electronic briefing book 87, 2003.

Weathersby, Kathryn. *Soviet Aims in Korea and the Origins of the Korean War 1945–50.* Cold War International History Project working paper 8, 1993.

Wendt, Alexander. *Social Theory of International Relation.* Cambridge: Cambridge University Press, 1999.

Wu, Anne. "What China Whispers to North Korea." *Washington Quarterly* 28, 2 (2005): 35–48.

Yeo, In-Kon. "Search for Peaceful Resolution of the North Korean Nuclear Issue." *International Journal of Korean Unification Studies* 15, 1 (2006): 53–65.

Zhang, Xizhen, and Eugene Brown. "Policies Toward North Korea: A Time for New Thinking." *Journal of Contemporary China* 9, 25 (2000): 535–45.

Index

About the Author

Christoph Bluth is a professor of international studies at the University of Leeds and is a founding member of the Korea Research Hub there and at the University of Sheffield. He was a visiting professor at Yonsei University, Seoul, in 2005 and a visiting researcher at the Korea Institute for Defense Analyses. The author of *Korea* (2008), among other books, Dr. Bluth lives in Bradford, West Yorkshire.